My STORY
in BLACK
and
WHITE

The Autobiography of
Jesse O. Thomas

Facilitated by Rosemary Braxton

Robert D. Reed Publishers

Robert D. Reed Publishers
P.O. Box 1992
Bandon, OR 97411
Phone: 541-347-9882; Fax: -9883
E-mail: 4bobreed@msn.com
Website: www.rdrpublishers.com

Cover Designer: Cleone Reed
Interior design and composition: Susan Leonard

ISBN 13: 978-1-934759-98-1
ISBN 10: 1-934759-98-8

Library of Congress Number: 2015948089

Designed and Formatted in the United States of America

Notes to the Reader:
My Story in Black and White

As our country approaches an elder boom, I have found myself wondering the kinds of solutions my granddad would have imagined. Jesse O. Thomas stimulated and inspired his environment. His wisdom was invaluable to me when I began working for the University of California, Davis as an Assistant Dean of Students in 1969.

He counseled me to have entertainment, investment and savings account categories in my monthly budget. I sought his advice when a crisis arose on my job and successfully emerged as Assistant Director of the Learning Resource Center, Coordinator of the Educational Opportunity Program and Director of the Summer Enrichment Program.

At that time many of the students were reading W.E.B. Du Bois and since granddad knew Du Bois we had several conversations about him. He described Du Bois as a nonconformist who sometimes paid for his decisions. For example Du Bois was not rehired as a professor when he married a student during the academic year. The school had a non-fraternization policy between students and faculty. In 1920 granddad was founder of the Atlanta School of Social Work (ASSW). Years later he hired Du Bois when he sought employment with the Atlanta University School of Social Work. Helping others was a hallmark of his life.

Jesse O. Thomas' life speaks to the importance of networking and making courageous decisions when life finds you in a position of influence. By 2035 there will be more than eleven million people over the age of eighty-five in the USA. That will put our country in the position of acquiring an enormous wealth of wisdom.

Fortunately my granddad has penned his career and decisions he made. His choices are applicable in today's work environment and can serve as an inspiration to those seeking excellence.

Granddad also made a wise decision when he proposed to my grandmother, Nellie Ida Mitchell, the daughter of Nelson Turner Mitchell and Ida Anne Scott. Nelson Mitchell was a linguist and Fisk graduate who taught at Wiley College in Marshall, Texas. His wife, Ida Anne Scott, graduated from high school and normal school. In this atmosphere my grandmother grew up with an appreciation for the importance of education. After obtaining her Bachelor's Degree from Tuskegee Institute she attended The John Robert Powers School of Charm in New York City. Her predilection for etiquette and the knowledge she gained helped her become one of Atlanta's most gracious hostesses.

Mary McLeod Bethune, Roland Hayes, and other distinguished African American visitors to the gate city (Atlanta) stayed at her home when "jim crow" was king and hotel accommodations were unavailable to people of color.

My grandparents had one daughter, Anne Amanda Thomas, named for her maternal grandmother Ida Anne Scott and her paternal grandmother Amanda Johnson. She is my mother. Mom married John Thomas Braxton and to that union my sister Nell Anne and I were born.

Following distinguished careers at historically black colleges, my parents retired as administrators with the Sacramento City Unified School District in Sacramento, California. My sister, Nell Anne Braxton, married Bertram M. Gibson and bore Bertram M. Gibson, III before the death of my grandfather. Tragically young Bert died in an accident August 2, 1992 the year after graduating from Franklin Marshall College. His younger sister, Erika Anne Gibson, is the first African American neuro-surgeon in Veterinary Medicine. My sister Nell has retired from an active life in social justice. She recently penned her memories in *Too Proud to Bend: Notes of a Civil Rights Foot Soldier.* Prior to my retirement I became a licensed (lay) preacher with The Episcopal Diocese of Northern California and currently preach at the Eskaton Monroe Lodge in Sacramento one Sunday a month representing Trinity Cathedral Episcopal Church.

As you read this book my hope is that you will be inspired to pursue excellence and creativity.

~ Rosemary Braxton

Special Thanks

I especially want to thank my mother, Anne Thomas Braxton; my niece, Erika Anne Gibson; and my friend, William Mooring for their help in getting this manuscript to the publisher.

~ Rosemary Braxton

Table of Contents

Foreword

*M*y *Story in Black and White* is an engrossing picture of Negro–white relationships as seen through the eyes of an active participant in the drama of race relations in America for more than half a century. The life story that Jesse O. Thomas recounts in simple and straightforward fashion is made vivid by well-chosen anecdotes skillfully told. Many of the important personalities that people these pages have gone from the scene; and the events involving them have been forgotten by many, or have never been known by some who will read this book.

This is personal history that will give its readers a kaleidoscopic view of the institutions and agencies, the patterns and attitudes, and the black and white people-to-people relationships that helped to shape the education and economic condition of the Negro in America during the decades when Jesse O. Thomas moved about on the national scene.

Whitney M. Young, Jr.
Executive Director
National Urban League

MY STORY IN BLACK AND WHITE

I

Family Life

In deciding to reduce to writing an analytical description of some of the things I have done and that have been done to me in the seventy-five years I have been going "to and fro—up and down this earth," I am very conscious of the fact that I have done very few things or very few things have been done to me, if any, that have not been done by or to millions of other members of my group of both sexes who were born and reared under circumstances substantially similar to those in which I grew up.

With this honest confession, the reader would logically wonder why one should take the time and use the amount of printer's ink and paper that have gone into this narrative to record his experiences in book form. The explanation is that I have been persuaded by friends of mine whose judgment I respect highly, whose confidence I have enjoyed and whose motivation I believe I understand.

Some thirty years ago, the late Dr. Charles S. Johnson, who was at one time President of Fisk University but who was then employed as Director of Research of the National Urban League and Editor of *Opportunity*, its official organ, said to me in my home in Atlanta, "Your experience has been in many ways unique, and you have a way of getting over your message to people which has earned for you a reputation as a public speaker and social worker which, if you should reduce it to writing, would be an inspiration to many other people who have and are encountering difficulties in their struggle to achieve. Why don't you write a book?"

Claude A. Barnett, of the Associated Press, on more than one occasion has said to me, "J.O., you should put something in a permanent record about your life and experience. You have an engaging vocabulary and unique mannerisms which enable you to bypass a lot of obstacles which would otherwise become insurmountable hurdles."

More recently my friend John Rice, of Houston, Texas, who has known me for more than a quarter of a century and has worked pretty closely with me when I was making a survey of the living, working, and housing condition of Negroes in Houston in 1929, and who also was a frequent visitor of the Texas Centennial when I was General Manager of Negro Participation in that Centennial, suggested that I write my memoirs.

No less insistent has been the counsel of my good friend "Comrod," Dr. C.A. Bacote, whose major is historical research, that I put some of the things "you know that nobody else knows as well where posterity might benefit by them." Dr. Bacote's approach has sometimes changed its complexion from admonition to reprimand.

In recent years, scarcely a week has passed that some person has not repeated the statements of these gentlemen. In spite of the fact, therefore, that to me my life contains nothing so particularly unique, my resistance finally broke down, and this chronological life story is the result.

I was born in Pike County, Mississippi, December 21, 1885. I was the second child in a family of six children—four boys and two girls. My parents were born during the days of slavery. As I recall, my father was eight or nine years old at the end of the Civil War, and my mother was two or three years younger than my father. I never knew too much about my grandparents on my father's side, never having seen either of them. I can scarcely remember my grandmother on my mother's side, but I knew my mother's father very well. I knew more about my mother's brothers and sisters than I knew about my father's brothers and sisters.

Because my mother was ill during most of my childhood, and because she had to conserve her energies, she spent much of the time, when she was not engaged in housecleaning and in preparing the family meals, in bed. This did not provide much opportunity for the normal family fireside chats and reviews of the family background. I have always envied children whose mothers lived until they reached young manhood and young womanhood and who had the benefit of the counsel and advice of a good mother. Because slavery ended before either of my parents reached adulthood, they escaped the horrors of involuntary servitude, and, therefore, had no stories of cruelty to relate to their children.

In the particular community where I was born the relationship between white and colored people was, for the most part, very cordial. Most of the white people were sharecroppers or tenants like most of the colored people. The sharp social distinction that characterized the relationship of many of the white and colored people occupying distinctive positions with respect to land ownership elsewhere did not seem evident in this community. The young white boys and girls, for example, would answer "Sir" to my father and would call him "Uncle Jeff." It was not an unusual thing to have the neighbors eat a meal with each other across the line of racial demarcation. While none of them had very much, if any, money at the end of the year from the sale of their share of the produce, they all had plenty to eat. Each family had an abundance of poultry and livestock. There was no law requiring a farmer to fence in his livestock. We lived near a river, and a considerable acreage on either side of the river was what we called swampland. Anybody's hogs could live in the swamp from early spring until late fall, when the crops were gathered; then each farmer would go to the swamp and call his hogs and turn them into the field. Now, that was before Dr. Carver started milking potatoes and peanuts, and the hogs found enough undug peanuts and potatoes to become "fat enough to kill." I don't believe my father ever knew how many hogs he had, because pigs without number were born to the female hogs in the interim between early spring and the late fall while the hogs were still in the swamps. We had so many cows that we had milk to feed to the hogs after the family had consumed all they wanted.

Because of the length of time we lived on this plantation and the obvious prosperity that everywhere seemed evident, I had every reason to suppose that we owned the land. I shall never forget the shock and frustration which I experienced when my father told us one evening in great distress and disappointment that one of our neighbors had gone to the owner of the land and entered into a negotiation to rent the land by offering to the owner a larger rental than our family was giving. My father was very much hurt that this neighbor would seek to take advantage of us, inasmuch as we had lived on the land for so long a time and had kept our contractual agreement with the owner in terms of liquidating our obligation at the end of each year, even though we had very little left after the debts were paid. I asked my father, "How can a neighbor cause us to move off our own land and out of our own home?" He said, "We do not own this land. We are sharecroppers." We finally had to move off the land we had occupied for more than two decades. This disaster created within me a determination never to permit that kind of thing to happen to me again. I developed an antisocial attitude toward living on premises that I did not own or could not buy if I wanted to.

II

Early Educational Experience

The school that we attended was known as the Cleveland School. It was typical of the rural schools of that day, and even of some communities at the present time—a one-room and one-teacher school. This teacher had to "hear all the classes from the first grade to the seventh grade." The term "hear" is the term that was in general usage at the time and, as I look back at it now, it was scientifically correct, because it was about all any teacher could do with seventy-five or one hundred students all in one room and comprising seven different grades. How she was able to classify the students I do not know. Most of the time, most of the teachers themselves had not gone beyond the seventh or eighth grade, and because they did not receive their appointments on the basis of qualifications, they had no claim to the job as such, and the turnover was very rapid. The superintendent, who I imagine, also had gone no further than the seventh grade or less, appointed his teachers—both white and colored—according to where he felt he wanted to send them, or some favoritism may have been brought to bear which would determine how long teacher X remained in Z community. There was no such thing as a certificate of graduation. A student went to school as long as he or his parents felt he was receiving any educational information from the particular teacher in question.

In any case, the school was about two and a half miles from home, and of course we walked that distance, through the woods for the most part, morning and afternoon. What I can remember most about my school experience at the Cleveland one-room and one-teacher school was my participation in the Friday afternoon spelling matches and speechmaking. The class would stand against the wall, and the one who spelled the most words remained standing the longest or went to the head of the class.

The other thing that I remember vividly concerning my school experience in this one-room, one-teacher school was that on Friday afternoons the upper classmen, if that term can be applied to persons above the fourth grade, were required and given an opportunity to memorize and "say" a speech. This meant that a teacher would assign to each student a poem or a piece of poetry or prose, and the student would memorize it and deliver it on this semiformal occasion on Friday afternoon.

As I think of it now, this must have been a survival technique employed by the teacher to keep these students, who would otherwise have been idle, occupied in learning their speeches. As I remember, you were on your own once the assignment had been given. There were no rehearsals and no coaching, except what you got from your parents. It proved to be rather a community-wide activity because, as a part of the homework, each prospective Friday afternoon speaker would get such support of his parents and other members of the family as might prove helpful in allaying the possibility of his having stage fright, on the one hand, and on the other hand, he could use the members of his family as a testing audience. The participants in these Friday evening recitations were somewhat graded or classified on the basis of their delivery and their accuracy in committing to memory the subject matter of the assignment. I earned the reputation of having a very good memory because I was able to memorize, without an error or inaccuracy, a speech that would require five or ten minutes to deliver. In retrospect, I get the impression that the degree to which I have been rated as a public speaker is traceable to my periodic appearances before my teacher and schoolmates in the one-room schoolhouse in Pike County, Mississippi.

If, perchance, a pupil's father and mother, or either parent, a sister or brother, had any educational background, he was most fortunate, and the majority of the children were no more fortunate in this respect than I was. I do not believe my mother ever attended any school at all. My father had three weeks' night-school training. He was limited, therefore, in the amount of academic assistance he could give to his children, although he had taught himself to read and write. He must have been a fourth-grade student. He reflected a perpetual hunger for knowledge and information, reading everything he could get possession of that was, in his language, "uplifting." What he lacked in education he made up for in basic character in terms of honor and upright living. He was a great churchman and a choir singer. He learned to read notes and taught all of his children how to sing by note. He was a deacon in the church and usually supplied leadership in the conduct of any official business which the officers of the church were called upon to handle.

Either my grandmother or grandfather, or perhaps both, on my father's side must have exercised a rather wholesome influence over their children, because three of my father's sisters, whom I knew, were rather outstanding citizens in their communities and enjoyed the respect and admiration of their neighbors. I never heard anything derogatory concerning their social conduct or community behavior. The only one of his brothers whom I knew was a minister. The Monday following every fourth Sunday during the month of August, he preached in the afternoon at Summit Baptist Church, of which my father was the head deacon. While he lived at Johnson Station, which was some eight or ten miles from Summit on the Illinois Central Railroad between Summit and Northfield, Mississippi, this anniversary occasion was a part of what was called "the Big Meeting" or "Protracted Meeting." People would come each year from as far as twenty or twenty-five miles in buggies and on horseback to celebrate, as it were, this "Big

Meeting" or "Anniversary Revival." The meeting would last from Sunday through Tuesday or Wednesday, with services morning, afternoon, and evening of each day. The participating ministers were supposed to be the "cream of the crop" of the area and would come from as far away as twenty or thirty miles.

Sunday, however, was the outstanding day of interstate significance because then an excursion would be run from New Orleans to Summit. It happened, of course, that a great many people had moved from the Summit community to New Orleans, and they looked forward with great anticipation to returning on the fourth Sunday in August to fraternize with their friends who would be coming from far and near to celebrate the occasion. Each family brought a basket, and there were perhaps twenty-five hundred or three thousand families with baskets. In each basket there were at least two kinds of meat: chicken, beef, and sometimes fish; and two kinds of cake (what they called pound and layer cake). Any person—whether he was personally acquainted with the family or not did not make very much difference—could go from one basket to another as long as he was physically able to take in food and enjoy the hospitality of the people who came to celebrate the "Big Meeting."

I always looked forward to the Monday afternoon, because then my uncle was to give his annual sermon. He indulged in very few preliminaries, and within five minutes after he had taken his text he had thrown himself and all that he had into his message and "at the sinners and backsliders." After a forty- or fifty-minute exaltation, he would come down out of the pulpit and "open the doors of the church." I can see him now standing over those who came either to join the church or to take their place at the mourners bench to be prayed for, with his collar melted down with perspiration and fanning himself with a large palmetto fan. The effectiveness of a sermon—as indeed the comparative significance of the message on the part of the speakers themselves—was largely determined by how many hitherto lost souls "confessed their sins" and became candidates for baptism. Any sermon that was not punctuated by "A-men" or shouts, or that was not followed by some "sinsick soul coming into the fold," was considered an ineffective sermon and delivered without the divine benediction of "His Lord." This fact was the influence that contributed to the competitive aspect of the theological competition on these significant occasions.

The situation described above was rather typical of what took place at all the churches of the different denominations in the community from Sunday to Sunday, beginning in the later part of July and extending to the last of August. The spiritual enthusiasm kindled by these periodic denominations of religious fervor was in some respect sustained by the parishioners or communicants for the ensuing calendar and sectarian year.

My father, like the heads of the other families in the community, assumed the responsibility for, in the first instance, getting his own house in order by building up attitudes of expectation and participation in his children and neighbors, and then as head deacon he looked after the business aspect of these meetings, including the expense to cover the cost of transportation of the visiting ministers and such other miscellaneous financial items as would be incident to the conduct of a meeting of this kind.

For weeks after the revival the whole neighborhood was alive with discussions of the pros and cons of what transpired during the meeting, touching every aspect of human behavior, as well as with evaluating the success of the meeting in terms of the number of persons who joined the church either as new converts or by letter or reaffirmation of faith.

Although, in terms of formalized information, my father was not a lettered man, measured by the extent to which the community looked up to him for leadership and sought his counsel, he was a useful citizen. He was of such a tranquil character that he was given the nickname "Uncle Peace." Out of every situation he was always striving to bring about understanding and goodwill. He had many very profound sayings, which linger with me until this day. He would never permit us to speak unkindly of anybody or make fun of people. He had a saying as he admonished us to be thoughtful in our consideration of other people, that "What comes to others may eventually come to us."

"Segregation" is a word that, because of its implication, I have come to detest. I not only hate the act of segregation; I have no use for the word. If I had the authority, I would delete it from the dictionary. The Supreme Court has held that segregation does not necessarily mean discrimination. That may be true as a judicial analysis, but in actual human experience, the only purpose of segregation is to discriminate. If I had to choose between horizontal and vertical segregation, I think I would take the vertical. That is to say, if you must have segregation, then have complete segregation—meaning that on all administrative levels, as well as the operational level, representatives of the same racial or ethnic groups would be in control. That is approximately what happened in the Cleveland School District. While the superintendent of the county schools was a white person, the board of trustees of this particular school were all colored. The students in the school never came in contact with any white person, on which account there was no opportunity for the impact of white domination becoming a part of their daily experiences.

In the case of my own immediate family, while we lived on a rented plantation we were for all practical purposes in complete control of the land and premises. As far as I know, my father saw the landowner once a year and made arrangement for the cultivation of the land for the ensuing year, and no further contact was necessary until the time for settlement at the harvest season. We never had to work for the local white people because there was adequate demand for our services on our own land. At no point, therefore, in my early experience did I sustain any relationship to the white world which would develop in me an inferiority complex. In addition there was a neighborly spirit that characterized the conduct of the Negro and white tenant families as well as the few Negro and white landowners who lived in the county or agricultural community. The children—white and colored—played baseball and other recreational games without any consciousness of inferiority or superiority.

My mother died when I was fourteen years of age—about the same time that the neighbor negotiated with the landowner to take possession of the land we had occupied for so many years, making it necessary for us to find a new place to live. The frustrating reaction to these two overwhelming losses that the family sustained was devastating to me. I could see no future for me as a part of a sharecropping unit or as a member of a tenant family. I noticed that the people who came up from New Orleans on the excursions to the "Big Meetings" on the fourth Sunday in August all seemed well dressed and reflected an air of security and prosperity which was intriguing. On my way back home from my mother's funeral, I decided to put what few things I had in a bag and disappear unannounced.

The distance from McComb, Mississippi, to Natalbany, Louisiana, is something like forty or fifty miles. How I got the railroad fare, I do not now remember. The only thing I recall is that on a Sunday afternoon I slipped unnoticed out of my father's house with my bag and got into town in time to catch the train going south. When the train pulled out from the station I said "Bye-Bye" to Pike County and to the sharecropping neighborhood and, except for infrequent visits, I did not go back.

III

Sawmilling in Natalbany and Strater, Louisiana

My first time to ride a train was the trip to Natalbany, Louisiana, which was a sawmill town. Another boy, a schoolmate of mine, named David Davis, and I took this trip into the unknown together. One can easily imagine the anxiety which characterized the experience of a young lad fourteen years of age arriving in a town where he knew only one person, and that person no more familiar with the surroundings and the people than he.

The population of this community was something like five thousand people—I should say, forty-five hundred colored and five hundred white. The whites, for the most part, represented the administrative and managerial element in the population: the foremen and bookkeepers, clerks and managers of the commissary, and owners and proprietors of other stores and business places in the town. The majority of the colored were unskilled and semi-skilled laborers. A small percentage of them were skilled workmen. They comprised the lumber graders, the straw bosses of crews of unskilled laborers, and a few mechanics.

We arrived Sunday afternoon, and Monday morning early we were out at the mill seeking employment. My companion was three or four years older than I, but not any larger and very little more mature. Fortunately for us, there was a shortage of labor and we had no difficulty in finding employment. We were given positions out on the yard stacking lumber and loading lumber in boxcars and other open freight cars. The wages paid for ten hours' work was ninety cents a day. The management operated on the theory that the way to keep Negro wage earners on the job was to keep them broke. One of the devices employed to this end was to encourage, if not coerce, each employee to spend a sizable percentage of his income in the commissary. Regardless of what his particular need was or how much money he may have had otherwise, he was suppose to go to the bookkeeping department and draw a coupon at least once every week. The more of his wages he took up in coupons, the more desirable an employee he was in the appreciation of the management because the less money in cash would he then draw on pay day, which was bimonthly, and so much the better. An employee who did not take up coupons was apt to be questioned as to what his reason was for not patronizing the commissary. The prices of the commodities in the commissary were from ten to twenty-five per cent higher than the prices of the same commodities in the open market.

Hammond, Louisiana, which was only three miles below Natalbany, was the largest city between Jackson, Mississippi, and New Orleans. It was possible to catch a train at the end of a working day, ride down to Hammond, and purchase enough supplies to last a week and get another train headed north toward Jackson and get back to Natalbany within three or four hours. Most of the colored employees and a number of white were unmarried; a large number of both white and colored were in common-law wife-and-husband arrangements. Some of the single men who lived in sawmill shacks boarded with the families, whereas others found it more economical to prepare their own meals before and after work. My boy friend and I chose the latter, and after the first payday we bought a stove and set up housekeeping.

Notwithstanding I was making money and handling it for the first time in my life, my first few weeks at Natalbany were very unhappy days. My father did not know where I was, and I was afraid to make my whereabouts known to him because I did not know what his reaction would be. If he had taken a train and come down to Natalbany and ordered me to leave and return home, I would not have had any alternative. I did not want to go back, and yet I was very lonesome and homesick. It occurred to me that the thing to do was to make a "peace offering." So the early part of the second month I went to the store, took up a coupon, and bought a supply of groceries—consisting of meat, flour, sugar, and coffee—and also included a couple of pairs of shoes for Father, and sent them to him by express. I wrote him a letter advising that there would be a package for him at the Express Office. I was greatly relieved mentally and also emotionally reconstructed when I received his letter of acknowledgement and thanks for my thought-fulness. In the letter were words of counsel and admonition to stay out of bad company, and the request that I take care of my money. It also contained the assurance that I would be welcomed whenever I wanted to come back to visit the home folks. This letter gave me a new lease on life, and I felt for the first time since I had "departed into a far country" that I had my father standing back of me. I at least had a home, even though I never expected to return to live in it again. From that time until my father finally passed away, I became the largest wage earner in the family in terms of financial intake and, by that token, the head of our family. From that time forward I was the main breadwinner in the family and the one on whose shoulders fell the responsibility of its upkeep.

It was the middle of July, as I remember, when I severed my connection with the agricultural economy and cast my lot with the mechanized culture of a sawmill community. On a plantation, if you got too warm you could go out at the far end of the row and cool off under a shade tree, but this was not possible in a lumberyard. I have never witnessed such hot days. That section of Louisiana, from the point of view of altitude, was much lower than McComb, Mississippi, my hometown community. I never encountered so many mosquitoes at night. We had to purchase mosquito netting to sleep under. In spite of the heat, however, and the unaccustomed exacting toil, which seemed to have taxed every ounce of my strength and rendered me sore all over for the first few weeks, I never lost a day of work.

Regardless of the management's desire and the accepted practice of encouraging every employee to take up most of his wages in coupons, I took a chance on inviting the disfavor of management by living as economically as I could and saving all the money I could possibly save. I was determined never to be caught in the position my father was when he was compelled to move off the land he had occupied for more than two decades, or to be caught with no financial reserve or accumulated buying power.

Because my father himself was active in the church and superintendent of the Sunday School, at home it became a matter of course for all the children to accompany him to church and to Sunday School. Notwithstanding the fact that he had only a limited opportunity for securing an education, he was head and shoulders above most of his neighbors, white and colored, from the point of view of his knowledge of the Bible and his ability to interpret the Scripture. The neighbors, therefore, regardless of their racial identity, came to him frequently to inquire as to where a certain passage of the Scripture could be found in terms of its chapter location in the Bible and as to the meaning thereof. Since we had very little other literature to read, we were encouraged to read the Bible. Under these circumstances, I developed a rather keen appreciation for the Scripture and, until this day, I have the habit of reading the Bible with some degree of regularity and with an understanding that would not have been possible otherwise. This background made it easier for me to identify with the church in the sawmill town where we had service at least once a month. The pastor usually had two or three other churches he was serving, so that he would get to us only once a month. Some local person was given the responsibility of being superintendent of the Sunday School and carrying on such other auxiliary activities as were common during the interim. My activities in the Sunday School and my regularity in attendance upon the job soon attracted the attention of the people in the community, because I had neither time nor desire to participate in the less wholesome activities, such as crap shooting and gambling. It is surprising and interesting how the refraining from participation in this type of enterprise distinguished a lad from the general "run of the mill" employees and made it possible for him to become very widely known as a unique personality. This fact helped to protect me from any ill will on the part of management following upon the fact that I did not comply with the general policy of drawing most of my salary in coupons and spending it in the commissary. In the course of events, I became well liked by the head foreman and pretty widely and favorably known by management—paradoxical though it may seem.

The history and development of these typical sawmill villages followed a certain pattern, which was familiar to the people who made sawmilling their means of livelihood. The custom was, and I suppose still is, to locate a sawmill in the center of densely populated timberland near a railroad track. As long as timber could be brought to the mill by water or by steam, and as long as the distance did not impose a cost which threatened the profit of the transaction, the mill remained in operation. When the radius of timber cutting had reached distance that threatened to exhaust the supply or that represented an unprofitable distance for transportation, this particular mill was closed down and machinery moved to another location of timberland. That explains somewhat the temporary character of the lumber mill itself, as well as of all other buildings, including stores, commissaries, hotels, and dwellings. The more important people, such as those in the white-collar division of labor, whose income would support such an economy, were housed in the better-constructed and more durable houses.

The unskilled and semiskilled workers lived in the more poorly constructed and inexpensive houses. The rent charged for a dwelling place depended upon the character of its construction and appointments as well as its location. The turnover in the labor supply was very rapid, and there was little or no security on the job, because labor was cheap and unorganized and the situation not only welcomed but invited exploitation.

When the sawmill finally moved away from such a town, the original location quickly became a ghost city, because all the other activities in the community were dependent upon the buying power of the employees connected in some way with the mill. During my second year at Natalbany, the location reached the saturation point in timber intake, from the point of view of profitable transportation, or the mill had so completely utilized all of the available lumber that it no longer represented a dividend-yielding enterprise, from a stockholder's point of view. I do not now recall whether the same management transferred the machinery from Natalbany to a place named Strater, Louisiana, which was nine miles below Ponchatoula and forty miles above New Orleans and located also on the Illinois Central Railroad, or whether a new investment corporation established the mill at Strater. I do know that, as information reached Natalbany that a mill-developing project was under construction at Strater, many of the people at Natalbany moved on to Strater as rapidly as housing accommodations—temporary or otherwise—could be found.

The wages for unskilled labor at Natalbany was ninety cents; at Strater it as a dollar and a dollar and ten cents, which was quite an attraction. Strater was the typical sawmill village or community, differing from Natalbany in two essential respects, so far as demoralizing facilities were concerned, but the motivation with relation to management sanction was the same. With the basic thought in mind of keeping the employees broke, the management encouraged a supervised game house where gambling was openly indulged in in a wholesome fashion. In this room, which measured twelve by eighteen feet wide, there was a table ten feet long with a velvet top built something like a pool table with a wooden framework around the edges which would prevent the dice from falling off the table. The man in charge of the game had a long rake which enabled him to reach the dice at the farthest corner from where he sat; it was his duty to call the dice, accept the bets from the bidders, and cut a percentage of what was won or lost as the income for the house. Any number of persons who stood by the tables or anywhere in the room could bet that the person rolling the dice did not make his point, or could bet that he would make it.

The other medium of separating the wage earner from his cash contained in his pay envelope on pay day, between Saturday night and Monday morning, was the encouragement on the part of management of women of easy virtue to come out from New Orleans to Strater on the afternoon train which reached Strater around four o'clock every pay day, and to remain until late Sunday night or early Monday morning. These were very attractive young women for the most part, white and colored—many more colored than white, because a larger percentage of Negroes than white men were unmarried, and there were more Negroes than whites among the unskilled laborers.

It was somewhat of a competitive enterprise on the part of these women. They were to contact and make themselves available to as many men as it was humanly possible to associate with from six o'clock Saturday night until six o'clock Monday morning. Between the game house and these female parasites, ninety per cent of the wage-earning population was as broke Monday morning as they had been Friday night. Not infrequently, two or three of the women of each excursion would "make good" with some of the men with whom they had contact and thereby become their common-law wives. They would return to New Orleans and move whatever household goods and personal belongings they might possess into the homes of their newly acquired husbands. These types of demoralizing influences had other by-products no less destructive. The venereal disease incidence was abnormally high, and scarcely a day passed that somebody was not either cut or otherwise beaten up as a result of disappointing experiences at the gambling table or of being double-crossed by these "transient harlots."

The resident male employee population encountered an additional hazard during the weekend following pay day, which was a bimonthly experience, as a result of the visitation of professional gamblers who scheduled their itinerary across the state, and even out of the state, so as to arrive at a sawmill community or railroad shop center on pay day or shortly thereafter. These usually took the winners. In other words, when the lucky neophytes had dispossessed their contemporaries, they were choice morsels for the professional "sharp shooters," who took them in their stride by mid-week. The lucky boys who came out of the gambling pool on Sunday night with their pockets bulging with their fellow craftsmen's earnings were soon themselves so impoverished that they became eager wage earners again with no more financial reserve or economic security than they had had the day before pay day. The tragedy of this situation was that nobody seemed to learn any beneficial lesson from their accumulated experiences, because the operation was repeated as often as payday arrived, with similar results.

By showing a disposition to learn all I could about my job, I found favor with a Mr. Doyle, who was one of the head foremen, and I was finally given the job of managing what they called, as I remember, the "hog." This machine was so constructed that it had blades on a revolving wheel which operated with such speed that they chopped up the slabs of lumber into very fine shavings and dropped them on a conveyer that carried them to a fire pit and dumped them in the fire. This was a semiskilled job, and I was given the remarkably high salary of a dollar and a quarter a day. I learned a good deal about machinery, in terms of when the wheels and pulleys were out of line and had burned-out bearings, and so forth, and as a result became somewhat of an assistant millwright.

In spite of the substantial progress I made in terms of income, security and status, the over-all environment was anything but satisfying and wholesome. The longer I remained there, the more restless and discontented I became, but I was very much undecided about what else to do or where to go. As has already been indicated, my father's educational opportunities were limited and the educational institutions in the county, as well as in the state, were inadequate. There was not a high school in the state, and only one class A college in the state—either tax-supported or privately controlled. The latter was not only true in 1899, but was still true in 1961. In my father's time there were, of course, no Negro college graduates in the community, a fact that had an influence on the aspirations any parent in the community might have for his children.

The only colored person that I had ever seen who had attended even a second-rate college was a cousin of mine by the name of J. E. Johnson. Professor Johnson was co-founder and principal of Prentiss Institute at Prentiss, Mississippi, of which institution he served as the executive head until his death. He was a good deal older than I, but during his vacation season he would occasionally visit our home and give my parents, particularly my father, the benefit of such knowledge as he had acquired at Alcorn College, the state college, which though named a college, was hardly equivalent to first-grade high school. Professor Johnson's father was, I believe, the only blood brother that my mother had. She had several half-brothers on both her mother's and her father's side and two half-sisters on her mother's side. I was fortunate in having a mother as well as a father who came from good stock, both of their families having been outstanding for their constructive citizenship.

Most of the money I earned was spent in assisting my father to operate the farm to which he had been compelled to move on a more economic or cash basis. I purchased fertilizer and supplied meat, flour, and other provisions so that he would not have to mortgage his crops before they were planted or harvested in order to secure these necessities. I got the impression that all the people who lived in town dressed well and were more intelligent than those who lived in the country; also, they seemed more prosperous otherwise than did the country folk. In order to harmonize with that impression and to conform to the tradition, I spent a good deal of my remaining money on my personal apparel.

I made periodic visits to McComb, my home town, from Strater because every Sunday an excursion train ran from New Orleans to McComb, and the round-trip fare from New Orleans to any point en route was a dollar. The train would pass through Strater around ten o'clock in the morning going to McComb and return around eight o'clock at night, which meant that one would have from around twelve o'clock noon to five or six o'clock in the afternoon in McComb to visit and fraternize with friends for a dollar. There would be some twelve or fifteen cars. All the cars became so filled with passengers that no more than fifty per cent of the people had seats, while others stood in the aisles and in the vestibules. Nobody expected to make the round trip without observing at least a half dozen fights and a dozen or more people being left behind in each important station on the return. This was simply a part of the weekly experience of the excursion rider.

It was in connection with one of my excursion visits to my home community that I called on a young woman in whom I had been interested. While there her brother told me that there was a school in Alabama by the name of Tuskegee Institute, about which I had never heard, where a student could work his way through school and select any trade or vocation of his choice. He showed me a catalogue that he had received from the school and gave me some detailed account of his plan to enter Tuskegee the next school year. I took down the name of the registrar, who at that time was J. H. Palmer, and wrote him for a catalogue, which I subsequently received. In the course of a few months my application to enter the school had been accepted and I was on my way to Tuskegee Institute with sixty-five dollars, plus railroad fare, in my pocket.

IV

Student Days at Tuskegee

I arrived at Tuskegee on Sunday morning, September 6, 1906. At that time there was a combination passenger, milk, and freight train that ran from the town of Tuskegee to Chehaw, Alabama, a distance of five miles. Chehaw is located about forty-eight miles from Montgomery on the main line of the Atlanta and West Point Railroad, running from Atlanta to Montgomery. As I recall, this Chehaw–Tuskegee train made two trips every day—morning and afternoon. Under these circumstances it would wait for passengers coming from both Montgomery and Atlanta, as the trains were sometimes an hour apart in arriving, in order to accommodate the passengers going to Tuskegee who came from the direction of either Atlanta or Montgomery.

Because of the large volume of traffic, including students and visitors from all over the United States and other parts of the world, forming a constant source of revenue coming to Tuskegee, Booker Washington was able to have the railroad track extended from the town out to the school campus, a distance of a mile. Whenever distinguished guests came to Tuskegee before the track was extended to the school, it was necessary for them to be met either at Chehaw with a carriage or a buggy or in the town of Tuskegee. I remember hearing Booker Washington in the Congress Hotel in Saratoga Springs one night inviting his hearers to visit Tuskegee. He stated that it was possible now for persons to ride a train from Chehaw up to the school campus. He said that while the railroad from Chehaw to the school was only six miles long, it was as wide as the New

York Central. There was a family of Pattersons who operated a hack service from the town of Tuskegee to the school for twenty-five cents per passenger.

As I read the catalogue, I was primarily concerned with the portion dealing with the circumstances under which an industrious student might, while working at his trade, earn enough money to pay his tuition, room, and board. I did not differentiate, however, between the earning possibilities of a day student and a night school student. One could not go beyond the b-middle class, which corresponded to the sophomore class in college, in night school. When a student qualified to enter the a-middle class, which corresponded to the junior grade in college, he had to enter day school; he only had to spend the senior year in the day school. Neither did I inform myself adequately, if at all, concerning the fact that students wore a uniform to classroom and chapel. The only time a student was not compelled to wear a uniform was on the days he was working at his trade or vocation; and he also was not required to be in uniform in such other social activities as he might engage in during that day. He alternated one day in the academic department pursuing academic studies with a day in the industrial or vocational department participating in the theory and practical application of his chosen vocation. If I had more clearly understood the matter with respect to the regulation for the wearing of uniforms, I would have spent much less money on civilian clothing.

I remember I was wearing a new suit that I had bought at Samuel Bonaparte on Rampart Street in New Orleans and a genuine Panama hat that I had paid five dollars for. That same hat today would cost fifteen or twenty dollars. I drove upon the campus and entered the Commandant's Office for registration smoking a Cremo cigar. Capt. C. B. Hosmer, one of the cadet officers from the State of Louisiana, took me aside and gave me a brief orientation concerning the rules and regulations with respect to students smoking cigars. That afternoon I attended a meeting of the Mississippi State Club. It was customary on Sunday afternoons for the students from the different states to meet under the auspices of the state clubs. As new students came in, they identified themselves with their respective states and enrolled as bona fide club members. This was purely a social organization where new students would have a chance to meet with their state-mates, who would seek to welcome the new ones and make them feel less homesick, giving such helpful information as would assist them in becoming acquainted with the rules and regulations. It was always possible to identify a newcomer. He was usually introduced and given an opportunity to state his particular section, give his name, the city or county from which he had come, and so forth. At the conclusion of the state meeting on my first Sunday afternoon on the Tuskegee campus, a young fellow by the name of Wysinger, from near Kosciusko, Mississippi, engaged me in conversation and pledged himself to assist me in any way possible in the selection of class, school day, or industry. He was a member of the junior class, which corresponded to freshman class in college, and suggested that I apply for admission to join his class and section. This suggestion proved most beneficial. The following morning I went into the office of the late Dr. David G. Houston, a classmate of Theodore Roosevelt and who later became principal of the Armstrong High School in Washington, D.C., who at that time was director of the Academic Department of Tuskegee Institute, and told him I wanted to enter the junior class. At that time the majority of the students entering Tuskegee, or any other Negro college, who came from a rural district had no transcript or certificate of graduation. As a process of adjustment they were assigned to a class, and on the basis of their performance they either entered the assignment given or were demoted or promoted. Frequently when doubt was entertained as to their educational background, they were given an examination. Mr. Houston was sufficiently impressed with my "brass" to assign me to a class—though one grade below that to which I requested to be assigned—without an examination. Had I been given an examination, I would have made a class at least two grades lower than the one to which I was assigned. This means that the suggestions of Wysinger saved me at least two years. I spent the first month or six weeks trying to familiarize myself with the subject matter and become sufficiently acquainted with the assignments given to make an intelligent evaluation and recitation. Once this difficulty was overcome I was able to make satisfactory progress.

I became actively identified with different campus organizations, such as the Debating Societies, the midweek Prayer Meetings, Y.M.C.A., the school choir, and the Glee Club, and participated in other extracurricular activities. I became such an important member of the bass division of the choir that the choir directress, Mrs. Lee, requested that I be excused from drill duty. This fact became significant when the Commandant, during my second year, made me a commissioned officer with the grade of Second Lieutenant without my ever participating in the military requirement of drilling. All male students on their school days were required to wear their uniforms and go through drilling exercises an hour before coming to class. They also marched to chapel in military formation on Sundays. When the other commissioned officers, including First and Second Lieutenants, Adjutants, and Captains, learned that I had been made Second Lieutenant, they registered a protest on the grounds that I never came out on the drill ground or participated in any military exercises or other military activities. The Commandant took the position that the influence that I was exercising on the total student body qualified me for the honor that he had conferred and that my presence honored the staff more than the appointment honored me.

In selecting my vocation I chose carpentry and architecture. I decided that I was going to be a contractor and builder. During my second year, I was elected to the presidency of the Y.M.C.A., and as a member of a glee club traveled through the New England States in the interest of Tuskegee. During the summer of 1907, which was the end of my first school year, I went to Birmingham to work in the blast furnace of the Tennessee Iron and Coal Company. An employee could put in as many hours per day as he desired. I was anxious to bring my sister to Tuskegee so that she also might have a chance for training in that environment, so I decided to work all day and half the night. Eight hours had not become a standardized working day at that time, so I worked ten hours—from seven o'clock in the morning until six o'clock in the evening—with half an hour off for lunch. I went back at seven o'clock and worked until twelve o'clock at night.

I ate a lot of poorly cooked, and undoubtedly, more poorly selected food, and developed a serious case of chronic indigestion. When I returned to school I had saved some one hundred and seventy-five dollars, which would be equivalent to four or five hundred dollars at the present time, but because of the treatment I had given my digestive organs I was unable to remain in school more than three weeks. A part of that time was spent in the hospital. Dr. Kenny diagnosed my case as chronic indigestion and advised me to leave school. This was a devastating decision, and momentarily it appeared that my whole ambition and desire for an education had come to a tragic ending. I was so depressed and discouraged that I felt I was approaching the end of the chapter.

I left Tuskegee without informing members of my family or anybody else where I was going, and for some six months my family received no word from me. Letters sent to the school were returned and the school officials were unable to give the sender any information as to my whereabouts. I somehow felt defeated and despondent. I finally secured a job with a physician driving his buggy as he called on his patients, for four dollars a week and board. It was also my responsibility to feed the horse and keep him well-groomed.

I had spent a considerable portion of the money I had saved during the summer for my bill from the doctor in Montgomery before I was able to find employment. This fact made it necessary for me to economize in every way possible once I found a job. Being able to find a room for a dollar and a half a week made it possible for me to deposit in the bank two dollars out of my four dollars-a-week income.

My indigestion had developed to the point where a glass of water gave me as much discomfort as eating a pound of steak or half a peck of potatoes. Through changing physicians, when there seemed no response to treatment, and making inquiries, I finally was advised to see a colored physician by the name of Dr. Dunjee. The first thing he recommended was that I stop drinking coffee and start drinking hot water before and after meals. Until this day, hot water is my choice beverage, and for many years I have drunk coffee only occasionally when I wanted to remain awake beyond my usual bed time hour or in the morning when I have been up unusually late at night, and then it has to be very weak.

I arrived in Montgomery around the first of October and remained under the constant treatment by one physician or another until the first of May the following year, which was 1908. I had sufficiently recovered by the last of May to return to Tuskegee to witness the commencement exercises. I entered night school and made sufficient progress by the time day sessions opened in the early part of September to rejoin the class with which I was identified before leaving school on account of ill health.

At that time, the tuition was ten dollars and the board was eight dollars a month. I received no financial aid from any source from the time I entered until I was graduated. In addition to paying my own expenses at the beginning of the school year, September,

1908, I had my sister enter Tuskegee, and I became responsible not only for her transportation to Tuskegee but for all of her expenses, including clothing, while she was in attendance at the school and until her graduation.

Through my participation in various extracurricular activities, I made rapid progress in the consideration given me by members of the student body when it came to the election of officers and appointments to important committees. The cabinet of the Young Men's Christian Association elected me to its presidency at the beginning of the school year 1908–1909. I had heard nothing about Student Council at that time, but it occurred to me that some organization composed of representatives of the upper classes should form some type of federation and become interested in and concerned about the academic and social behavior of the entire student body. With that as a background, I organized the first Student Council on the Tuskegee campus. This Council developed to such a point in the appreciation of the administration that we were permitted to pass judgment on the ill behavior of the students and to make recommendations to the Executive Council for disposition. I do not recall a single instance—there certainly were not many, if any—where the Executive Council did not accept and approve of the recommendations of our committee on discipline.

The one thing that I was able to do which attracted Booker Washington's attention and gave me important status in his consideration was to break up what was called a "Flag Rush." I did not know the history of this enterprise, but it had become unnecessarily brutal and even hazardous, and in my judgment it did not require or reflect any additional attainment or cultural imagination. It operated in this fashion. On the last week in December, leading up to the first of January, some members of the senior class would hide away in the attic of either the academic building or Rockefeller Hall of the Dining Hall. On the morning of January 1 they were to hoist a flag, under which the members of the junior class were suppose to be compelled to march if they went either to the Dining Hall or to the Academic Building. Students would defy the members of the Commandant's staff or the faculty in participating in this annual flag-raising project. Members of the junior class—on the other hand—were to see that this flag was not, hoisted by the seniors. The occasion was characterized by physical fights and sometimes with deadly weapons. On one occasion a member of the junior class had hidden away in a classroom in the Academic Building with a shotgun, and when the members of the senior class came out on the roof of the Dining Hall to raise the flag, sometime between midnight and day, a shot was fired and a member of the senior class was slightly wounded.

Mr. Washington was always fearful that some student would be killed in the annual "Flag Rush." I decided to break it up and was successful in doing the thing that would seem almost unbelievable. There were one hundred and fifty members in my class. I called them together and got them to agree that the members of the junior class on New Year's Day, instead of following the tradition of participating in a flag-raising episode, would go over to Dorothy Hall, the building that housed the girls' industries, and have a New Year's breakfast and dance. All of the members of the class—boys and girls were to leave their dormitories as early as five o'clock in the morning—it was still dark, of course, at that early hour in January—and come directly to Dorothy Hall, which meant that they would get out of the building before any members of the senior class had an opportunity to observe their movements.

In order to make this arrangement official, I had to get the approval of the Dean of Women. I had an interview with Miss Susie Porter, who was Dean of Women at the time, and lay the proposition before her. She was in disagreement with the idea. She took the position that I, as president of the class, should simply issue a decree and that the class should adhere to it. I took an appeal from her decision to Mrs. Booker Washington. Mrs.

Washington was in sympathetic accord with my idea and advised me to proceed, saying that she would stand between Miss Porter and me if any complaint was made by Miss Porter to the Executive Council. The incident ought to have been sent to Ripley for his "Believe It Or Not."

This wholesale operation was carried out as planned: not a single member of the junior class had provided a leakage of any information concerning the contemplated plan to any member of the senior class. The seniors became the laughing stock of the whole school community, because they had hoisted the flag and stood on guard to see that it was not interfered with by any member of the junior class, who would have been compelled to march under it if he went into the Dining Hall, because the flag was hoisted before the main entrance of the Dining Hall. When not a single junior entered the Dining Hall for either breakfast, lunch or dinner on New Year's Day, 1910, the seniors were so humiliated that they left their flag hanging and had to be requested by the Commandant to take it down.

This manner of disposing of the "Flag Rush" greatly pleased Mr. Washington and brought a sigh of relief to Mrs. Washington. From that time until his death, Mr. Washington seemed to have a rather peculiar interest in and regard for the person who was then president of the junior class.

The question of food in any educational institution is always one around which you can mobilize mass action and stimulate widespread protest. There was almost universal criticism of the food that was being served to the students. An occasional formalized expression of protest was made, by sending committees to the steward. During the school year of 1909–1910, this food issue became so acute that it culminated in a student strike. Finally a committee was appointed to submit a list of minimum demands in terms of quality and quantity of food to the steward of the dining hall, asking the steward to indicate which of the demands he had the authority and resources to satisfy and which ones would need to be presented to the Business Agent's Office for consideration. The steward would always receive committees making complaints and agree to improve his services both qualitatively and quantitatively, and for the first two or three days after the committee had waited on him there would be recognized and appreciable improvement as above indicated. By the third or fourth day, his services would always drop back to what they were when the protest was registered.

My committee made out a list of demands which we decided were the minimum and took them to the steward, asking which of these he could guarantee to satisfy, and he in his own hand placed an "O.K." opposite each item and promised that he would comply therewith. My committee was composed of seven members. I asked each member to take a day, on which he would make a list of all the food served, so that we had a complete list of every item of food served on seven consecutive days. It was noticeable on the first two or three days that the food was more plentiful, but beginning on the fourth day a reduction in food, according to the steward's tradition, became obvious, and by the seventh day we were served no more, and perhaps less, than was being served the day before we made the complaint.

Mr. Washington was away during most of the summer. When he returned, he called the students together in a body and talked with them about their general health habits and then, as if to drop dynamite in the meeting, he asked if they were getting plenty to eat. This question brought every student to his feet in a resounding chorus of "No" reverberating in the assembly room of the Carnegie Library. He asked them why they did not appoint a committee to bring their complaint to the steward, and the answer was that a committee had been appointed and had seen the steward. He asked the committee to stand. We stood. He excused the committee from work that afternoon and requested that it make its report to his office at four o'clock. We were there at the stipulated time. After hearing our report, Mr. Washington sent for the steward and said to him, among other things, that "this school is run for the students primarily, and it is a very serious thing for a teacher to fail to keep his word with the students." The final outcome was, that the steward was transferred from the dining hall to the Bookkeeping Department and his former position was, filled by a graduate of Tuskegee Institute by the name of Edward L. Snyder. Mr. Washington had asked me if I knew a graduate of Tuskegee who I thought could handle the dining hall. I had suggested Snyder. It happened that Snyder was then at Tuskegee attending summer school, and Mr. Washington requested that I go and find him. Snyder was brought in for a conference with Mr. Washington, and at the end of thirty days he was appointed to the post.

I had chosen as my vocation carpentry and architecture and had decided to become a building contractor. I was moving calculatively in that direction. At that time the student body numbered around thirteen hundred. Our dining hall was on the ground floor of what was known as the old Alabama Hall, which had a seating capacity of around nine hundred. This meant that when the dining hall bell would ring, especially on cold days or rainy days, every student would do a "Jesse Owens" (a hundred-yard dash) in order to get into the dining hall before its seating capacity was reached. It reminded you more of a subway experience in New York than anything else I know. Those who could not get in on the first serving had to wait outside in good weather; when it was raining or cold, they would have to go to either the office building or the academic building and wait for the second shift.

Mr. Washington was able to secure sufficient funds from philanthropic and public-spirited citizens to build a dining hall known as Thompkins Hall, which had both a teachers' dining hall and a students' dining hall. The student's dining hall had a seating capacity of twenty-three hundred. The students in the upper classes were given an opportunity to compete for the privilege of representing the student body in the dedicatory exercises. In the competitive effort my paper was selected. At that time the Trustee Board was composed of such persons as Theodore Roosevelt, William G. Wilcox, William J. Schiefflien, George Foster Peabody, Julius Rosenwald, the Masons of Massachusetts, and the like. The Trustees came down to witness the dedicatory program. I attempted to do two things on that occasion: first, to express for the total student body its appreciation for having a dining hall with large enough seating capacity to permit the total student body to sit down in comfort all at one time and enjoy their meal; second, I tried to point out what technical skills or mechanized culture the students in the different departments had acquired in the construction of the new hall. The brick masons excavated the foundation and erected the walls; the carpenters hung the doors and windows and built the stairways; the tinsmiths made the roofing; the steam-fitters and plumbers installed the heating system; the electricians wired the building and the painters gave color to the situation.

The composition of my paper and its delivery so impressed the Trustees that several of them wrote notes to Mr. Washington while I was still speaking, inquiring as to how long I had been in the school, what my classification was, and so forth. When Mr. Wilcox returned to New York he sent me a check for fifty dollars. Students of this generation would not appreciate what that meant. Nobody on Wall Street had anything on me when I opened the letter and found this check. That experience caused a complete change in the course of my life.

Mr. Washington said to Dr. Emmett J. Scott, "This is the type of young man we want to represent Tuskegee in making friends for the institution in the North. When he graduates we want to select him as Field Secretary." I was graduated the last of May 1911, and on the first of June I became Field Secretary and was authorized to establish headquarters in Rochester, New York. I have not seen a hammer since.

During the summer of 1910, the writer was in charge of the school's choir of some fifty voices. This group of singers was excused from their respective assignments three or four times a week for an hour or more for the purpose of rehearsing the music scheduled for rendition during midweek Prayer Meeting and at the Sunday morning chapel hour. Reverend Whittaker, the school's Chaplain, stated for the record that the summer choir of 1910 rendered the most satisfactory musical program of any summer choir during his official connection with the institution, which covered some twenty-five years.

Because of the leadership which I seemed to have supplied for the various activities and the esteem in which I was held by the students and faculty, for the first and only time, as far as I know, a reception was tendered a student by the students and teachers while he was still a member of the student body.

V

Booker Washington Held
in High Esteem

Students and teachers alike idolized Booker T. Washington. In all of my experience I have never seen any one person who was so universally admired, respected, and loved, as was Booker Washington. The attitude was expressed not only by the people in the school community, but also by the people in Greenwood Village, the town of Tuskegee, and the County of Macon.

The student body was composed of some thirteen hundred students, ranging in age from fifteen to fifty and representing all parts of the United States and such foreign countries as the West Indies, the Virgin Islands, and Cuba and the Continent of Africa. Among them were ministers who had had experience in pasturing churches and were increasing their theological equipment at the Phelps Hall Bible Training School. There were politicians, men who had held political jobs, many who had been heads of families, others who had been housewives or persons whose employment covered a multiplicity of categories, as well as representatives of the younger element of the population. Many of these people had had the kind of experience which would have enabled them to penetrate deception and hypocrisy. This fact gave added significance to the statement made above with respect to the universality of the reaction of the total community toward the "sage of Tuskegee," affectionately referred to as "Pa Booker."

Dr. Washington spent a good deal of his time away from the school responding to the demands made upon him by all kinds of organizations and agencies to deliver addresses, to give counsel and advice as a member of the boards of trustees of different Negro colleges, and to supply leadership for many foundations concerned with the educational, social, and economic status of Negroes. Sometimes he would return to the institution unannounced. You could always tell, however, when his homecoming was anticipated. The people in Greenwood Village would mow their lawns if the grass had perchance grown unattractively. Students and teachers would busy themselves picking up all paper from the grounds and removing any unsightly object that might detract from the beautiful appearance of the Institution. It was the general agreement among all parties concerned that everything must be in "shipshape order when Pa Booker arrives tomorrow."

This cooperative response on the part of the people on the campus and in the community was motivated not by fear, but rather by a passionate desire on the part of everyone to please and make glad the heart of the community's benefactor. I never heard a student or teacher question any decision Mr. Washington made, even though it might involve the suspension or even the expulsion of a student or the severing of the official connection of a teacher. There seems to have been an agreement or a feeling on the part of all concerned that whatever decision Mr. Washington made, it was non-prejudicial and was predicated, as far as was humanly possible, upon the actual or alleged facts in hand.

One of his admonitions to students was not to take more food upon their plates than they were going to eat in order that no food would be wasted. I have known students to have completed a meal—so much as they had planned to eat—leaving some food on their plates. If suddenly Mr. Washington would appear at some point in the dining hall, that information would quickly gain circulation throughout the dining hall and, as if a new appetite had been created, students would with dispatch and precision quickly consume every morsel of food that had been taken on their plates.

Mr. Washington was critical of any aspect of untidiness. His homecoming meant replacing buttons on all garments to be worn where he might observe and seeing that shoes were properly shined. As further evidence of the assertion that this behavior was not influenced by fear it is only necessary to describe what frequently happened to houses adjacent to a highway where Mr. Washington would travel. Going into churches or schoolhouses in the rural areas of Macon County or some other county in the state, he urged people to beautify their premises. If they did not have paint, he would suggest they whitewash their houses, including their barns and outhouses. It was not an unaccustomed experience to discover that a farmer had whitewashed his house or barn on the side facing the direction from which Mr. Washington's party would approach his house, and to find that on the other side of the house not a drop of paint or whitewash had been applied.

It is difficult to describe in mere words the influence this one person exerted upon the behavior pattern of all the people, white and colored, with whom he came into intimate contact.

Booker Washington's Cabinet

It was the custom of Booker Washington at the turn of the century, and continuing until his death, to travel through some one Southern state every year. He usually chartered a Pullman for the transportation and comfort of his party. The trains on the main trunk lines would sidetrack his car onto a spur in the city where a meeting was scheduled for a given date.

In order to develop a community of fellowship, Dr. Washington handpicked one or more outstanding, well-known Negroes in each of the several Southern states. A sizable percentage of this cabinet, through alteration, would become a part of the Booker Washington party each year as it moved through the chosen state.

Included among his cabinet for the State of Florida was a man by the name of Charlie Anderson, of Jacksonville, and James H. Blodgett, a contractor; from the State of Alabama: Victor Tulane, of Montgomery, and Dr. J. Mason, of Birmingham; from Mississippi: I. T. Montgomery and Charles Banks, of Mt. Bayou; from Louisiana: Wallie E. Cohen and Whitfield McKinley; in Arkansas: Judge Scipio Jones, John Webb, and J. E. Bush; in Texas: Dr. R. L. Smith of Waco; in Tennessee: J. C. Napier, Henry Allen Boyd of Nashville, and Thomas Hayes, of Memphis; in South Carolina: W. T. Andrews, of Sumter; in North Carolina: Dr. J. I. Leavy, C. C. Spaulding, and Berry O'Kelley; in Virginia: R. R. Moton; in the District of Columbia: Judge James Cobb; in New York State: Dr. E. P. Roberts, Honorable Charles W. Anderson, and Fred R. Moore; in Massachusetts: David Crawford and Dr. J. E. Courtney.

Very few important decisions of nation-wide significance did Booker Washington make without consulting some one or several of the members of his cabinet. Once a decision was made, he could rely almost one hundred per cent upon the support of his cabinet.

Mr. Washington insisted that there be no racial earmarks, that anything done or taught at Tuskegee or appearing in the buildings and on the ground not suggest that they were occupied by or in control of Negroes.

The question of time as an element of decision and action was emphasized. It did not matter how the elements behaved, he insisted that programs should start at the scheduled time. He would accept no excuse for a job being poorly done or a person being late because of the condition of the weather or otherwise. In other words, events moved on schedule with the same clocklike precision as the Pennsylvania Limited. Any teacher or student associated with an unfinished task or under the control of a job half-done or poorly performed found himself in a most uncomfortable position in the presence of Booker Washington. As the institution grew and extended the borders of its influence, Booker

Washington was called upon by persons in all parts of the nation to pass judgment upon or give sanction to agencies and enterprises of various types and character calculated to enhance the welfare of Negroes in particular and the entire community in general.

The first farm demonstration agent appointed by the Department of Agriculture was a graduate of Tuskegee Institute from the Department of Agriculture: Thomas M. Campbell. In cooperation with the United States Department of Agriculture, Tuskegee Institute provided headquarters for Mr. T. M. Campbell and a school on wheels. This school consisted of two well-groomed mules, a wagon, and a plow. With this equipment Campbell would go from one farm to another and teach the farmers how to plow their land, as well as the importance of growing sufficient feed so that their animals might be well-fed and in condition to satisfactorily carry their rightful share of the load in the conduct and management of a well-managed farm. The success of this school on wheels persuaded the United States Secretary of Agriculture to expand the program by employing additional farm demonstration agents, both white and colored, and subsequently to add women in the category of home demonstration agents.

Members of the senior class of the Institute were sent out in the county to do practice teaching, which represented a type of extension service that revolutionized the educational procedure in the rural schools for a radius of ten, fifteen, or twenty miles from the institution. Farmers were taught and encouraged to grow livestock and poultry for their own home consumption and for the commercial market. A new day dawned, for the citizens of Macon County at first and finally for the State of Alabama, with the establishment of Tuskegee Institute.

Booker Washington manifested a keen and sensitive interest in every phase of community development and every department of the institution. He kept in daily touch with Tuskegee Institute both when he was on the campus and when he was away. When he was off on his money-raising trips and fulfilling the demands for him to speak or associate himself with some important enterprise away from the school, he required that his secretary send him an institutional digest every day.

In 1898 Dr. Frederick Ludwig Hoffman, in his book entitled "Race Traits and Tendencies of the American Negro," prophesied that, because of the abnormally high death rate of Negroes from tuberculosis, that tuberculosis alone would solve the problem of the Negro in a hundred years. As the information in this book gained currency, insurance companies rejected Negro risks or loaded the premiums so that there was a differential between what the Negro paid and what his contemporaries in the white community paid for the same protection. The Negro's reaction to this book manifested itself in many different ways. Letters of protest were written to Dr. Hoffman, indignation meetings were held, and resolutions were passed denouncing Hoffman as an unfriendly representative of the white community, if not an enemy to the Negro. Booker Washington took a different attitude from that of the majority of the members of his race. He employed a person who had majored in research at Chicago University, by the name of Monroe Work. Dr. Work was assigned the task of actualizing tables supplying comparative data on the mortality and mobility rates of Negroes and the white race, particularly in the area of tuberculosis. Work's research revealed the fact that Negroes were dying two, three, four, and sometimes five times faster than white people from tuberculosis. However, he suggested that the death rate had more sociological than biological significance. Negroes had not been exposed to the sources of health information, and their low earning power did not enable them to provide themselves with the kind of medical care that was available to a sizable percentage of the members of the other group. He convinced Booker Washington that there was a close relationship between mental mobility and physical mortality.

With this background information Booker Washington initiated what came to be known as National Negro Health Week. During the month of April each year Negroes in every city in the United States where their numbers were conspicuously large were encouraged to observe this Negro Health Week. The campaign for better education began on one Sunday with a sermon from the pulpit of every church and terminated the following Sunday with a summary of what had taken place during the week. Physicians, teachers, social workers, and lay citizens were invited to speak at all types of meetings. Dr. Work would supply the sponsor of these meetings with factual information concerning the comparative death rates and on the positive side gave some information as to how to acquire and exercise good health habits, including mental hygiene. This Negro Health Week demonstration became so universally accepted and its results became so manifest that in many cities and communities the white people participated in the "clean up and paint up" campaign, and many business concerns gave prizes to the city or community that did the best over-all job in providing a better physical environment for good living. Finally the Negro Health Week program was taken over and financed by the federal government as a federalized institution.

Significantly enough, forty years after Hoffman wrote his book, and largely as a result of this intensive health education campaign conducted by civic leaders all over the nation, the Negro death rate was lower than the white death rate was when Hoffman wrote his book. This is one example, and there are many others, which suggest the wholesome and helpful influence that Tuskegee Institute exerted on the welfare status of Negroes in particular and the total community in general.

The National Negro Farmers Conference attracted Negroes annually to Tuskegee from all over the South for a two-day workshop experience, with crop rotation, soil conservation, and cooperative marketing among the themes, which engaged the attention of farmers and their families for two full days. The first day was headlined as the "farmers' conference"; the second day, as the "workers' conference." In the former group were "dirt farmers" for the most part; the latter group was composed largely of farm demonstration agents, home economics workers, teachers of agriculture, and landowners. Improvised housing arrangements were provided for the farmers who came distances that made it impractical for them to return and come back the next day. For two days these hundreds, and ultimately thousands, of people were guests of Tuskegee Institute. They received free housing accommodations and free food. In addition to the above, through Booker Washington's contacts and resourcefulness, Tuskegee Institute became the first interracial forum where white people from the North and white people of the South and Negroes from both North and South could meet and discuss problems common to all of them on the basis of complete equality. Thus Tuskegee became not only an institution of learning, but an idea—it was more than an intercultural clinic, it was an intersectional, interracial, and international forum.

Extracurricular, Off-the-Campus Leadership of Booker T. Washington

A good deal has been written and said about the circumstances under which Booker Washington passed his entrance examination at Hampton Institute. Because of his hitchhiking method of traveling from West Virginia to Hampton Institute—sleeping on the ground, under bridges, and otherwise gathering dust and dirt—when he arrived at the Registration Office at Hampton, he presented anything but an inviting appearance. A Miss Mackey, a white person in charge of the registration, who was sympathetic with anyone who was seeking an education, through brief inquiry discovered that he had little or no background of an academic nature. As a process of elimination she assigned him a task of sweeping and dusting a room. When he completed the assignment he returned to the office of registration. When the teacher went into the room to check on his performance, she was surprised to find that even with a white pocket handkerchief she could find no dirt or dust remaining. She returned to her desk and acknowledged her surprise by saying, "I guess you qualify for admission."

A good deal has been written and said about this method of matriculation on Booker Washington's part. One other thing, though, placed concurrently with this action, has not been published. Booker had one name when he arrived. As he listened to other students registering, he discovered that most of them had at least two and some three names: John Fillmore Anderson, for example. He made up his mind that since he had an opportunity of giving himself a name, he would choose the biggest name in the world as far as he knew. Instead of naming himself Booker T. Smith, Jones or Thomas, he chose Washington. George Washington was the biggest name he had ever known.

This attitude toward bigness was demonstrated again when it came to the purchasing of land on which to build Tuskegee Institute. When Harvard University was founded in 1636, the overseers had adequate money to buy all the land that they thought they needed. They purchased one and one-eighth acres of ground. Booker Washington had no money; he borrowed the money to purchase the land from the Treasurer of Hampton Institute, and with it he purchased twenty-three hundred acres. We are led to suppose that he said in giving himself a name, "I am going to give myself the biggest name in the world." When he purchased the land for the building of the school, he must have said, "I am going to build the largest Institute of learning in the control of Negroes in the world." He could not think in small terms.

When Tuskegee was founded, the State of Alabama appropriated two thousand dollars for the purpose of paying teachers' salaries. For forty years after the Institute's foundation, the legislature was still appropriating two thousand dollars. This fact made it necessary for Booker Washington to spend the major portion of his time traveling through the North and East raising money with which to meet the current operating expenses of the Institute and money to build dormitories to house the students and an academic building where they could be taught. These duties were sufficiently exacting and inescapable to occupy the full time and attention and engage all of the energies of any normal person. In spite of these ever-present obligations of an acute financial nature, Booker Washington concerned himself with every phase of Negro development and achievement. In 1900 he founded the National Negro Business League, in the city of Boston, Massachusetts. Up to that time there was no coordinating relationship between a Negro businessman in Alabama and his contemporary in Mississippi, Florida, Virginia, or Massachusetts. Affiliated with and participating in the program of the Business League were representatives of professions, insurance executives, and heads of financial institutions. As the number of representatives of these affiliated organizations grew, it became more difficult for a representative of each of them to have adequate scheduled time on the program of the League in its two-day annual sessions. Under these circumstances and in the light of the condition indicated, Booker Washington encouraged Perry W. Howard in the organizing of the National Negro Bar Association. He influenced C. C. Spaulding in the organizing of the National Negro Insurance Association. He suggested to B. J. Franklin, of Chattanooga, Tennessee, that he organize the National Funeral Directors Association. Almost simultaneously with this effort he released J. R. E. Lee, who was head of the Academic Department of Tuskegee Institute, from his duties at the school to travel across the South and organize Negro teachers into a national organized entity.

In 1895, five years prior to the organization of the Negro Business League, Booker Washington asked Dr. I. Garland Penn to spearhead the movement. Dr. Penn organized a National Negro Medical Association in the City of Atlanta. Three years later Mr. Washington influenced Dr. A. H. Kinnebrew to organize a State Medical Association of Negro Physicians in the State of Alabama. Thus the influence and active concern of Booker Washington for the total development of the members of his group can be traced to the beginning of the National Negro Farmers Association, the National Negro Medical Association, the National Negro Teachers Association, the National Negro Insurance Association, the National Negro Funeral Association, and the National Negro Bar Association. He established the Phelps Hall Bible Training School for the training of Negro ministers. Some one or several of these organizations touched the development of the Negro at some point in every section of the country and on every cultural level.

In 1908 Booker Washington had a conference with a Quaker lady of Pennsylvania who inquired of him in the course of the conversation what in his judgment was the greatest need in the rural South in the area of Negro education. Booker Washington replied that in his opinion some type of pre-vocational training and some measure of standardization would fall in the category concerning which Miss Annie T. Jean was inquiring. In accepting Booker Washington's appraisal of the need, Miss Jean placed at the disposal of Booker Washington and Dr. Hollis Burks Frissell, who was then president of Hampton Institute, one million dollars, the interest on which was to be used to employ what came to be known as "Jean's teachers." A Jean's teacher was given the work of supervision and the responsibility of a county representative in Negro communities under the supervision of the county superintendent. In the course of events, for all practical purposes the Jean's teacher became an assistant county superintendent of education. Dr. Washington recommended Dr. James H. Dillard, a white person who was then a member of the faculty at Tulane University in New Orleans, as the first Director of the Jean's Fund. Dr. Dillard worked out an arrangement with the county superintendent whereby the Fund would pay the salaries of the teachers on condition that the county pay their travel expenses until a demonstration could be made of the real value of the program and the assistance given to the superintendent in the selection of the teachers and in a supervisory relationship to the school program. When that was done to the satisfaction of the local superintendent, he was able to get the county to assume responsibility for part of the Jean's teacher's salary. Progressively, therefore, the Jean's fund contributed less money for the salaries of the teacher, and the counties themselves contributed more. The last count I had of the number of Jean's teachers then employed had increased from one in Hancock County around 1909 to 1910 to four hundred seventy-five in 1952.

Booker Washington persuaded Julius Rosenwald[1] to make a demonstration of a rural school in which the principal and his wife would live with and thereby take advantage of that fact to teach the students who came from homes with little or no educational background something about proper homemaking. An acre or more of land was purchased near the school so that the students could be taught how to grow vegetables, and the like. Rosenwald was so pleased with the results of this investment of three thousand dollars that he agreed to give a dollar to any county for every dollar it raised from any source toward the building of a school. These schools eventually came to be known as Rosenwald Schools. Subsequently he extended the offer to the State of Alabama and finally to every state in the South. By 1930 approximately thirty-three per cent of all Negro children attending rural schools were housed in Rosenwald Schools.

---

1 An American businessman and philanthropist.

In the early 1900's the Y.M.C.A. leaders of the City of Chicago set out to raise two million dollars with which to build branch Y.M.C.A. buildings in different sections of Chicago. Notwithstanding the fact that Rosenwald was a Jew and could not at that time become a member of the Y.M.C.A., knowing his liberal attitude, the committee approached him for a contribution. He had a Gentile secretary by the name of Graves. Mr. Graves knew of the close friendship between Dr. George Cleveland Hall[2] of Chicago and Booker Washington. He stated to Hall that he believed that if Booker Washington could reach Mr. Rosenwald before he made a decision as to the amount he would contribute to the Y.M.C.A., it might be possible to get a branch Y.M.C.A. for Negroes. Hall called Booker Washington by long-distance telephone and gave him the story, and Mr. Washington in turn talked with Mr. Rosenwald by telephone. As a result, when the committee returned to get Mr. Rosenwald's final answer, and he inquired what they had planned to do for Negro men and boys, they admitted that they had made no plans as such. He agreed to give two hundred fifty thousand dollars upon the condition that they would allocate twenty-five thousand dollars of it toward the building of a Negro Y.M.C.A., to which their central fund should put in seventy-five thousand dollars. He extended this offer to many other cities with large Negro populations until he had influenced the building of Y.M.C.A.'s for Negro men and boys in the cities of Pittsburgh, Pennsylvania, Detroit, Michigan, Indianapolis, Indiana, Baltimore, Maryland, New York City and Brooklyn, New York, the District of Columbia, and Atlanta, Georgia.

In 1906 Andrew Carnegie came down to Tuskegee to witness and participate in the dedicatory program of a Carnegie library, the cost of which he had contributed through Booker Washington. The day following the dedicatory program he was just browsing around and stumbled into the office of the Treasurer. There he

---

2 A noted physician and Negro Life historian.

became interested in the salary schedule. He was alarmed to discover the relatively small salary being paid the teachers, including Booker Washington himself. On returning to New York he said to Mr. Washington that the next time he was in New York, he would like to talk with him. In due course Mr. Washington made one of his periodic trips to New York and sought an engagement with Mr. Carnegie. Mr. Carnegie was emphatic when insisting that the teacher's salaries were too low and that Mr. Washington's salary was relatively lower than all of them in terms of his job and in view of the fact that his constant appearance before the public was important. He then stated that he had decided to give Mr. Washington for his own personal use one hundred thousand dollars. Mr. Washington thanked him for the consideration and the suggestion of security, but advised that he could not accept it because he said, "it would hurt my work." Mr. Carnegie said that this would be a private matter between the two and that the public need not know about it. Mr. Washington insisted that the public had a way of finding things out, and that under those circumstances he still could not accept it. Mr. Carnegie inquired, "Don't you think anything about yourself and family? I have never seen anybody who gives no consideration to himself and an inadequate consideration to his family in the zone of economic security." He finally said, "I'll tell you what I am going to do. I am going to set up a trust fund of one hundred thousand dollars, the interest upon which will be your salary." From that day until his death Mr. Washington drew no salary from the Institute as such. The number of persons who would refuse a hundred thousand dollars as a personal gift under the circumstances described above do not go in droves; like lawyers going to Heaven, they pass one at a time.

The publicity, incident to the dedicatory program of the Carnegie Library at Tuskegee Institute, resulted in other Negro schools approaching Mr. Carnegie in an attempt to get him to contribute toward the establishment of a library on their respective campuses.

Among these institutions were Wilberforce University in Ohio and Livingston College in Salisbury, North Carolina. In response to the requests on the part of Dr. Scarborough of Wilberforce and Dr. J. C. Price of Livingston, Mr. Carnegie advised them he would be glad to give the requests favorable consideration upon the recommendation of Booker T. Washington.

When this matter was brought to the attention of Dr. Washington by both Dr. Scarborough and Dr. Price, Dr. Washington sent his secretary, Dr. Emmet Scott, to Wilberforce and Salisbury to evaluate the situation. Upon Dr. Scott's report, Dr. Washington advised Mr. Carnegie that in his judgment a contribution toward the building of libraries on the campuses of these two institutions would greatly enhance the educational potentials of the students in attendance, as well as of the teachers and citizens of the campus communities.

Mr. Andrew Carnegie gave favorable consideration to the requests of these two institutions upon the recommendation of Booker Washington.

How the Experiment Station at Tuskegee Came into Being

Because of the wide publicity accompanying the graduation from Iowa State College at Ames, Iowa, of George W. Carver, who when he entered the institution was not permitted to eat in the dining hall with his contemporaries of the Caucasian persuasion, Booker Washington sought and finally secured his services as Assistant to the Director of Agriculture at Tuskegee Institute. The head of the Agriculture Department was George Bridgeforth. At the end of the school year Bridgeforth reported to Mr. Washington that he had been dissatisfied with his experience with Dr. Carver and recommended that he not be re-employed in the capacity of his assistant. Pinpointing his evaluation of Carver's incompetence, Bridgeforth alleged, among other things, that Carver spent much more time explaining to students how many ways a sweet potato could be prepared as a breakfast diet than he spent in teaching them how to produce potatoes. Bridgeforth further alleged that Carver was giving more time and consideration to explaining to students how peanuts could be processed into face powder, milk, or peanut butter than he spent in teaching students how to grow peanuts. With this unfavorable evaluation before him, Booker Washington called in Dr. Carver to get his side of the story.

Carver affirmed Bridgeforth's indictment as being technically correct. In defense of his methodology he gave some demonstrations of the number of ways a sweet potato could be prepared as a breakfast diet and the many by-products that might develop from the processing of peanuts. It was not difficult for Booker Washington to recognize the comparative significance of the thing that Carver was attempting to do and teach. Carver suggested to Booker Washington that if he could secure from the United States Department of Agriculture the authority to establish an Experiment Station at Tuskegee, to be conducted under the auspices of the United States Department of Agriculture, he would further explore the potentials of peanuts and potatoes and the chemical analysis of the soil.

In compliance with Carver's request Booker Washington wrote to Secretary Knapp of the United States Department of Agriculture, requesting that an Experiment Station be established at Tuskegee Institute. The Secretary rejected the request on the grounds there was only one Negro in the United States that he considered qualified to conduct an Experiment Station that would meet the requirements of his department. He informed Booker Washington that that man was George Washington Carver, and that he was employed on the faculty of Iowa University. Booker Washington's reply to the Secretary brought the intelligence that the George Washington Carver referred to was no longer a member of the faculty at the University of Iowa at that date but had for more than a year been employed as Assistant to the Director of Agriculture at Tuskegee Institute. When the information concerning the relocation of Carver came to the attention of the Secretary of Agriculture, he readily agreed that the federalized agency sought by Booker Washington to be directed by George Washington Carver might be established on the campus of Tuskegee Institute.

With this Experiment Station, Carver became the proverbial "rabbit in the briar patch." His experiments with potatoes, with peanuts, with clay, with all sorts of insects, and with vegetation earned him the reputation of being the outstanding analytical chemist of his generation. Paradoxically enough, it might be observed that if in terms of relativity Carver had given more time to teaching students how to grow potatoes, the students at Tuskegee Institute, and the people of Alabama, America, and the world, would have been denied the opportunity of becoming the beneficiaries of this ex-slave's scientific imagination.

Dr. Emmet Scott "Sees the Promised Land" but is Not Permitted to Enter

In terms of the land of promise flowing, not with milk and honey, but with a throbbing multitude of young people in quest of knowledge and a corps of learned people representing a multiplicity of institutions of learning, this land seemed destined to be entered by Dr. Emmet J. Scott, at the death of Booker T. Washington, as the Executive Administrator.

Speculation as to Booker Washington's successor ran rampant immediately following the passing of Dr. Washington—friend and foe alike were nominating their candidates. The person, however, who held the inside track until the night the Memorial Exercises were held for Dr. Washington in the Chapel on the campus of the Institute in 1915 was Dr. E. J. Scott.

The two strongest men on the Trustee Board had agreed on Dr. Scott and had planned to go into the meeting of the Trustee Board Monday morning following the Sunday night Memorial Program and place his name in nomination. One of these persons' relative strength resulted from his financial prestige and the reputation he had earned as an international philanthropist. The other's relative strength was a result of his national political position, military achievement, and international diplomatic recognition. One of Dr. Scott's sponsors was Julius Rosenwald; the other was ex-President Theodore Roosevelt. A rather peculiar chain of circumstances associated with an unexpected—and until this day unexplained—tragedy manipulated by an unmerciful fate robbed Dr. Scott of what was conceived to be his unchallenged "birthright."

On the program for the Memorial Exercises were the Mayor of the City of Tuskegee, the Governor of the State of Alabama, and several members of the Board of Trustees, among them ex-President Theodore Roosevelt, who was the "keynoter." The concluding remarks of ex-President Roosevelt will linger in the memory of those who heard him and many who read his Memorial statement, "Mr. Washington was one of the few men to whom I turned for advice, as President of the United States."

Scheduled to speak for the Institution was Mr. Warren Logan, Treasurer and Vice-President of Tuskegee Institute. On that fateful Sunday afternoon, seven hours before the Memorial Exercises were scheduled to begin, Mrs. Logan, the wife of the Treasurer and Vice President, committed suicide by jumping out of a window of the Academic Building. The Trustees, motivated by compelling sympathetic frustration, decided that it would be unkind, unreasonable, and well-nigh inhuman to ask Mr. Logan to take his place on the scheduled program as representing the Institute in eulogizing his chief and the school's benefactor. They decided, under the circumstances, to ask Dr. Scott, who had been intimately associated with Dr. Washington as his private secretary for eighteen years and who had for a great portion of that time, served as Secretary of the Board of Trustees, to take the place to which Mr. Logan had previously been assigned and to evaluate the loss the school had sustained by the passing of its founder.

Dr. Scott, who knew he was being considered to succeed the man with whom he had been so intimately associated for almost two decades, seized upon this opportunity to preach his "trial sermon" instead of paying the kind of tribute to Booker Washington that no one else could pay, predicated upon his day-by-day association with him on and off the campus of Tuskegee Institute. He had intimate knowledge of the relationship Booker Washington had sustained with private citizens, responsible public officials, and top-ranking representatives of many governments, including the United States of America. For example, no colored person received governmental appointment from a President of the United States, from the time of President Cleveland in 1896 to that of President Taft in 1908, without the approval of Booker T. Washington.

In 1908, when the Republic of Liberia was facing threats of insolvency because it could not liquidate the obligation it had incurred with the Governments of the Republic of France and the United Kingdom, it sent a committee to the United States to seek a loan from the Congress of the United States. President Taft referred the application to the Senate Appropriations Committee. This Committee granted a hearing to the Liberian representatives, but they were unable to persuade the Appropriations Committee to recommend a loan to satisfy the emergency which the Liberian Republic was then facing.

The Committee informed the President that the Liberian Commission was not able to actualize information on the dividend-yielding resources of the Republic of Liberia, which would enable that political country to repay the loan it was seeking within a stipulated time. The chairman of the Committee said, however, that the Committee was in great sympathy with the position Liberia found itself in, and in consideration of the fact that it was founded in 1847 by the American Colonization Society, the Committee would recommend the loan if the President would send Booker T. Washington to Liberia to make a study of the dividend-yielding resources of the Republic and, based upon the findings, recommend that the loan be made. The President inquired of the Committee as to how long in their judgment this contemplated research project would make it necessary for Booker Washington to be out of the country. The chairman replied that he thought that it could be done in ninety days. President Taft's reaction to the recommendation was unfavorable, because he did not feel that the United States Government could spare Booker Washington out of its political and geographic jurisdiction for ninety days. Today, a president himself may go out of the Continental United States if and when an occasion in his judgment makes it necessary, and he may remain as long as necessary without in any sense jeopardizing the administrative control of the affairs of state. President Taft agreed to appoint whomever Booker Washington would recommend. Booker Washington selected his efficient secretary, Dr. Emmett J. Scott. The President approved Booker Washington's recommendation and Dr. Scott was sent to Liberia on a battleship. Upon Dr. Scott's return, Mr. Washington made a recommendation that the loan be granted and that the appropriate authorities of the United States of America give favorable consideration to Dr. Scott's recommendation. The loan was granted and Liberia's solvency remained in tact.

Nobody knew this inside story better than Emmett J. Scott. Instead of Dr. Scott devoting his time on the program to telling what he knew about his former chief, he went somewhat off on a tangent, giving his philosophy of education. While he was speaking, ex-President Theodore Roosevelt turned to Mr. Rosenwald and said, "Absolutely impossible." The following day at the meeting of the Board of Trustees, the two men who twenty-four hours prior to the Board meeting had been prepared to lead the campaign for Dr. Scott, reversed their position. The Board made no choice at this meeting.

Dr. Robert R. Moton, who was then Major Moton, Commandant of Hampton Institute was a runner-up in the line of proposed successors to Booker T. Washington. The Trustees wired Major Moton to come aboard their train at Richmond and ride with them to Washington.

Julius Rosenwald returned to Chicago through Birmingham, Nashville, and Evansville, Indiana. Upon the return of ex-President Theodore Roosevelt to his home at Oyster Bay, New York, he sent Mr. Rosenwald a telegram substantially as follows:

> You will recall that you and I had agreed that the logical successor to Booker T. Washington was the man who had been his private secretary and secretary to the Board of Trustees for almost two decades. After listening to his address on the occasion of the Memorial Exercises of Dr. Washington, I became convinced that he was an absolute impossibility.
>
> The Trustees wired Major Moton to join them in Richmond and ride to Washington. They were impressed, but did not reach a final conclusion. If we do not agree on Major Moton, we shall have to look all over the United States to find a suitable successor, because Dr. Scott is absolutely an impossibility.
>
> *Signed:* THEODORE ROOSEVELT

If Mrs. Logan had not died under the unfortunate circumstances described above, there is no question as to who would have been Booker Washington's successor, Emmett Scott, by this token, became the "Moses" of his generation. He was permitted to see the promise land, but he died in the wilderness of disappointment and disillusionment.

The Founder of Tuskegee General Alumni Association

In March of 1916, when Dr. Moton was president-elect of Tuskegee Institute, upon advice of Mrs. Booker T. Washington, he spent three weeks with me in western New York. During this period he fulfilled a number of speaking engagements which I arranged for him and had conferences with many of the citizens of wealth and influence in that section of the state.

During this period I suggested to Dr. Moton that a general alumni association—if its membership included active members of the alumni family across the nation—could be of immeasurable assistance to him as he assumed the administrative leadership of Tuskegee Institute as the successor to Booker T. Washington. I gave him some impression of the type of approach I felt could be made toward bringing into existence such an auxiliary to his administration. My thought was that we could set up an organization with officers and chairmen of important committees which would give every section of the nation where a sizable number of Tuskegee graduates might reside an opportunity to be represented in the cabinet or executive family of the association.

Dr. Moton thought well of the idea and asked if I would assume the leadership responsibility of bringing such an organization into existence. In my anxiety to give every possible assistance to the new president, I began almost immediately to correspond with key alumni in localities where there were a sizable number of graduates employed by institutions or business enterprises or self-employed.

The plan agreed upon was to hold annual meetings of the association in different sections of the United States two years in succession, and every third meeting on the campus of the Institute. In the opinion of the organizer, this approach would have two significant avenues through which information could be channeled to the larger community with respect to the course offerings at Tuskegee Institute; second, it would give both the president and other representatives of the Institute's official family a chance periodically to come into personal contact with educators, lay citizens, and public officials in the cities where these meetings would be held and provide an opportunity for graduates, ex-students, and former teachers of the Institute to attend meetings held in communities near enough to where they were employed to make it possible for them to attend with a minimum loss of time from their places of employment. Many graduates living in Detroit could attend a meeting in Cleveland in the evening after working all day and be back in Detroit on the job the following morning. The same would be true for persons living in Cincinnati and other cities within a radius of one hundred miles of Cleveland, without losing any time from the job, whether they were employed in the public school system or in private industry. This would not be true to the same extent of a meeting held at Tuskegee Institute.

We received enthusiastic response from the graduates, and the General Alumni association was organized on the plan indicated above. We held a number of very successful meetings, but a suspicion was generated which finally reached Mrs. Moton and convinced her that the purpose of the meeting was to build up sentiment against Dr. Moton which ultimately would remove him from his position as president, even though Dr. Moton himself insisted that he did not share Mrs. Moton's thinking in the matter. He could not, however, dissuade her from the position she had assumed when she replied to a letter that the writer had sent to Dr. Moton inviting him to speak at one of the evening meetings assembled in Memphis, Tennessee, indicating that on the day Dr. Moton spoke to an alumni group off the Tuskegee campus, on that day she would file for a divorce.

In this climate of confusion and indecision, the General Alumni Association, as originally designed, never came to full fruition. It has been limping along on decentralized crutches ever since. In lieu of the original portfolio, as a substitute there were organized Regional Alumni Association meetings.

VI

Field Director

The day following my graduation, the last week in May, 1911, I was called into the office of Dr. Emmett J. Scott and given my assignment as Field Director of Tuskegee for the states of New York and Pennsylvania. My headquarters was to be in the city made famous in Negro culture because it was the home of that great American, Frederick Douglass, and where a monument of Douglass built with money raised by citizens across the nation, white and colored, had been erected in front of the New York Central Railroad Station. The dedicatory address at the opening of this office had been delivered by the Honorable Theodore Roosevelt, who was then Governor of the State of New York. Dr. Scott could give me only a general outline of my job assignment, because he had not any experience in the type of job I was to do. While I had lived on the Tuskegee campus for four years, with the exception of the time I was away in quest of health restoration, I had acquired sufficient knowledge of the institution and its history for personal consumption, but when it came to telling other people about Tuskegee, it suddenly dawned on me that I needed to find out something more about it specifically.

I spent about two weeks, after accepting the job, familiarizing myself with the different departments, the accomplishments of many of its graduates, and the number of schools headed by its graduates, as well as those founded by the graduates of Tuskegee, called the "Off Shoots," such as Utica Institute at Utica, Mississippi, Voorhees Institute at Denmark, South Carolina, Calhoun School near Sanford, Florida, and many others.

With this equipment I left Tuskegee in the early part of June en route to my headquarters in Rochester, New York. I was to be met in New York by Mr. Frank Chisholm, who was senior field director of Tuskegee at that time. I spent a day with Mr. Chisholm getting something of an "orientation briefing." For some reason I do not recall, Mr. Chisholm thought my first assignment should be in Albany instead of my going directly to Rochester. Up until this time, my total training and experience and association had been with and under the supervision and control of colored people. As Field Secretary of Tuskegee, my total job responsibility would bring me into contact with white people almost exclusively because of the large sums of money I needed to raise. In such a task one's time would be injudiciously spent if much of it was invested on or among colored people. On one occasion, in order to complete the payment on a heating plant that was in process of installation, we were called upon to raise ninety thousand dollars in thirty days. With this type of objective, there would be no point in wasting one's time with "after collections" in Negro churches.

Booker Washington had worked out a system of money raising which gave the job a dignity which it would otherwise not have had. The Field Directors were not employed on a commission basis, but on a fixed salary plus living and traveling expenses. The procedure was to seek conferences with persons who enjoyed the reputation of being listed among persons of wealth, to appear before organizations of various kinds whose membership was composed of people of means, and to tell an honorable, accurate, logical, and convincing story of the costs of operation of Tuskegee, including its annual budget, the amount of money it received from student fees, the amount, if any, it received from the State of Alabama and the County of Macon, and the difference between this income and the income from sources suggested above. In addition, some information was given as to the number of graduates that had gone out, where they were, and the kind of job they were doing.

It was his procedure not to ask for specific amounts unless the proposed contributor requested a suggestion as to the amount he should contribute.

The accident of my position gave me an opportunity of associating and working with some of the most wealthy philanthropic and public-spirited citizens in the States of New York and Pennsylvania. The day-by-day contact I had in this personal and official fashion was equivalent to securing a college education. The training that I had received at Tuskegee with respect to punctuality served me in good stead in my new assignment. I soon learned that, in the matter of public speaking, when one is given ten minutes or thirty minutes, he was not supposed to speak eleven minutes or thirty-one minutes. I also discovered that the people who gave substantial amounts, for the most part, gave systematically with respect to time. A contributor who made his contribution in June, 1911, would not expect to be solicited again before June, 1912.

In 1916, Thomas Jesse Jones under the auspices, I believe, of the Phelps Stokes Fund, made a study of Negro schools which was published and circulated pretty generally among people who were known to be heavy contributors toward Negro education, as well as to school libraries and among other interested individuals and organizations. Prior to the Jesse Jones study, the prospective donor was frequently limited in his knowledge of a particular Negro institution to the description and information given by its representatives. Philanthropy had not at that time been organized in terms of foundations, which subsequently became the pattern.

There was a feeling among many of the Negro heads of institutions that Jesse Jones was more critical of his evaluation of institutions manned by Negroes than he was of institutions whose executive heads were white, even though members of the faculty might be both Negroes and whites. The report pointed out the need for certain physical improvements, and it called attention to the alarmingly high percentage of the student body in the Negro colleges composed of those in the high school department. In most Southern institutions, there were either no accredited high schools or very few. It was, therefore, necessary for Negro parents, whose taxes went to the support of public high schools which white children could attend, to send their children to a Negro college at an additional personal sacrifice, which meant that though they had the least income and buying power, they had to pay double in order that their children might receive even a high school education.

With the Jones report in the possession of the proposed contributor, it became increasingly necessary for the solicitor to be in a position to indicate the extent to which the school had changed the condition complained of in the report or to which it was complying with the recommendation set out in the report. Prior to 1916, when Thomas Jesse Jones made the survey of Negro colleges, and before philanthropy had become organized and expressed itself through established foundations, it was possible for impostors who carried their institutions in their pockets to fleece individual philanthropists out of sizable amounts of money in the guise of Negro education. Many institutions with limited financial resources employed field representatives on a commission or percentage basis.

The institutions in question had no way of determining the amounts of money its representatives raised except what he himself might have reported. This unsupervised and free-lancing procedure made possible a lot of dishonesty and downright fraud in many instances. I have known persons to turn in one hundred dollars a year to an institution when they may have solicited three or four thousand dollars a year, which the institution never heard about. The head of the institution took the position that the one hundred dollars was more than they were going to get without the representative. Therefore, they justified the procedure on the theory that whatever they got was more than they would have received otherwise. Some persons represented two or three different schools as they approached prospective contributors. Whichever school this particular individual decided that his prospect would be interested in was the school whose claims he presented. I ran into a number of communities where some person had appeared a few days prior to issue a public statement to the effect that there was only one bona fide representative of Tuskegee in that state and giving his name.

I had the opportunity of speaking in most of the large churches whose membership enjoyed the reputation of affluence in the cities of Kingston, Newburgh, Poughkeepsie, Hudson, Albany, Detroit, Schenectady, Amsterdam, Utica, Syracuse, Rochester, Buffalo, Niagara Falls, Watertown, Jamestown, Elmira, Binghamton, New York, and many of the smaller cities, as well as Scranton and Wilkesboro, Pennsylvania. In addition to the important church groups in these cities, I also spoke before the members of the Kiwanis, Rotary, and Civitan clubs in these states.

The first year of my employment, according to the Treasurer of Tuskegee, Mr. Logan, I was successful in raising more money than any other Field Director, even though some of them had been out on the job twelve years. Mr. Washington remarked that in addition to the amount of money sent in, he was interested in the large number of persons on whom I called from month to month, as evidenced by the number of contributors as well as by the grand total. For me, it became quite a study of personalities. It was a great satisfaction to observe how persons would increase their contribution as a result of becoming more intelligently concerned about the institution. A person for example, in the first interview might contribute ten or twenty-five dollars and in five years might include twenty-five or fifty-thousand dollars in his will for Negro education.

I was successful, in cases without number, in getting the children and grandchildren committed to continuing to support the causes in which their wealthy parents or grandparents were so vitally interested. I was frequently impressed with the spirit of sac-rificial giving which characterized the response of some persons who were not included among the people of wealth, but who would be in a congregation or an audience to which I made a speech, and at the conclusion would invite me to their homes to receive a contribution. I have known many cases where people were in very meager circumstances, and some cases where it seemed to me they were worse off than the students at Tuskegee, who were anxious to contribute to those students' expenses at great personal sacrifice.

In the course of events it was my good fortune to form some very worthwhile and abiding personal, as well as professional, friends. Some of the best friends and finest people I have ever known, I met in this benefactor-and-beneficiary relationship. It would take too much time and space to refer in detail to all of the generous, public-spirited, and rare personalities with whom I have formed a most intimate and helpful relationship. It will have to suf-fice to refer in a very personal way to a few of them. In Rochester, New York, there was an outstanding attorney. He looked after the legal business of the late George Eastman, of Kodak fame. His name was Walter S. Hubbel. He was the teacher of the Hubbel Bible Class in the Baptist Church, of which he was a member. This class had the reputation of being the largest men's Bible class in the world.

At least once a year the writer was invited to speak to this class of business executives, educators, and professional men, and in response to my message they always made a substantial contribu-tion toward the support of Tuskegee Institute. On one occasion I told the men, without consultation with anybody, that I wanted them to give a permanent scholarship to Tuskegee in consideration of the fine spiritual leadership Mr. Hubbel had given the class and to designate it the Hubbel Scholarship. When I completed my remarks, the seven or eight hundred men rose to their feet and gave unanimous assent to the idea. Mr. Hubbel was so overcome that he wept like a child. From that time until his death, he was one of the closest friends that I have ever had.

There was another person in Rochester by the name of Mr. Hiram W. Sibley. I always looked forward to my annual interview with Mr. Sibley. His granddaughter, Mrs. John Glenn, who was an employee of the American Red Cross some years ago, reminded me that on a number of occasions she had served me tea on her grandfather's lawn when she was quite a child. She is the daughter of Mr. Harper Sibley, whom I was able to get to take up where his father left off, continuing the Sibley family support toward Tuskegee Institute. In these annual conferences I had had with Mr. Hiram Sibley, he always terminated them in this fashion after we had been talking for perhaps an hour, more or less: he would excuse himself and in a few minutes would return. We would resume the conversation, and within a comparatively short time his secretary would appear with a check of a substantial amount made payable to Warren Logan, Treasurer of Tuskegee Institute. He always seemed so happy for the opportunity of having this annual review of what was going on at Tuskegee and to punctuate it with a contribution.

In Albany, New York there was a family of the Huycks: three brothers, Edmund, John, and Francis. They were engaged—and held controlling stock, as I recall—in a felt mill in Rensselaersville, New York, which is across the river from Albany. I knew all three of them very well and was able to enlist their financial support for Tuskegee Institute. When I left Tuskegee and accepted the principalship of Voorhees Institute in Denmark, South Carolina, they included Voorhees among their benevolences and gave substantially toward its support. On one occasion I went in to see Mr. Edmund Huyck during a periodic visit to that section of the state. He expressed interest in a young colored boy named James Thompson, whom he had engaged as a caddy on a golf course at Camden, South Carolina. Mr. Huyck spent his winter vacations at Camden. Part of his daily recreation was playing golf. He was impressed with the fact that this young lad, unlike the other caddies, did not gamble and risk his money in a game of chance. Another thing that impressed him about Jimmy, he told me, was the fact that whenever he missed the hole it hurt Jimmy worse than it did him. Jimmy seemed to be much concerned about the result of Mr. Huyck's golf playing and so disappointed when he did not accomplish his objective that Mr. Huyck became personally interested in Jimmy and inquired as to his educational background and outlook. He discovered that while the boy was around fourteen years of age, he could scarcely read or write and had only a smattering of education.

With the degree of self-control exercised by Jimmy in refraining from throwing his money away through games of chance, in contrast to the other caddies, and as a result of his dependability as well as the interest he exercised in his job, Mr. Huyck felt that he had the elements essential to a foundation for character building and education. On this particular occasion he said to me that "if you will find this boy and take him to Denmark, I will pay for his education." When I got back to South Carolina, I made a trip up to Camden from Denmark and spent a day trying to find the boy from the meager description which Mr. Huyck was able to give me. I went from one school to the other and talked with the principals, with physicians, with people in barbershops, but was able to pick up nothing that I could use as a lead. A few minutes before it was time to take a train back to Denmark, I decided to talk with a Reverend Boykins to see if he could give me any information concerning a boy who fitted into the general description which I had received from Mr. Huyck. This hunch proved a logical procedure.

From the information I had, Reverend Boykins had no difficulty in identifying the person sought. Mr. Huyck knew only that the boy's name was Jimmy, and that was all I had to work on. Reverent Boykins added "Thompson," and said that boy was out in the country picking cotton. I left money to cover railroad fare with Reverend Boykins and asked if he would, through some member of his church, get in touch with the boy, clear with such parents or guardian who might have any legal jurisdiction, and either send the boy to Denmark or advise me what other steps I would need to take to make it possible for Jimmy to take advantage of Mr. Huyck's offer.

It was only a few days before I received word from Reverend Boykins that the boy had been located and permission given by his sister (since both parents were dead) for him to come on to Denmark within the next ten days prepared to enter school. When Jimmy arrived, he was enrolled in the Practice School. This was an elementary school on Voorhees' campus which served the whole county but received only a very small appropriation from the county. The majority of the teachers were paid by Voorhees Institute, and the young women in the senior class who chose teaching as their profession, did their practice teaching in this school under the supervision of the teachers.

When Jimmy was graduated from this school, he entered Voorhees Institute proper. When I finally resigned from Voorhees and accepted a position with the National Urban League as Southern Field Director and established headquarters in Atlanta, Jimmy had become so attached to my family that he wanted to transfer his quest for scholastic competence to the "Gate City of the South." He became a member of my family, lived in my home, and entered Morehouse College, from which he was graduated. He then decided that he wanted to take up steam fitting and went to Tuskegee, where he spent two or three years and received a certificate in steam fitting. He returned to Atlanta from Tuskegee and identified himself with a plumbing organization, and still later went into business for himself in the City of New York.

During all these years—sixteen to be exact—Mr. Huyck gave financial backing that made it possible for Jimmy to equip himself to take his place as a productive and useful citizen as a graduate steam fitter at Tuskegee Institute, which was a long way from his status as a caddy with less than a third-grade education. This gives some glimpse of the great heart that motivated the anxiety concerning the economic security, educational outlook, and moral and spiritual growth of a lad who was discovered in a blind alley.

I talked with many people in Albany about Mr. Huyck. As I remember, once he was chairman of the Board of Directors of the Community Chest. All the member agencies seemed to have the impression that they would get all they deserved if they had their cases reviewed by Mr. Huyck. I never heard anybody express any apprehension over his fair-mindedness or Christian stewardship. At Mr. Edmund Huyck's death it appears that he bequeathed his interest in the educational welfare of colored youth to his wife Mrs. Edmund Huyck. Mrs. Huyck seemed also to have inherited his interest in Jimmy, plus her own concern about Jimmy's development, because even to this day she expresses the most motherly concern as to Jimmy's whereabouts and his welfare.

In the past forty years, eight different young colored women have had their educational opportunities enhanced through Mrs. Huyck's generosity as a result of my bringing their special cases to her attention. Whenever I have found a girl whose academic record and citizenship status justified an investment in her educational ambition and brought the case to the attention of Mrs. Huyck, without any further information or investigation beyond my own evaluation, Mrs. Huyck has provided the money necessary to cover the over-all expenses for a one or two-year period, as the case in question may indicate. My judgment in each instance has proven sound and Mrs. Huyck and I, in this type of partnership, have not pulled a single "rotten apple." Every person that I have recommended for her financial assistance has proven to be a good student in terms of academic classification and a good citizen in terms of community leadership and unit production.

There is no way to measure the result of inspiration, aspiration, or outlook on life or emotional urge. On this account Mrs. Huyck will never know how much she has contributed toward the economic stability, educational advancement, moral steadfastness, and spiritual vitality of members of the Negro community through the financial aid she has made available to this group of young people who have been the fortunate beneficiaries of her cheerful generosity. I am very happy to have served as party of the first part in this reciprocal arrangement.

There was another citizen in Albany whose confidence I shared and who served as a great inspiration to me. My chronological experience with him was very unique. His name was Mr. Charles Gibson. He was a large stockholder and an executive officer in a drug business that operated a number of drugstores in the State of New York. He was a man of considerable wealth and very liberal. He gave generously to both home and foreign missions for the support of educational institutions. His pastor told me on one occasion that Mr. Gibson instructed him to inform him at the end of the church calendar year of all the money that members of the church had given to foreign missions and he would give a check to equal the aggregate amount of what all the rest of the members had given.

With this background, I approached Mr. Gibson in the interest of securing a contribution for Tuskegee Institute. He received me very graciously at his office and expressed a great deal of interest in Negro education in general and in the work that was being done at Hampton and Tuskegee in particular. He had, on more than one occasion, I believe, visited Hampton and knew at first hand some of the things that were being done at Hampton for the educational advancement of Negro people. I was sure that with this reaction to my approach I would receive a generous contribution when the conference was terminated. I was very much disappointed, however, when he finally indicated that he would have to bring the conference to a close. As he arose, he expressed great satisfaction at having me come in and bring him some fresh information as to what was being done in an educational way for Negro people at Tuskegee, but stated that he felt he had already made commitments sufficient to absorb all he felt he could give for education.

Each year, for some three or four years, I would call on Mr. Gibson with a hope that I would be able to break through his defense, but with exactly the same results. During the summer months I followed the custom of going up into the Adirondacks, where the wealthy people of New York City and New Jersey had large estates where they spent their summers. Getting off a boat at Westfield, I usually rented a horse and buggy and drove through the mountains and winding roads up to these large summer mansions. Many of these people you could not see at their offices in New York, New Jersey, or Boston: because of the heavy official traffic coming in and out of their offices and places of business every working hour of the day, they were not disposed to be interrupted for the purpose of being solicited for financial support of an educational institution a thousand miles away.

These same people, in their summer places however, would be less protected by an army of secretaries and sub-executives, and, as a result, would welcome a visitor, even though he was in quest of financial support, as a means of breaking the monotony of prolonged inactivity. It was on such an occasion, one rainy afternoon that I drove by the summer home of Mr. Gibson. When I first approached the entrance, I noticed the name on the mailbox. I drove about a quarter of a mile from this entrance before I came in view of the house. I parked by nag, went up on the porch, and rang the bell. The butler came to the door and I inquired whether this was the summer home of Mr. Charles Gibson of Albany, New York. He said it was. I gave him my card and asked him to present it to Mr. Gibson. In a few minutes Mr. Gibson came to the door and invited me in. We went through our usual cordial chat about Tuskegee and its needs and so on. I always watched for a facial expression or a statement that would indicate that the person being interviewed was ready to terminate the interview. When I recognized such a signal on this occasion, I arose and expressed appreciation for having the opportunity of talking with Mr. Gibson again and started toward the door when he halted me by saying, "I cannot let you leave empty-handed." He went into his study or office and wrote a check to Tuskegee for ten dollars. That was the opening wedge to a friendship akin to comradeship that developed in subsequent years between Mr. Gibson and myself.

When I became principal of Voorhees Institute, Mr. Gibson gladly consented to serve as a member of the Board of Trustees and gave generously toward causes in which I was interested. His interest in those causes was sustained after his death by his son, Mr. Will Gibson, and his daughter, Mary Gibson. On one occasion when Mr. Gibson was visiting in China, an important Chinese citizen asked him how many Chinese there were in Albany. Mr. Gibson was embarrassed to admit that he did not know. He had given generously to foreign missions and China was included in the benevolent budget of his church. He came back to Albany and had a survey made to determine how many Chinese there were in Albany. Shortly after his return I had a conference with him. He said that if he were asked how many colored people there were in Albany, he would be just as embarrassed as he was when the question was raised about the number of Chinese there were in Albany.

For fear that question might be asked and in consideration of the fact that he had given to foreign missions, which included Africa, and had contributed toward educational institutions in the United States on behalf of colored people, he felt that he ought to at least exercise a little more concern than he had done with respect to the number of Negroes in Albany and their living, working, and housing conditions. He agreed that he would finance such a study if the National Urban League would permit me to make it. The arrangement was made for the study and it was financed by Mr. Gibson, so that as long as he lived he was always in a better position with respect to a knowledge of the Albany Negro population than when the question was originally raised.

The Gibson and Huyck families will be hard to duplicate in Albany or any other political subdivision, and both of them will be long remembered for their contribution toward the sum total of human welfare.

Booker Washington indoctrinated his field representatives with the idea that they were going out from Tuskegee as its representatives to sell an idea which, in the last analysis, was a measure of social security, in the same fashion as an insurance agency sold insurance policies: "Don't let anybody give you the impression that you are beggars; nor should you assume that attitude. A beggar is an individual who is seeking alms on his own behalf. A solicitor, on the other hand, is a person who gives the relatively stronger members of society an opportunity to contribute toward the type of social reform or group improvement that will enhance their own welfare."

He emphasized the fact that any individual, organization, or foundation that contributed toward the educational advancement of any member of the community who, by reason of any misfortune wholly beyond his control, had been rendered illiterate, was making a contribution toward the sum total of literacy. "The more people," said he, "who are productively literate and functionally intelligent, the greater the sum total of literacy and intelligence that obtains in a community." He pointed out that if an industrialist or investor, in terms of ownership of stock and other securities, in New England or New York invested in the education of a Negro in the most remote section of Alabama or Mississippi, he would enhance his own investment in proportion as he increased the productivity of this Negro, increased his wants, and also increased his buying power. The Negro in Alabama, as a result, would want more creature comforts, would be able to purchase more, and thereby would consume more of the manufactured goods produced in Massachusetts and ultimately would increase the volume of turnover of the businesses in which the investor owned stock or other securities. That point of view and equipment gave dignity to the position and produced an attitude, which undoubtedly contributed very largely to the success of the field representatives.

With the Booker Washington admonition still dominating my perspective, in September, 1913, I went in to see Reverend John Appleby, Pastor of one of the large and influential Unitarian churches in the City of Syracuse, New York, seeking an opportunity of speaking before his congregation. I might give a brief background as to the history of this church in relationship to Negro America. Before and during the Civil War the territory in and around Syracuse was occupied by a number of "Underground Railroad Stations" and inhabited by many of the outstanding abolitionists of that period. One of the leaders in this Abolitionist Movement and a conductor of the Underground Railroad through that area was Reverend Samuel J. May, who was one of the earlier pastors of this same Unitarian Church. After his death a new church was built and named the May Memorial Church in honor and memory of Reverend Samuel May. Between the pastorates of Reverend May and Reverend Appleby another minister supplied the ministerial leadership of the flock, by the name of Reverend S. R. Calthrop. The daughter of Reverend Calthrop was a member of the Hampton faculty for a number of years.

Reverend Appleby discouraged my appearing before his congregation. It was his opinion that I would be wasting my time. He said to me, "It will do no good for you to speak to my congregation. In the first place you would not be able to interest them, because they are accustomed to hearing the best speakers. In the second place, we do not permit any extra offerings to be taken in our church and, therefore, no appeals for financial assistance are made from our pulpit for special contributions. In the third place, we budget our benevolences and my membership has already made its commitments for this calendar and fiscal year. Therefore, you could better invest your time by going somewhere this condition does not obtain. My advice to you, therefore, is not to waste time talking to my people."

Even though the reason Reverend Appleby gave seemed somewhat non-prejudicial and logical, I had heard an excuse or reason of the same kind a number of times before which was no more convincing than Reverend Appleby's admonition. I finally said to him, "I have something to say that your people ought to hear, and I will not do them any harm in five minutes; on the contrary, I think I will do them some good." After a repeated attempt to dissuade me from seeking a hearing, he seemed convinced that I was not inclined to accept his evaluation of the situation, and he reluctantly agreed that I could have five minutes. On Sunday morning at the scheduled hour I arrived at his study and he and I went into the pulpit together. He went through the usual devotional exercises, and just before he was to preach the sermon, he arose and described to the congregation exactly what had happened as an explanation for my presence in the pulpit. He gave a detailed account of my initial interview with him, what he said to me, and what I said to him. He then said to the congregation, "I am presenting him to you under these circumstances with the understanding that he is to occupy only five minutes." I took exactly four and a half minutes to be sure that I did not go a second over time, and said all that was humanly possible for me to say in those four and a half minutes. When I concluded, he arose and made no reference to anything that I had said, saying. "The services will continue by singing Hymn 576." Following the hymn, he delivered his message. At the conclusion of the services it was his custom to go to the rear of the church to greet the members of his flock and permit the assistant pastor to pronounce benediction. He invited me to accompany him to the door, where he shook hands with each member as he went out. I had some literature that described the work being done at Tuskegee and also indicating its cost of operation, the assured income, and the amount of money necessary to be raised each year over and above the interest on the endowment and money received from students' fees, and so forth. A majority of the people to whom I gave this printed material thanked me and gave a contribution and made some complimentary reference to the speech I had made in the interest of Negro education. Some of them gave silver money but the majority of them gave a dollar bill. One man and his wife stood back until all the rest of the members had retired and the pastor had gone back to his study to leave his robe. Then this man and his wife came and commended me for the message that I had given, the man giving me two bills which I thought were one-dollar bills. After he had gone out, I took the opportunity to examine the two bills and discovered that they were both ten-dollar bills. I had had enough experience by that time in raising money to know that a person who gave that much money had more than twenty dollars left. The following morning I went to the First National Bank and told the president, who was a friend of mine, what happened. He asked me to describe the man, and I did to the best of my ability. He asked, "Was the woman short, and the man a tall, heavy-set person slightly gray?" I answered in the affirmative. He then replied, "The woman is my daughter, and the man is my son-in-law. His name is Irving S. Merrell. He is connected with the Merrell–Sewell Company." This firm manufactured the "None-such Mince Meat" product and "Klim." They first called the latter powdered milk, but the Pure Food people insisted that milk had water in it. Under these circumstances, since there had been no chemical change taking place, except that the milk had been driven through a disk with such speed and velocity that the water was dried out of it and it became a powder, they reversed the name from "Milk" to "Klim".

In order for the substance to become milk it was only necessary to add water.

I went to the City Directory and looked up the name of Irving S. Merrell and sent the money to Tuskegee, associating his name as the donor. In due course, he received an acknowledgment from Mr. Warren Logan Treasurer of Tuskegee, which he later said was one of the surprises of his life. He wondered how I had found out his name and his address.

As it was my custom to reappear in each city in a corresponding month in each year, when I retuned to Syracuse the following year I made a beeline to the Merrell–Sewell Company office and sent my card in to Mr. Merrell via the switchboard operator. He returned in company with the young woman and extended a very cordial welcome for me to come into his office. He gave me something of his background, so far as Negro education was concerned. In his early childhood he was a member of the Sunday School of the church in question, and largely as a result of the information brought to the Sunday School by Miss Calthrop and other interested persons, the Sunday School contributed a fifty-dollar annual scholarship to Hampton Institute. He told me that he had heard many persons speak in the interest of Negro education, including Booker Washington and Major Moton, of Hampton Institute, but that he had never heard anybody say as much as convincingly on behalf of Negro education in five minutes as I did in the pulpit of his church on the Sunday morning mentioned above.

I learned another important lesson from that experience. I learned that any effort conscientiously exercised may be of history-making potentiality. After recounting his surprise at receiving the acknowledgement from Mr. Logan and complimenting me on my honesty and industry, he stated that the reason he gave the twenty dollars as he left his church the Sunday morning I spoke was that both he and Mrs. Merrell resented the treatment accorded me by their pastor. This seems to be a paradox. If the pastor had been more kindly disposed toward me, I perhaps would never have met Mr. and Mrs. Merrell. Because of the subsequent friendship that developed between the Merrells and the Thomas family, I would rather not have received a penny from anybody that morning and have met the Merrells than have received one thousand dollars and not met the Merrells. From that day to this, Mr. Merrell has been listed in the Thomas's book as the best friend the Thomas family has. He not only became a member of the Trustee Board of Voorhees Institute and remained an active member as long as I was its principal, but he transferred his interest to the National Urban League when I became its Field Secretary. Within a period of twelve years while I was an employee of the National Urban League, he gave six thousand dollars toward its current operating expenses. He and Mrs. Merrell became the godparents of my only daughter.

In 1913 Booker Washington sent me a telegram asking me to come to Tuskegee during the commencement season and to remain for a conference with him on a matter of vital importance. It developed that the installation of a new centralized steam heating plant was nearing completion. It was Dr. Washington's hope to make it a pay-as-you-go job by organizing sufficient finance by the time it was completed to pay the last dime, liquidating all obligations in connection with its installation. To do this it was necessary to raise ninety thousand dollars in thirty days. He somewhat parceled out territory in the New England States, New York, Pennsylvania, and Illinois and divided it among the different Field Secretaries, giving each Field Secretary a number of introductory letters to important people residing in the territory to which each was assigned.

My assignment included New York and Pennsylvania. Among the people to whom I was given an introductory letter was a person by the name of Mrs. Mary Louise Bok. She was the wife of Mr. Edmund Bok. Mr. Bok became internationally known as the author of the fifty-thousand-dollar Peace Prize following World War I. In his memory there was built the Bok Tower, an historical landmark in southwest Florida, to which there is a constant pilgrimage by people from all over the world daily.

On the day I made the initial attempt to see Mrs. Bok I arrived at her home, which is about sixteen miles from Philadelphia, a few minutes prior to her leaving for an engagement in the city of Philadelphia. I gave the letter to her secretary, who took it up to Mrs. Bok's dressing room and informed her of its contents. Mrs. Bok expressed great interest but registered regret for her inability to see on account of a pervious engagement, but suggested that I reduce to writing the nature of my errand. I went back to Philadelphia and wrote her a letter describing as best I could the urgency of the appeal and suggested that she send her reply to me in care of General Delivery, Pittsburgh, Pennsylvania. Two days afterward I arrived in Pittsburgh and went to the post office to receive my mail, because I had written another person in Philadelphia a similar letter. Among the mail awaiting my arrival were two letters with the Philadelphia postmark. When I opened them I was very much gratified to discover that in each of them was a check for one thousand dollars. One of them of course was signed by, Mary Louise Bok. Three years afterward, when I became principal of Voorhees Institute at Denmark, South Carolina, I decided to get married, but I encountered one difficulty as the result of inadequate housing facilities for the principal and his bride. I talked the matter over with Mrs. Bok and suggested that I would like to have an eight-room cottage built for the principal, and I would like to name it the Bok–Strawbridge Cottage. I wanted her and Mr. Strawbridge who was connected with the Strawbridge Clothing Company of Philadelphia to assume the financial obligation involved in the construction of this cottage. She asked me to talk with Mr. Strawbridge and indicate to him her willingness to assume at least fifty per cent of the cost—more, if Mr. Strawbridge felt he could assume less than the remaining fifty per cent of the cost of the construction—and then have my architect draw the plan for the building and submit it, if Mr. Strawbridge found himself in agreement with the idea. When I talked the matter over with Mr. Strawbridge, he cheerfully assumed fifty per cent partnership in the project, and the building was constructed. It was named, as originally suggested, the Bok–Strawbridge Cottage and remains until this day the home of the principal or president of the Voorhees Junior College.

In 1928 I wrote Mrs. Bok and informed her that I had been elected official delegate to the First International Conference of Social Work to be held in Paris, France. Mrs. Bok acknowledged receipt of my letter and enclosed a check for three hundred dollars with the statement, "This will help pay for your habits."

Mrs. Bok was an annual and substantial contributor toward the support of the work of Voorhees Institute as long as I occupied the headship of the institution. When I resigned and became Southern Field Director of the National Urban League, she transferred her interest to the organization, and for a great many years she was one of the most generous donors toward the support of the annual budget of the National Urban League. The fact is that she continued her support of the Urban League until she decided to endow the Curtis Institute of Music in Philadelphia and make it her major and primary benevolent enterprise. She discontinued her financial support to most other institutes and organizations in order to guarantee the perpetuity of the institution named for her grandfather.

In addition to supporting institutions and organizations with which I became identified after Mrs. Bok's interest had accumulated in my efforts, as has been indicated above, Mrs. Bok contributed toward the educational welfare of some six young people whose names I submitted to her as worthy of consideration and in need of financial assistance. Until the Curtis Institute of Music absorbed her major financial interest, she never turned down a single request I made on behalf of any deserving individual or cause. Mrs. Bok has not only been a constant and abiding friend through all these years, but she has been a great inspiration to me as well as an educational influence. With all her wealth and family background, her behavior in my association with her was characterized by simplicity and sincerity.

Some years ago I was in Philadelphia and read in the paper that Judge Bok was to preside over a case that was to be heard that day. Upon inquiring, I learned that this judge was the son of Mr. Edmund and Mrs. Mary Louise Bok. I changed my schedule of events for the day and went and sat in the court. Somehow, I felt a fatherly interest in the judge's judicial behavior. When the court adjourned, I went up and told him of my friendship with his mother and how he had grown up and achieved the distinction of the status of judge since I had seen him some fifteen years ago as a lad. He seemed quite pleased to recognize my gratitude to his mother and my satisfaction in the way he handled the cases that came before him on that occasion. It is interesting how, in human relationships, our interest will spill over into areas where people who are connected with the benefactor may reside.

Mr. Merrell was a graduate of Massachusetts Tech, in the Department of Engineering. He gave generously of his advice and counsel to the Trustees of Voorhees Institute in matters touching the installation of the steam heating plant. His contributions to Tuskegee in the same area, was no less far-reaching in terms of the economy resulting in the price of coal. If the two institutions had paid for the type of scientific information given, the amount of money involved would have been almost prohibitive as we think in terms of their limited budgets. Protracted ill-health made it necessary for Mr. Merrell to retire from business and, finally, to retire from membership on the Tuskegee Board. During the twenty years of his active life, after we had become such close friends, there were few important decisions I was called upon to make, whether affecting the institutions and organizations with which I was connected or my own personal family life, in which I did not seek his advice, which I always found fundamentally sound. During this period both Mr. and Mrs. Merrell saw the Thomas family at least once a year. Their coming to wherever we were located was always an occasion of history-making significance because we usually had a number of the local citizens meet them and participate in a reciprocal social hour.

In the last four years that I was Field Secretary of Tuskegee and during the life of Booker Washington, whenever any person who was to represent Tuskegee in the area of public relations or any other institution with which Booker Washington was connected as Trustee, he always suggested that such a person spend as much time with me in an orientation training experience as in my judgment was necessary before approaching the general public. This had become such a tradition that at his death when Dr. Moton, his successor, was President-Elect, Mrs. Washington suggested to him that, in light of Dr. Washington's evaluation of my methodology in the zone of public relations, he spend some time with me in western New York familiarizing himself with what she called the "Jesse O. Thomas Technique." Acting upon this advice, Dr. Moton, who then was known as Major Moton, spent three weeks traveling with me across the State of New York participating in interviews with outstanding public-spirited citizens and in sharing jointly my previously arranged speaking schedules and in serving as the principal speaker at other meetings planned specifically as a medium introducing him to people of finance, prestige, and social position in that area. At the conclusion of the itinerary, Dr. Moton expressed himself as profiting from the experience and learning of many things about Tuskegee that he did not know, as well as forming the acquaintance of many important people whose interest in Tuskegee Institute would enhance its position in American culture.

The position of Field Secretary for Tuskegee Institute provided an opportunity for me to secure much of my larger education. In such a relationship one can learn things that one could never be taught out of books, because it is not written in books. Early in my job experience I learned to organize whatever I was going to say in such a manner as to say it in the time allotted. It dawned upon me very early that when people in charge of large organizations with great responsibilities ask you to speak fifteen minutes, it does not mean twenty minutes; nor does it mean sixteen minutes. I also learned that the possession of money in itself does not always, if ever, indicate that its possessor is a person of character and good breeding. I found many people rich in finance and all of the power and influence that finance represents who were poverty-stricken in terms of human brotherhood, simple human dignity, and ordinary everyday civil behavior. By this measurement, some of the richest people I came in contact with were among the poorest individuals I ever met.

Some people would thank you for giving them an opportunity to improve the educational status of the segment of the population that has been denied the opportunity, which every child ought to be given in a democracy. Others would seek to humiliate or embarrass you. Some persons would indicate that they were interested in the nature of your errand and have you come back a half dozen times and then finally terminate the interview by describing some awkward conduct of some Negro. At that time, Jack Johnson was the ready-made exhibit. Others would go through the same type of dilly-dallying and then end up with a lecture on what the Negro ought to be satisfied to be, and what he could never become. Early in the game I was frequently led up the blind alley by a prospect who would ask if I had gotten permission to solicit funds in "X" town from the Board of Trade or the Chamber of Commerce. When I replied in the negative, he would advise that this be done immediately if I expected to have success in raising money in that town. The implication, of course, was that he wanted to assist me in qualifying so that I would run into no difficulty with the law or otherwise and, in the second place, that once the Chamber of Commerce had legitimatized my right to solicit, he would feel free and justified in making a contribution. Sometimes the committee on the Convention Bureau or the convention in charge of such matters would not meet for two or three days, or the chairman was out of town. After a week or more, when clearance had been secured from the Committee or the Board or the Chamber of Commerce, I would return to my original contact, feeling sure that the supporting evidence from the Chamber that I was a bona fide representative of Tuskegee Institute would bring a sizable contribution.

Imagine my disappointment when I was dismissed with a statement to the effect that, "I am not in a position myself to make a contribution, but I want you to get the proper credentials because the people in this town are skeptical about outside solicitors, etc." I soon discovered that that type of technique represented an escape complex. I had letters with the Tuskegee stamp and the signature of Booker Washington, plus always a letter from some local citizen who had given the school the authority to use his name, as reference. Strangely enough, no person who ever raised a question about the Chamber of Commerce or Board of Trade certification ever gave a penny after such certification was secured. I was not only successful in raising a great deal of money and in securing the equivalent to a university education, making friends for Tuskegee Institute and the cause of Negro education, but was successful at the same time in discovering some of the finest men and women and the noblest spirits with which God had blessed this earth, who became my personal lifelong friends.

In 1915 when Booker T. Washington was removed from the scene of action, I shared the frustration that characterized the expressions of people in all walks of life with respect to the future of

Tuskegee Institute and the leadership of the Negro race. Although Mr. Washington had no disposition, as I discovered, to style himself as the leader of the Negro race, he was so regarded by many. From 1895 when he delivered his now famous speech in Atlanta, Georgia, at the Cotton Exposition, up to the time of his death, he was accepted by a larger percentage of people in the United States and abroad as the spokesman for the colored people in the United States than any other single individual. As one example of his spokesmanship, during that period beginning with President Cleveland in 1896 and continuing to President Taft in 1908, no colored person received an important federal appointment without the approval of Booker Washington. As one of the speakers on the Booker Washington Memorial Exercises in the Chapel of Tuskegee in December 1915, ex-President Theodore Roosevelt stated that Mr. Washington was one of the few men to whom he turned for advice as President of the United States.

Many people prophesied Tuskegee's failure because it had to depend so largely upon Booker Washington's personality and financial appeal for its operating expenses of upward of a half-million dollars a year. The school had a little over two million dollars in endowment, but the difference between the interest on the endowment plus the intake from students, tuition, board, and other fees was so large that it was felt that no other person or group of persons could secure from the general public the amount of money necessary. Shortly after Dr. Moton's induction into office, the trustees agreed to launch an endowment campaign under the sponsorship of Tuskegee–Hampton Trustee Boards for both institutions. Dr. Moton, Dr. Washington's successor, supplied the leadership which resulted in increasing the endowment fund to approximately seven million dollars.

With my chief no longer at the steering wheel, I found myself for the first time in my employment history in the frame of mind to evaluate other job possibilities. Booker Washington was such an understanding employer, always ready to hear the other side of a story, that it was somewhat disconcerting to contemplate maintaining my status with another employer. One illustration will suffice to emphasize some of his humane qualities, as well as his sympathetic understanding of the vexing experiences, which any colored person may encounter, or which may become a part of his personality. When I arrived in Buffalo in the fall of 1911, I sought and secured accommodations with a nationally known clubwoman, Mrs. Talbot, who was a very close friend of Mrs. Booker T. Washington and a leader in the Federation of Negro Women's Clubs. I talked with her about the possibility of getting before the wealthier people of Buffalo. She told me that there was an executive secretary of the Y.M.C.A. of Buffalo by the name of Whitford who knew all of the people of Buffalo of any financial distinction or reputation. She suggested that I seek to have Mr. Whitford arrange a meeting at the "Y" where I might speak to such of the people of wealth as he might invite to this meeting. Following her suggestion, I approached Mr. Whitford. He arranged to have the meeting, and the date was set. As Mrs. Talbot had indicated, at Mr. Whitford's call the wealth of Buffalo assembled. When I returned to the home of my hostess and informed her that I had succeeded in getting Mr. Whitford's consent to call this meeting, she congratulated me on the success that I had obtained and remarked that Mr. Whitford and the "Y" ought to do something for colored people, since colored men were not accepted as bona fide members of the Buffalo Y.M.C.A. She suggested that she did not believe that the people who supported the "Y" knew that the management denied membership to Negroes.

My older brother was a more conciliatory make-up than I, to the extent that he would not defend himself against attacks from the "gang" with whom he came in daily contact on his way to and from school. He was especially docile if I were absent. That is the only explanation I can give for my inner urge to defend the underdog and to speak against any encroachment on the rights of another. I found myself in an attitude of apprehending the offender and measuring out such penalties as in my judgment the offense warranted. I have always had difficulty in restraining myself from moving in unsolicited in any area where someone seemed to be suffering from the imposition of another. Whether that other was an individual, an organization, or an institution did not matter. With this somewhat engrained attitude accumulating from childhood, I took advantage of the opportunity, which Mr. Whitford's meeting afforded to refer to the fact that Negroes were not accepted as bona fide members of the Young Men's Christian Association of Buffalo. Obviously, this was an unfair advantage to be taken of my host, but being young and inexperienced and sensitive to differentials predicated upon race, I yielded to the temptation to commit an almost unpardonable sin.

The meeting was largely attended and the response was overwhelmingly generous. I was able to make a great many friends for Tuskegee on the occasion. While Mr. Whitford made no reply to my attack that night, he subsequently wrote Booker T. Washington and reported the matter to him in some detail. In about three months I received the following letter from Booker Washington, which I consider priceless:

My DEAR Mr. Thomas:

Any person who becomes sincerely interested in improving the Negro's position in American culture will recognize daily a multiplicity of avenues in which the need makes itself manifest.

If, however, he yields to the temptation of trying to satisfy every need, he will so dissipate his energies as to render them well nigh ineffective.

I believe that in the long run if one will confine his activities to the area in which he has jurisdictional responsibility, he will make the most substantial contribution toward the objective mentioned above.

Signed: BOOKER T. WASHINGTON

During the many times that Booker Washington and I were together, alone after that he never mentioned Buffalo specifically or by inference. If he had been a smaller person he would have threatened my job or advised me that I was not employed to solve the problems of the Y.M.C.A., and so on. He might have so crushed my spirit as to impair my usefulness to the institution and otherwise re-direct my focus, which would have been no less disastrous. He undoubtedly was in agreement with the motivation, but through this "Sermon on the Mount" he sought to dramatize that in the whole effort toward democratic participation as a full-fledged citizen, success would be achieved through a division of labor on the part of people concerned with and devoted to justice, equality, and fair dealing.

VII

Principal of Voorhees Institute

In the spring of 1916, nine months after the death of Booker Washington, I accepted the position of Principal of Voorhees Industrial School, located at Denmark, South Carolina. This institution was founded by Miss Elizabeth Wright, a graduate of Tuskegee Institute. Like many other institutions founded by Tuskegee graduates, it was dubbed an "Off Shoot" of Tuskegee. In some quarters it was referred to as the "Tuskegee of South Carolina." It was named in honor and memory of its largest benefactor, a family of Voorhees, residing in the State of New Jersey. It was controlled by a Board of Trustees, and occupied some fifty acres of land and had an endowment fund of a little more than one hundred thousand dollars. Although at the present time this institution, which is now a junior college, is operated under the auspices of the Episcopal Church, at that time it was nonsectarian, receiving no stipulated support from any church—or from Bamberg County or the State of South Carolina.

The turnover of principals or executive heads of the institution following the death of its founder was unceremoniously rapid. The treasurer was a man who had only one arm and an impediment in speech. He also was a graduate of Tuskegee Institute and had taken shorthand and typing instruction while a student there. He developed a rapid speed of manipulating the typewriter, so that he could write as fast with one hand as most people write with both hands. He married the founder, Miss Wright, a few months before she died and upon her deathbed. It was the general impression of the people in the community that he had married her under the circumstances described above in order to become the heir to her throne of administrative control of the institution.

Although the treasurer was never elected principal or president, he exercised greater influence over the conduct of the institution than he had permitted any of the founder's successors to exercise prior to my election as the principal. He was the treasurer and paymaster, and it was important that every employee ingratiate himself with this miniature "Hitler."

The Trustee Board was composed largely of nonresident members, with a chairman—who, as I understand, had never seen the school—living in Boston, Massachusetts. The vice-chairman, an ex-Senator of the State of South Carolina, lived within a mile of the school and, for practical purposes, served as president. The treasurer kept in daily contact with the vice-chairman of the Board and thereby built up a relationship, which made it difficult for any principal to dislodge him or to exercise administrative control over his official behavior.

I suppose that the handicap that this man experienced all of his life emphasized his insecurity and made it seem logical for him to employ unorthodox methods in order to achieve security or recognition. I never saw a person who seemed more suspicious of others or who expressed so little confidence in his fellow men; nor have I ever known a person who was so universally disliked by the people with whom he associated daily or who had so few real friends. I recall having heard very few people speak kindly of this man. He had a reputation for being untruthful and dangerous, because it was the impression of the people on the campus that this treasurer would resort to any tactics to bring the displeasure of the white community upon any colored person who provoked his animosity.

Upon accepting the headship of the institution, I was warned by friends concerning what I was going into and the kind of man with whom I would be called upon to deal. I had some advantage over my predecessors in that I had made some helpful contacts with men of both influence and affluence, both white and colored, in many sections of the nation. As a result of these contacts, I was able to begin at once to utilize some of their resources in adding to the equipment and facilities of the institution. Between the time I was inaugurated, May 16, 1916 and September 15, the beginning of the school year, I had raised sufficient money and met the contract for installing the school's first steam heating plant, which would permit all of the buildings to be heated from a central point.

By the time the Board of Trustees held its fall meeting, I had secured the consent of two outstanding successful businessmen, in the persons of Mr. Irving S. Merrell of Syracuse, New York, and Mr. Charles Gibson of Albany, New York, to serve on the Board of Trustees. In examining the constitution and by-laws, I discovered that the treasurer was given constitutional authority to have the final word as to who should be employed as a member of the faculty. The language of that authority was as follows:

The principal shall have the right to employ teachers with the approval of the Treasurer.

When this matter was brought to the attention of the newly constituted Trustee Board it was their collective judgment that that article should be amended to give the principal final authority in the hiring and firing—if necessary, with the approval of the Board—every member of the faculty, including the treasurer. I had spent a great deal of time in the South, but since there are no uniform customs and every community is apt to have some colloquialisms different from those in every other community, I was surprised to find that the matter of a colored man extending his hand to greet a white man at a time of introduction was not the accepted pattern in the Demark community. One afternoon the

son of the vice-chairman ex-Senator came out to the school and
was introduced to me by the treasurer. I extended my hand to greet
him, which he acknowledged, and we shook hands, but later on
the treasurer commented that I had violated a Southern tradition.
Neither the vice-chairman nor his son mentioned the matter to me,
but Mr. Merrell spent the night at the Mayfield residence following
one of our regular Board meetings and discovered that I had not
received the wholehearted approval of the Mayfields because the
treasurer had not only magnified this incident with the Mayfields,
but had sought to build up in the community an antisocial attitude
because the constitution had been so amended that his authority
with the members of the faculty had been impaired.

We not only added to the physical equipment of the institution,
increased its financial resources, and added important persons to
the Board of Control, but we were able so to enrich the curricu-
lum that it became possible for the graduates to receive from the
office of the Superintendent of Education of the State of South
Carolina certificates to teach in the public school system in the
state without having to take an examination. We did not limit our
interest and activity in the state to the campus of the institution,
but we were appointed and served as a member of the Hoover
Food Conservation Committee. The discharge of the responsibility
of this assignment took us all over the State of South Carolina
speaking in the interest of increasing the production and the conservation of food.

Very shortly after my inauguration as administrative head of
the institution, requests began to come in from educational institutions, churches, and business organizations across the State of
South Carolina for me to be their guest speaker. In response to
one such request, I accepted an invitation to speak on the Men's
Day Program in the Friendship Baptist Church in Aiken, South
Carolina, which is located forty miles from Denmark. The chairman of the program committee and the person through whose

influence my services were made available was Cyrus Campfield, who was Principal of the Scofield Normal School in the City of Aiken. This school was another one of those private institutions founded and developed by a Northern philanthropist. Through it Negro youth received the only accredited high school education that was obtainable in the County of Aiken.

A sizable percentage of the audience was composed of white people, including the Mayor of the city, whose name was Jackson. I do not remember at this date what I said on the occasion, but I must have impressed Mayor Jackson as having some courage and platform ability. Some months afterward the citizens of Aiken organized an interracial committee to sponsor a Liberty Bond Rally, which was to be held in the City Auditorium. It was the hope of this committee that the auditorium would be filled with people who would be interested and in a position to purchase bonds following the platform presentation by the speakers. It was hoped that it would be an outstanding success from a financial point of view, as well as from the point of view of education.

The white speaker chosen was Colonel Dunn, an able lawyer and very popular as a public speaker. He was the best drawing card in the white community, so far as white people were concerned, as a speaker and was frequently chosen when any important message was to be given to the white section of the community. The Negro members of the community, however, were reluctant to accept Colonel Dunn for the occasion and expressed their apprehension that he would say something, which would embarrass, if not humiliate, the colored section of the audience. As a result no financial cooperation could be expected from the colored people in terms of bond purchases. Colonel Dunn did not enjoy the best reputation among the colored people. Negro members of the committee stated that Colonel Dunn had sent more colored people to the chain gang than all the other lawyers in Aiken County.

Among the white members of the committee was Mayor Jackson, and the meeting was held in his office. He remembered the speech I had made on the Men's Day Program at the Friendship Baptist Church some weeks previous. He said to the committee, "I think I have a solution for your problem. If you can get this man Thomas, Principal of Voorhees Institute, and put him on the program behind Colonel Dunn, he will take care of Colonel Dunn in such a way as to neutralize any unsavory remark Colonel Dunn may make." Acting upon Mayor Jackson's suggestion, the committee came up to Denmark and went over the whole situation with me and asked if I would accept a place on the program under the circumstances mentioned above. I was happy to do so. I went down to Aiken on the day the meeting was scheduled. Long before the hour for the meeting to begin the auditorium was packed. This was the first time that Negro citizens had been part of the audience in the new auditorium. The occasion taught me a great lesson which I will never forget. Colonel Dunn was the first speaker. He was a real orator in the Chautauqua sense of the term and, to my disappointment, he made a very fine speech. It may be that he had been briefed by some member of the committee, because he did not utter a derogatory statement, or say anything that would embarrass any member of the audience. Since I had anticipated that the Colonel would say many derogatory things that would rub the fur of certain members of his audience in the wrong way, I made no preparation other than carrying a pencil and pad to write down any statement he would make to which I had planned to take exception. This meant, of course, that my inexperience with a thing of this kind left me with no alternative in terms of an offensive approach. Toward the end of Colonel Dunn's speech, I discovered that I had been disarmed. It meant that I had to draw quickly on the resources of my imagination in order to have something to say comparable to what the Colonel had said and, at the same time, verify the prophecy of the Mayor who had heard me on a previous occasion and had assured his committee that Colonel Dunn would be matched in every department of his culture. That was a painful lesson. I have never since that time depended upon someone else to make my speech.

A rather amusing incident characterized my experience with a Mr. Emerson, the executive officer of the Standard Oil Company, whose office was in the Fidelity Building in Buffalo, New York. My secretary at Denmark was a person who insisted on everything being correct. He knew that I had been a student officer at Tuskegee with the rank of First Lieutenant. The difference between the cost of current operations at Voorhees and the amount of money raised from students from board, lodging, and incidental fees was so large that it was necessary for the Principal periodically to make trips through the North and East to supplement the income that came in response to letters of appeal which went out daily from the Treasurer's office. I had had some business cards printed with "Jesse O. Thomas, Principal of Voorhees Institute, Denmark, South Carolina." When this supply of cards had been almost exhausted, I asked my secretary, Mr. Goins, to have some more cards made, as I would need them on the contemplated trip to western New York. He remembered that I had been a Lieutenant and, in his attitude of having things "just right," he had the cards printed with "Lieutenant Jesse O. Thomas, Principal of Voorhees Institute, Denmark, South Carolina." I had left a few of the original cards that I had had, and in order to have a sufficient number to last until my return, I also took some of the cards which my secretary had printed and must have inadvertently put them in different partitions in my card case.

I went to see Mr. Emerson, and the receptionist inquired my name and the nature of my errand. In response I gave her one of the lot that I had printed myself, with my name and official position, minus the Lieutenant, printed on it. The receptionist took the card to Mr. Emerson, who happened to be in a conference at the time, and was told that he asked me to wait ten or fifteen minutes, as he was very anxious to see me. A Mr. Schoellkopf had an office in the same building, with whom I expected to call on after I had concluded my interview with Mr. Emerson. I therefore advised the receptionist that I had another appointment to keep, but would return within the time limit Mr. Emerson suggested he would be occupied. After I had seen Mr. Schoellkopf, I returned to Mr. Emerson's office. Another young woman was temporarily relieving the receptionist, and as she went in to inform Mr. Emerson of my return, I gave her another card as a means of identifying myself. It happened that the card given the second young woman was one that my secretary had printed with "Lieutenant Jesse O. Thomas." Mr. Emerson had a very keen sense of humor. Upon receipt of the second card, he came rushing out of the office asked me to hurry in, because, he said, "I thought I had better see you at once because if I kept you waiting another half hour, you would be a Brigadier General."

When I resigned the principalship of Voorhees Institute and accepted a position with the Department of Labor as State Supervisor of Negro Economics for the State of New York, my successor was not a person who had any contacts with people of means in the North or elsewhere. Many of the people who had contributed toward the support of the school while I was principal did so in response to a personal appeal from an individual with whom they were acquainted and in whom they had confidence. These persons discontinued their support when that relationship no longer obtained. A few years thereafter, the school was experiencing such financial difficulty that it sought or accepted a somewhat subsidiary connection with the Episcopal Church. It is no longer a privately controlled institution of a nonsectarian character.

VIII

Negro Economics
Examiner-in-Charge of United
States Employment Service

In 1917 I took a leave of absence from the principalship of Voorhees Institute to accept a position as State Supervisor of Negro Economics for the State of New York and Examiner-in-Charge of the United States Employment Service in New York City under the auspices of the United States Department of Labor. The duties and responsibilities of this dual administrative tie-up evolved from the task of building industrial morale on one hand, and encouraging the absorption of the total employable population by emphasizing the comparative significance of available jobs in relationship to the war effort. Some people were persuaded to transfer from less essential to more essential industry. When America first entered the war, many persons in high official positions in government, both state and federal, proclaimed the war "a white man's war" and America "the white man's country"; therefore colored soldiers were not at first drafted or permitted to volunteer. Obviously, in the back of some people's mind was the idea that if the Negro learned how to fight and defend himself according to the most modern methods of warfare in Cherbourg, France, he could transfer that skill to his own defense in Jesup, Georgia, or Brookhaven, Mississippi.

When the going got tough, however, the bars were let down and Negroes were admitted into the military organization. A separate officer's training camp for Negroes was even set up near Des Moines, Iowa. The record of bravery and military prowess, which characterized the behavior of the Negro solider in World War I fully justified the prophecy of his leadership concerning the account he would give of himself if given a chance to bear arms in defense of his country. The military demands grew so highly upon the white male population that it produced a shortage of labor in many of the war industries and other industrial organizations throughout the North and West. This gave the Negro his first opportunity in the history of the United States to find employment in large numbers in industry on unskilled, semiskilled, and highly skilled levels. The job opportunities offered by the steel industry, railroads, and other industrial organizations attracted upward of a million colored people from the South to the North and West.

Traveling over the State of New York in the discharge of my assignment, I came into contact with a great many of the people whose acquaintance I had developed as Field Secretary of Tuskegee Institute. When I was associated with them as an official of Tuskegee Institute, providing an opportunity for them to contribute toward the support of that institution and, by the same token, toward the training of Negro youth, they had expressed themselves as being intensely interested in not only the educational development of the Negro, but also in his economic advancement. Many of these people were heads of business organizations and industrial plants and financial and educational institutions. In the original relationship one could easily have gotten the impression that these people who were giving money toward training Negroes as bookkeepers, stenographers, clerks, electrical engineers, steam fitters, and so forth, would be delighted to provide employment for the beneficiaries of their philanthropy, if only those persons should find it necessary to seek employment in the home community of the industries manned by these generous benefactors. It was quite a shocking disappointment, therefore, to find when the personnel director of any one of the above-named organizations or institutions was interviewed and informed of the availability of trained Negroes to replace white members of his staff who had been drawn into the military organization, or who had found more lucrative employment in the war industry, that even though there were vacancies, the organizations were not ready to fill them with Negroes, however competent they might be. I suppose the whole attitude could best be summed up by quoting a president of one of the universities in western New York, who said to me, "We have a very brilliant young woman in our graduating class. In fact, she is a straight-A student and has maintained a higher average in her four years of college work than any other member of her class. I have suggested that she apply to Tuskegee or Hampton. She would make a wonderful teacher and leader of her race."

It happened that there were a number of vacancies on the faculty of this university which were going to be filled by some members of her class who, the president himself admitted, had not shown in the four years of their association that they were her equal in terms of scholastic attainment or scholarship actuality as well as potentiality. By the same token, these heads of industries and business concerns, who had been giving money toward Hampton, Tuskegee, Fisk, and Atlanta University, were interested in the training of Negroes for positions in the community of the school or in the South but were not prepared to avail themselves of the skills which their resources had helped develop. It was the foreign mission approach. I heard some years ago that a woman, becoming so much interested in and concerned about the need for missionary work on the Continent of Africa, sold a slave in order to increase her contribution toward Foreign Missions. I knew a case of a young woman, a graduate of the University of Georgia living in Elberton, Georgia, who went down to Talladega College to a student interracial conference. This was her first contact with her contemporaries in Negro colleges. She became so shockingly surprised at the similarities of the subject matter and classrooms, their dress, and their eating habits, as well as their aspirations in general, that she decided upon graduation to seek employment in a Negro institution. She wrote a great many letters to the presidents of Negro colleges, whose names she had secured through her contacts with Negro students. When the answers to these letters came to her home, her parents soon discovered that they were from Negro colleges, as they were familiar with the names of a number of the colleges. This fact threatened a very serious family disintegration because the father could not take it and made it clear to his daughter that if she identified herself with a Negro school she would be disinherited and could no longer retain residence under his roof. In the midst of this frustration she received a letter from a member of the educational board of the Congregational Church, in reply to an inquiry, advising that there was a position open on the faculty of a school in Portuguese West Africa supported by the Congregational Church. When this information was made available to her father, he became completely reconciled and gave his daughter a bon voyage reception preliminary to her departure for Africa.

Just as it is possible to find people who respond generously to an appeal for foreign missions but who give "sparingly" toward home missions, there are persons who contribute liberally toward the education of a colored person in Alabama or Tennessee but would not give that same person in whom they had invested money for his education a job in the business concern over which they exercised administrative control. It was a little difficult for me at first to harmonize these conflicting attitudes. I recall several instances of people in whose homes I had been a guest on repeated occasions, who reflected no inhibition in our social relationship, upon whom I could always count for a generous contribution and who would frequently go out of the way to make contacts by telephone and letter to introduce me to their fellow Rotarian or Kiwanis or Civitan members, but who would not employ a Negro other than as a janitor.

I had another rather interesting experience in the zone of paradoxes. Business concerns of every character and kind would requisition large numbers of men from the Central United States Employment Office, and the Central Office would allocate a quota to the several branch offices. My office was located at 139th and Seventh Avenue, and all the people seeking employment in that geographical district were encouraged to register at my office. Sometimes the quota for that office was as high as a thousand persons. We gave each registrant an introductory card to be presented to the Personnel Director of the industry in which he was seeking employment, and when employed the card would be mailed by the industry back to our office. Frequently, when we would send out as many as five hundred or a thousand men, fifty or sixty per cent of them would be back the next day, indicating that they had not been accepted. This percentage of rejections seemed to me to be abnormally high in the light of the urgency of the nature of the request. I finally decided to follow up on one of these assignments, and I made a trip to a plant in Bayonne, New Jersey, where we had been requested to send a large number of men. I was admitted through the gate, after identifying myself at the office of the personnel director. I noticed that only about one in every five persons who were interviewed by the staff were accepted. I was close enough to hear the questioning, so it was evident that the people who were rejected were not necessarily less competent than those accepted. At noonday, I went up to one of the interviewers and told him that I had sat and observed what had gone on, and I explained to him that the reason I had come out was that our placement record against the referral was so low. He asked me not to betray his confidence or expose him for giving the facts in the case. He said, "The reason we turn away as many or more men than we employ is that it is the policy here for the men who are employed to know that there are at least two persons outside waiting for each employee's job. With that knowledge he will stand more pushing around than he would if he thought he was the only person available for the job he occupies."

In each community throughout the state we attempted to set up an interracial advisory committee composed of the civic-minded, public-spirited citizens who were prominently known so as to assist in interpreting to the community the nature of the job we were attempting to do in support of the war effort as related to the best use of the manpower. On the committee in New York City was a socially minded, very wealthy Jewish woman by the name of Mrs. Erdman, who was also a member of the Board of Directors of the National Urban League. She became very much impressed with what she evaluated as my community organization ability and leadership potentialities. To this, she added, "dynamic personality." With this impression she convinced the Board and Executive Secretary of the Urban League that when the war was over, the League should make a bid for my services. Upon the strength of her submission, I was offered the position as Southern Field Director of the National Urban League. It took me some time to make up my mind to resign my position with the federal government and identify myself with the National Urban League. While in that quandary I asked Mr. Merrell if I might have a conference with him on occasion of his next visit to New York. His reply was in the affirmative. On the stated occasion I gave him the facts on both sides of the equation and asked his advice. I never shall forget the conversation. He said to me, after considerable deliberation and asking me questions, "Mr. Thomas, I would suggest that you resign the government job and accept the job with the Urban League. In the very nature of the case, the government job is political, so that it would seem that at least every four years you would need to be concerned about the change of administration. The Urban League job is less glamorous, but always remember that a person who holds a political job can work with only one hand—it takes the other hand to hold the job."

I accepted Mr. Merrell's advice and resigned from the job with the United States Department of Labor and accepted the Southern Field directorship of the National Urban League.

IX

Field Secretary of the National Urban League

I resigned the position of State Supervisor of Negro Economics for the state of New York and Examiner-in-Charge of the United States Employment Service, New York City, in the spring of 1919 and entered the New York School of Social Work preliminary to establishing the Southern Office of the National Urban League in Atlanta, Georgia.

In October of that year I opened offices of the League in the Odd Fellows Building, 250 Auburn Avenue, Atlanta, and began conferences with the Negro and white leadership as a basis for evaluating the practicability of organizing the first branch of the Urban League in the Deep South with a paid staff.

When I first began my work in Atlanta, most of the churches had what they called a Social Service Department. The department functioned somewhat in this fashion. Each Sunday the pastor would take up an "after collection," and during his pastoral visits the following week he would divide the amount among the shut-ins or those on the sick list. This represented his conception of a social service. The establishing of the Atlanta Urban League brought to Atlanta, to the extent that Atlanta was the Gateway of the South, a new conception of social work. It was not long after the Atlanta Urban League got to functioning and had an opportunity to demonstrate a more scientific approach toward supplying the unmet needs of persons who were ill-housed, under-fed, unemployed or under-employed, or suffering from some other manifestation of maladjustment, that these Social Service departments of churches automatically disappeared.

Prior to my employment with the Urban League, my predecessor, Dr. Haynes, had followed the policy of organizing committees composed of volunteers and giving them the name of Urban Leagues. Through this method organizations could be set up more rapidly, but they gave the people a misconception of the real function of an Urban League, and myself. The cities of Augusta and Savannah are two cases in point where the people once got the impression that they could have an Urban League without raising a budget to engage as employed staff. It has until this day, I believe, been difficult to change their thinking to the point where they have been willing to attempt to raise a budget to cover the cost of carrying on the work of the E.K. Jones type of local branch of the National Urban League. Getting that region to agree to the point where it was willing to underwrite the budget of a local branch of the Urban League seems to me to be one of the significant accomplishments of the Southern Field Office. The extent to which it demonstrated the possibility of securing sufficient financial support from both Negro and white people to enable the organization to survive until it had demonstrated the need for such an agency—to the extent that the Community Chest accepted it as a member agency—was an accomplishment.

The first meeting to consider organizing the Urban League was called in November, 1919 in the office of Herman Perry, President of the Standard Life Insurance Company. Prior to that time the citizens of Atlanta had very limited knowledge of the Urban League program and less disposition to have a branch of the League in Atlanta. The one person in Atlanta who had been associated directly and officially with the Urban League movement was Dr. John Hope, who was a member of the Board of Directors of the National Urban League. He was not keen on my establishing the

Southern headquarters in Atlanta. In the meeting of the National Board, when he was advised that I was soon to come to Atlanta to establish headquarters of the National Urban League there, he asked me in the presence of the other board members why I did not establish the headquarters in Nashville. Now, that did not mean that he was unsympathetic with the League coming south, or even to Atlanta. In view of the fact that Dr. George Haynes, who had been the Southern Field representative, was a member of the faculty of Fisk University, and up until this time the Southern Field activities had been centered in Nashville, it was Dr. Hope's thinking that perhaps I might capitalize on such goodwill and understanding as Dr. Haynes might have built up, as he indicated that no such knowledge of the League or such association with it characterized the experience of the people in Atlanta. He was nevertheless very cooperative in giving suggestions as to the people to be interested, as I established my headquarters in Atlanta and began to explore the possibility of establishing an Atlanta branch. Since my headquarters was going to be in Atlanta, I felt it logical to organize the first branch of the League in that city.

The League was organized and its Board of Directors selected, with Dr. Plato Durham, Dean of Emory University's School of Religion, serving as chairman, before the knowledge of the League's existence was brought to the attention of the Committee on Church Cooperation. In December, preliminary to launching the financial campaign, I was invited by Mr. J.C. Lindsey, who was then District Manager of the Atlanta Life Insurance Company, to a joint meeting of the Committee on Church Cooperation in the assembly room of the Butler Street Branch of the Y.M.C.A. At the appropriate time, Lindsey presented me to the members of the committee and stated that he had already organized in Atlanta a branch of the National Urban League. In the brief time at my disposal, I attempted to indicate the kind of job the Urban League would attempt to do and something of the mechanics it would employ, emphasizing the fact that it was to operate under the supervision of an interracial board and that several members of the Committee on Church Cooperation had indicated a willingness to serve on the Board, including Dr. Plato Durham, who was to serve as chairman. One member after another of the committee, both white and colored, stated that, inasmuch as the Committee on Church Cooperation was limited in its function, because of lack of staff, to discussing situations making for disharmony, it could not go beyond the passing of resolutions and seeking conferences with responsible people, and they asked whether the Urban League could become their agency for social action. They would seek no authority in directing activities or in controlling its policies; they would simply allocate to the Urban League from time to time problems and situations that required the kind of follow-up which the committee had no facilities or resources to do. They agreed to contribute a substantial amount toward the operating budget of the League if we would undertake to serve them in the capacity above indicated. I promised then that I would take the matter up with the Board of the Urban League, which I did. The Board unanimously agreed to accept the committee's proposition.

The committee then voted to underwrite a portion of the League's budget to the amount of four thousand dollars –two thousand to be raised through the colored churches and contributed by the colored division of the committee, the other two thousand to be similarly raised and contributed by the white section of the committee. It appears that the colored committee failed to sell its part of the responsibility to the Negro church membership, and therefore, the colored section of the committee did not pay one penny of its pledge. The white division kept its contract and paid two thousand dollars in twelve installment payments of one hundred sixty-two dollars and sixty-six cents. This means that only two thousand dollars was received from the Committee on Church Cooperation. The other eight thousand seven hundred dollars was raised by Negro and white citizens through voluntary contributions during the year of 1920. During the years 1921, 1922 and 1923 the budget was raised from the Atlanta citizens, independent of any money from the Committee on Church Cooperation—either the white or the Negro division.

The first person to make a substantial gift was John Manget, a cotton broker and a member of the white division of the Committee on Church Cooperation. With a check for five hundred dollars from Mr. Manget in my possession, I approached Mr. Charles Bailey, who was the senior member of the Bailey family who operated a chain of theaters in Georgia and Tennessee. Inasmuch as the major intake in these theaters came from Negro communities, and in view of the fact that I had some background information as to the financial ability of Mr. Bailey, I approached him for a contribution. After listening to a description of the type of organization the Urban League represented and some of the things we were contemplating doing toward improving the living, housing, and working conditions of the Negro and stimulating a better relationship between the two races, Mr. Bailey indicated an interest in giving financial support. He buzzed his secretary at this point and, when she responded, instructed her to draft a check for one hundred dollars. Unceremoniously at this point I interrupted and said, "I cannot accept a hundred dollars from you, Mr. Bailey." He seemed shocked at this refusal and inquired, "What do you mean? I repeated what was said above. He then asked, "What do you expect me to give?" My reply was, "Five hundred dollars!" Mr. Bailey could use profanity with eloquence. He said, "G - -D-—it, if you got that much nerve to demand five hundred dollars the first time we have seen each other, I will give you five hundred dollars." He re-instructed his secretary to write a check payable to the Atlanta Urban League, John Eagan, Treasurer, for five hundred dollars.

Some years later the City of Atlanta, by a resolution of the Aldermanic Board or City Council, directed that theaters adhere to the "blue law" with no operation for commercial purposes on the Sabbath Day. Mr. Bailey, my five-hundred-dollar benefactor, had a bright idea. He called a meeting of his staff and suggested that his man Thomas, of the Urban League, be invited to formulate an arrangement whereby the Bailey Theaters would agree to give the net proceeds from their Sunday entertainment to charity, placing the Atlanta Urban League at the top of the list. From that day until the present time, I believe, the Bailey Theater Cooperation has contributed at least one thousand dollars annually toward the current budget of the Atlanta Urban League.

The Southern Field Headquarters of the National Urban League was established in Atlanta to serve at least two significant purposes. The second edition of the Ku Klux Klan was reorganized in 1916 on Stone Mountain, ostensibly to serve as a reception committee for Negro soldiers upon their return from the Continent of Europe. It was alleged that Negro soldiers had enjoyed a fraternizing relationship with the French people, including the female element of the population, on a social parity. In the Klan's book, it was contended that upon his return to the United States, the Negro soldier would reflect this unrestrained social behavior and freedom from social inhibition in his association with the women of the United States regardless of their racial identity.

Without waiting for the returning Negro soldiers to substantiate the allegation, the Klan leadership launched an anti-mass campaign calculated to create an unfriendly attitude toward Negroes, Jews, Catholics, and foreigners. Any effort toward improving race relations was opened to indictment for disturbing the social pattern and threatening Southern tradition. A section-wide campaign was launched against "outside interference and Northern infiltration." By locating its Southern regional office in Atlanta and selecting a South-wide advisory committee as a consultant administrative staff, the League invalidated in a large measure any charge of Northern control or outside interference.

In the second place, the expense involved in railroad transportation from New York to any community south of the District of Columbia, and certainly to urban centers of Georgia, Alabama, Texas, and Louisiana, would involve the expenditure of a sum of money much larger than would be necessary to maintain an office in Atlanta, and thereby reduce the supply line, as it were. In other words, in twenty-four hours one could travel by train from Atlanta to any city south of Washington and east of St. Louis.

During the time that the Southern headquarters of the National Urban League was located in Atlanta, the Community Chest and the Council of Social Agencies had not yet been organized in that section. This meant not only that the initial budget of the local League had to be raised through unorganized voluntary contributions, but that the sponsors had to contemplate organizing the subsequent financial campaign of the chapter in the same manner.

In later years, after the larger cities and urban communities in the South had become affiliated with the Community Chest movement by the organization of a local unit, a policy was enforced which made it necessary for any new agency that was brought into existence after the Chest had been organized to move on its own steam for at least two years before it could become a participating member of the Chest. It was the theory of the Chest officials that if the newly created agency could not command enough support to survive two years and thereby demonstrate that it was supplying a community need, then it would prove just so much dead weight, or excessive baggage, for the Chest.

The responsibility for raising this demonstrative budget for local Leagues fell very largely upon the shoulders of the Field Secretary. In Northern communities where a large number of Negro migrants were attracted by local industry, their unaccustomed behavior and unprecedented numbers created a climate of anxiety akin to frustration among the leaders, so that it was comparatively easy to raise sufficient money from corporations and individuals to cover the operating expenses of a local unit. In the Southern community the traffic of a large number of Negro people did not produce the same type of psychic or emotional vibrations, so that an appeal to the community based upon the behavior of a large number of colored people would not receive the same response. In many Southern communities, ten thousand or more Negroes could leave the city and not be missed outside of their immediate relatives or neighbors. In a Northern community, one white person could assume the leadership for improving living, housing, and working conditions of Negroes. In a Southern community, by contrast, it would be inadvisable for any one white person "to poke his neck out" if he had any political ambitions or if his social position in the community was not well-nigh impregnable. As a protective device, the usual custom was to get several white people to become identified with the League. Even to secure this group support, it was always necessary to initiate the effort among Negroes and make a "self-help" demonstration as a basis of appeal to the white community for support.

Since the establishment of the Community Chest and Council of Social Agencies throughout the South, there have been some basic changes in this picture as relates to setting up a local chapter of the Urban League. Seven persons have succeeded the writer as Southern Field Director of the National Urban League working out of Atlanta. No one of then has had to assume the responsibility for raising a budget before a local branch of the League could be established. The establishing of the headquarters in Atlanta and securing the sponsorship of outstanding men and women of the South as members of the Advisory Committee did not satisfy Jacksonville that Northern influence might not be exerted in the conduct of the unit in that city. After we had agreed upon a budget, upon the program, and upon board members of the Jacksonville organization, I received a hurried telegram from the district manager of the North Carolina Insurance Company, who was supplying leadership for the organization of the Jacksonville Urban League, to come to Jacksonville at once. Upon arriving, I found that some white members of the Board had discovered that the National Urban League headquarters was in New York City, and they were afraid that white members of the community might charge them with being identified with or dominated by Northern influence, and they asked if the name of the League could not be changed to "Negro Welfare League." I was so disgusted that I replied that they could change it to the "Jacksonville Sunday School Union" if they wished as long as they carried out the program. It took fifteen or twenty years to get the name of the Jacksonville organization change to Urban League.

I did not encounter the same reaction to "outside influence" in Tampa or St. Petersburg. Of all the local branches that I assisted in organizing, none of them experienced so many disastrous threats in the executive administration as the Tampa branch. The first Executive Secretary was a very able woman whose husband was killed by an alleged chauffeur. This situation created an administrative environment, which so impaired her usefulness that her services had to be terminated forthwith. At the time I was attending the National Conference of the Urban League in New York, and I received a telegram to come to Tampa at once. I had been very friendly with the family, and the most difficult decision I have ever had to make was my submission to the Board as to what, in my judgment, was the best thing to be done for the survival of the organization. The second Executive Secretary was Mr. Benjamin E. Mays, who is now Dr. Mays and President of Morehouse College.

There was a program, participated in by Negro students in the high school and sponsored by the Negro supervisor of schools, that was rendered on the stage of the City Auditorium. The downstairs was reserved for white people only, and the upstairs for Negroes only. The downstairs seats were about half occupied, whereas the upstairs was occupied to the full and crowded, with people standing around the walls and others unable to get in. Executive Secretary Mays wrote an article in criticism of this arrangement entitled, "It Cost Too Much in Terms of Manhood and Womanhood." Before he submitted the article to the Tampa *Bulletin,* he read it to the Ministers Alliance, of which he was a member, and received unanimous approval. The president of the Board of Education was a member of the Board of Directors of the Urban League. When the current issue of the Tampa *Bulletin* hit the streets with this article on the front page, it created quite a sensation. The Negro supervisor of schools took the article to the president of the Board of Education and convinced him that the article was not only directed at her, but was an indictment against the Board of Education. The chairman of the Board of Education consulted with the director of the Community Chest and reached a collective mind that Mays had to go.

Mrs. Mays was employed as a case worker for the Urban League and had adopted the unprecedented practice of referring to her clients as "Miss," "Mrs.," and "Mr." and Dr. Mays had further irritated the community's sensitivity by referring to his wife as "Mrs. Mays" when reporting her cases to the Board. The accumulation of these cross-currents found a common denominator in the demand for Mays to leave Tampa.

The National Conference of Social Work met in Memphis in 1928, and Secretary Mays came to Memphis for a conference with me to determine what course he should follow in the equation. I suggested that he return to Tampa and not wait for the Board to call him in question, but to call a meeting of the Board and give a complete chronological review of the whole situation, pointing out that by virtue of accident of his position he was expected by the Negro community to speak on its behalf whenever and wherever its welfare status appeared in jeopardy. I suggested also that he call attention to the fact that he submitted his article to the Ministers' Alliance, which was composed of the accepted and accredited leadership of the Negro segment of the population. It happened that the president of the Alliance was the vice-chairman of the Urban League Board. When this procedure was followed, Father C.E. Culmer, Vice-Chairman of the Urban League Board and President of the Ministers' Alliance, substantiated the submission of Dr. Mays and motioned that he be given a vote of confidence, and this motion was carried. In spite of the Board's action, I received a wire from the executive secretary of the Community Chest to come to Tampa. Upon my arrival, I was advised that Dr. Mays had precipitated a situation that made it advisable for him to be relieved of his position.

A short time after this Board action, Mr. Mays drove into a filling station to have his car serviced, and was greeted by an attendant who inquired, "What can I do for you, boy?" In an attitude of resentment, Mr. Mays backed his car off the filling station platform and drove away. When he finally arrived at this office, he addressed a letter to the proprietor of the station in which he described the treatment accorded him by the attendant and registered formal protest.

The Tampa Urban League was a participating member of the Tampa Community Chest (a Red Feather organization), which fact made it possible for the proprietor to seek economic reprisal by including Mr. Mays' letter with a statement expressing his displeasure in the behavior pattern of Mr. Mays in this connection. Upon receipt of this communication, the officials of the Community Chest decided to add to the newspaper story described above the letter of criticism received by the proprietor of the filling station in question, which would become a part of Mr. Mays' record. With this additional supporting evidence of what was adjudged the unorthodox behavior of the Executive Secretary of the Tampa

Urban League, the Executive Secretary of the Community Chest (a Mrs. Ruth Atkinson) requested the Southern Field Director of the Urban League to come to Tampa at once. In response to this telegraphic request, I made immediate plans to make an official visit to Tampa. I wired Mr. Mays, informing him of the scheduled time of my arrival. I spent the evening with Mr. and Mrs. Mays prior to the day the conference was to be held with the Community Chest officials.

Mr. Mays drove me down to the office of the Community Chest, thirty minutes before the conference was scheduled to begin. We went directly to the office of the Executive Secretary, Mrs. Atkinson, and when the time came for us to go into the office of the President, who was also President of the Bell Telephone Company, Mrs. Atkinson suggested to Mr. Mays that he not accompany us into the office of the president. Mr. Mays complied with her request and remained in her office during the fifty minutes the conference was in progress.

Participating in the conference were: President Brorein, of the Community Chest, Superintendent Anderson of the Public School System, Mrs. Atkinson, Executive Director of the Community Chest, and the Southern Field Director of the National Urban League. When the bill of particulars as indicated above, including the article "It Cost Too Much in Terms of Manhood and Womanhood" written by Mr. Mays, which appeared in the Tampa *Bulletin*, and the letter from the filing station proprietor, was concluded, an agreement obviously had been reached between the President of the Community Chest and the Superintendent of the Public School System that Mr. Mays' services as Executive Secretary of the Tampa Urban League should be terminated at once.

After considerable discussion of the matter I took the position that, in the first instance, the Board of Directors of the Urban League at its special session called to evaluate Mr. Mays' action in connection with the *Bulletin* article had by majority vote sanctioned his action. Referring to the letter in question, I took the position that I had some criticism of the letter, but it was not from the point of view emphasized by the filing station proprietor or the superintendent of the Public Schools and the president of the Community Chest. Mr. Mays described in some detail the number of different educational institutions from which he received his education, beginning with the Orangeburg State College and including Bates College, of Maine, and Chicago University. He also mentioned the number of degrees he had received and from which institutions he had received them: his Bachelor's and Master's degrees, and the work he had done toward his Doctorate. My position was that Mr. Mays was not a boy in the first instance, and that he was entitled to civil considerations, not because he had graduated from several institutions and received a number of degrees, but because he was an adult citizen, and that I wanted for every other adult citizen, who may have never entered a college or university, all of the consideration that Mr. Mays was demanding. And in consideration of that fact, I would take no official cognizance of the conduct of the Executive Secretary of the Tampa Urban League. The meeting adjourned on that note. Mr. Mays remained in Tampa as Executive Secretary of the Urban League for several months, if not years, until he voluntarily resigned to accept a position with the Young Men's Christian Association.

To my surprise, in 1939, perhaps eight or ten years after Mr. Mays had resigned from the Tampa Urban League to go work with the Y.M.C.A., and was then employed by Howard University as Dean of the School of Religion, the Tampa episode was again brought into focus when Dr. Mays was being considered for the presidency of Morehouse College. The writer was then serving as Acting Executive Secretary of the National Urban League during the acute illness of Mr. Eugene Kinkle Jones. I received a long distance telephone call from Dr. Ira DeA. Reid, informing me that Dr. Mays was being favorably considered for the presidency of Morehouse College; that a roadblock had been thrown in his pathway in the form of his Tampa Urban League work history. He asked me if I would meet with the interested persons in the office of Dr. Jackson Davis, a representative of the General Education Board, and give my interpretation of the chronological history of the Tampa controversy.

Subsequent developments would suggest that my analysis satisfied the persons sitting in judgment that Dr. Mays' action had been provoked by the extenuating circumstances given in my evaluation, and the vote of the Trustees of Morehouse College, I believe, was unanimous.

In the City of New Orleans, you have decentralization of cultural leadership that is divided on the basis of geography and on the basis of religion or theology as well as on the basis of race. Colored people, who live below Canal Street, have had little do with colored people living above Canal Street, as a dividing line of demarcation. The city is primarily a Catholic community in which the Negro Catholics felt they owed nothing to Protestant leadership; then you had the free-born French ancestry, and the descendants of the freed men who came into New Orleans from Mississippi and Alabama. President James Lewis, of the Peoples Insurance Company of New Orleans, who was a member of the organization committee of the Urban League—as well as many other citizens less well-known—regarded the complexion of the sponsoring committee and the Board of Directors of the Urban League as a distinct achievement. On the Board were white and colored people from below and above Canal Street. Prominent Protestants, Catholics, and Jews were included in the membership. You had Samuel Sumurray, Edgar Stern, and Rabbi Feibelman, Father Jacobi, Archbishop Rummel, and Father Murphy of the Catholic persuasion, and Dr. Revus Frederick, A.W. Dent, James Gayle, Emile Labat, C.C. Dejoie, and S.E. Green, to mention only a few of the colored people representing various religious denominations in different sections of the city.

I believe it will be conceded by any unprejudiced person that the stand taken by the representatives of the National Urban League, operating out of the Southern Field Division, on all matters interracial gave to Negro people throughout that section backbone and a spirit to fight. Always, when there was a difficult situation to be met, by unanimous consent the Field Director of the Urban League was called upon to take a responsible, if not the leadership, position in the equation.

In 1940, while in New Orleans directing a campaign to raise the third year's budget of the New Orleans branch of the National Urban League, I received a telegram from President L. Hollingsworth Wood advising of the serious illness of the Executive Secretary, Eugene Kinkle Jones, and requesting me to come to New York prepared to assume the position of acting Executive Secretary of the National Urban League. This was an unenviable position, because I was very much in the position of a strikebreaker.

It developed that between Mr. Jones and T. Arnold Hill, his boyhood friend and closest administrative associate, there had developed a schism akin to mistrust and suspicion. Information accumulated while Mr. Jones was serving as advisor to Mr. Rober, Secretary of Commerce, made it appear that Mr. T. Arnold Hill, who was second in authority at national headquarters, was seeking to undermine Mr. Jones and replace him as Executive Secretary. This impression became sufficiently convincing for Mr. Jones to resign the position in Washington and return to New York and assume his position as executive head of the organization.

When Mr. Jones became seriously ill, it seemed logical to take the position that if Mr. Hill was trying to take his job while he was well and giving part-time supervision to the organization, he would be more successful if he were put in charge while Mr.

Jones was seriously and dangerously ill. It was in that kind of situation that I became acting Executive Director of the National Urban League.

I never held a job where I exercised less of my imagination and where I was less aggressive in the discharge of my functional responsibilities. This was true for two reasons: (1) I knew there were persons in the office who would keep Mr. Jones informed of what was happening, and I did not want to militate against his recovery by giving any basis for his informant to become suspicious of any ambition that I might entertain of becoming Executive Secretary; (2) I knew of the possibilities of a reconciliation between these two erstwhile boyhood friends, in which event I would find myself "a lost ball in high weeds." On this account, I adopted a middle-of-the-road policy and did the best job possible under the circumstances.

In New Orleans, the cooperative relationship and community togetherness greatly enhanced and increased with the consolidation of New Orleans and Straites universities into Dillard University. Dillard University was named for Dr. James H. Dillard who at one time was a member of the faculty of Tulane University and later became the Executive Director of the Jean's Fund.

The upgrading of Xavier from a high school to university status attracted students and teachers from other states and political subdivisions. These two developments so infiltrated the community culture that community-wide efforts could more easily cross the denominational lines and penetrate geographic boundaries.

While there was a great deal of intrigue to be encountered in the Urban League movement, such as one may expect in any group regardless of racial identity or geographic location, nevertheless I spent some of the most pleasant years of my public life on the organization's payroll and was thrown into association and contact with some of the finest people I have ever known, both on the national board and staff and on the local boards and staffs, and other people interested in or connected with the organization in various capacities.

For many years the Urban League had the largest group of trained colored people in the field of social work of any organization in the country. In later years the Department of Public Welfare and other public and private agencies have employed Negroes in an increasingly large number, so that today the Urban League no longer has the largest number or necessarily the best-trained Negro social workers.

I cherish the memory of my association with such persons as L. Hollingsworth Wood, Eugene Kinkle Jones, Elmer Carter, Mrs. Phyllis Joyce, John Dancy, John Clark, Nimrod Allen, Wylie Hall, Clarence Laws, J.A. Thomas, Ed Lewis, and Clifford E. Minton, to mention only a few persons with whom I was associated in some particular enterprise touching the program activity of the Urban League on both national and local levels.

I could give a sweeping statement to include the total staff personnel of all local branches, without a single exception, as well as all the people at national headquarters, by saying that for more than two decades it was my pleasure to enjoy the most sustained and animatedly cooperative relationship with this large company of persons who, under the banner of the Urban League Movement, had found a common denominator.

X

Extracurricular Activities in the Gate City

When the primary responsibility of the Southern Field Director was to organize local branches of the Urban League, his leadership was frequently invited into other community activities, and it very often became necessary for him to assume responsibility for creating or making available facilities and organized resources in areas of the social work field. An attempt was made to get the Traveler's Aid Society to employ two colored women in the Negro waiting room in the Terminal Station in Atlanta for the purpose of giving out information and assisting the traveling public in the manner peculiar to this agency. The Traveler's Aid representatives in Atlanta expressed sympathy with the idea, but advised that they had no funds to cover the salaries of additional staff. The Field Secretary assumed the responsibility of raising the money for the salaries of two people if the Traveler's Aid organization would agree to appoint them. Two women were appointed: Mrs. Brinson on the day shift, and a Mrs. Richardson on the night shift. From 1920 until 1922, when the Community Chest came into existence in Atlanta, the monthly salaries of these two women were raised by the Field Secretary.

In 1919 no Public Health Nurses were employed by the Board of Education to work with Negro children. The Field Secretary went before the City Council and got an appropriation to cover the salaries of Miss Josie Starks and a Miss Charity Collins, who became the first two Negro nurses in the public school system. He also secured an appropriation from the City Council to employ

135

a Negro physician for the first time to give medical attention to the indigent members of the Negro community who were unable to pay for medical care. Dr. E.I. Robinson, who now resides in Los Angeles, California, an ex-President of the National Medical Association, was appointed.

In 1922 while Dr. Singleton, Pastor of Big Bethel A.M.E. Church, was in Columbia, South Carolina, for the purpose of inviting the Bishop's Council to hold its next meeting in Atlanta, a fire of unknown origin in Big Bethel gutted the church and seriously damaged the roof. By coincidence, the insurance on the building had expired a few days before Dr. Singleton had left for Columbia. The Field Secretary went before the City Council and the County Commission, emphasizing the fact that Big Bethel at the time was not only serving as a place of worship for the members of the A.M.E. Church religious denomination, but also providing a meeting place for every civic movement and, in that respect, was the "People's Church." Wheat Street Baptist Church in the same community had been destroyed by fire in 1917 and was in process of reconstruction. As a result of the presentation of Big Bethel's claim to the City Council and County Commission, each of these bodies appropriated five thousand dollars toward the rebuilding of Big Bethel. Reverend Singleton dubbed the writer "Assist Pastor" and stated publicly on more than one occasion that the writer, though a member of the Congregational Church, with no official connection with Big Bethel or any denomination with which it was connected, raised more money for Big Bethel's reconstruction than any other person with the exception of the pastor himself.

In the State of Georgia there were two organizations composed of Negro teachers. One was led by the late H.A. Hunt, former President of Fort Valley College, known as the Georgia Education Association; the other was led by the late Professor W.D. Thomas and was known as the Georgia Teacher's Association. At each state convention there were two badges: one for the "Hunt-ites" and the other for the Thomas followers. Hunt would preside over one session and Thomas over the other; or Hunt would reside one day and Thomas the following day. As a result of a newspaper article written by the Field Secretary pointing out the duplicity and waste of time and money in the educational duplex, he was asked to take the chairmanship of a committee to work out a basis of con- solidation. As a result of the committee's recommendation, these contesting units were consolidated under the name of the Georgia Teachers and Educational Association. By this token, the writer is the organizer of the Georgia Teachers and Educational Association. The one other person who is living that I can identify, who was a member of the organizing committee is Mr. R.W. Gadsden, of Savannah, Georgia.

Prior to establishing the Southern Field Office in Atlanta, it was not the customary thing for colored people to travel through the South in Pullman cars. Our office became the reservation center for colored persons coming into the South from other sections of the country or going out of the south, as well as for those going further into the South. Before I left Atlanta it was comparatively easy for any well-appearing colored person to get reservations out of Atlanta to most anywhere.

I began to file suits against roads and threatened to file them against others when I discovered I was refused reservations when through telephonic communication it was revealed that there was unoccupied space. In filing suits I would indicate the number of unoccupied berths, lower and upper, on the train departing from Atlanta or from some other city in this section. Finally, the super- intendent of Pullman Service in this region decided that, in order to stay out of the courts, they had better let me have Pullman accommodations. They adopted a method that became operative on all roads leaving the south in selling me a lower berth in the drawing room designated "Lower 13" at the same price that a lower berth could be purchased in the body of the car. This meant that I had a whole drawing room for the price of a single berth.

Information gained currency that Jesse O. Thomas was able to secure Pullman accommodation to any section of the country. In the course of events, my office became equivalent to a sub-Pullman ticket office.

This, of course, was before the Supreme Court ordered the Interstate Commerce Commission to illegalize segregation on public carriers. Even though I would make reservations for other colored people, the accommodations would have to be reserved in my name. For years Forrester B. Washington, after he became Director of the Atlanta School of Social Work, whenever he wanted to leave Atlanta sought reservations through my office. The same thing was true when Dr. Mays established headquarters in Atlanta as representative of the Young Men's Christian Association. I finally took both of them down to the ticket office and introduced them to the district passenger agent, stating that their positions required them to travel a great deal and that it was not always convenient for them to wait until I returned to the city, in the event I was away on a business trip, in order to secure Pullman accommodations. Thereafter, they were able to secure Pullman accommodations without any difficulty.

The Standard Life Insurance Company, under the leadership of its founder, Herman Perry, attracted the largest number of college-trained Negro men ever assembled in any one community. There were a number of subsidiary organizations, which offered employment opportunities of administrative and sub-executive rank to men of high caliber, such as the Citizen's Trust Company, the Service Construction Company, the Service Laundry, the Service Printing Company, and the Service Drug Stores. Each of these subsidiary organizations had an administrative head and one or more assistant executives.

There was no civic organization providing a forum whereby these top-ranking Negro educators could pool their thinking. It occurred to me that this group of people could supply a kind of sounding board and spearhead for the less informed element of the population. With this as a background, I called together a small company of insurance executives, physicians, and educators and organized what became known as the "27 Club." The group drew up a rather explicit set of by-laws and a constitution under which the club would be organized and would function. The Constitution provided that the membership should consist of twenty-seven men, ranging in ages from twenty-seven to fifty. It also stipulated that for one to qualify for membership in the "27 Club," he must have resided in the City of Atlanta or Fulton County, for at least two years; he must have achieved some distinction in his chosen vocation or profession; and he must be able to contribute to scientific discussions. The wives of the membership had to be socially compatible. The club would have six business meetings during a calendar year and six social meetings. The business meetings were held at the home of a member, at which time a formal dinner would be served. The membership would appear in formal attire and two papers would be read. These business and social meetings would alternate so that there would be sixty days between each. One paper would be on current events; its author would be expected to list and report on the outstanding happenings of historical importance and current significance anywhere in the world during the interim of sixty days elapsing between the meetings. The paper on current events would occupy no more that fifteen minutes. It would be followed by a discussion of fifteen minutes, at which time the total membership might add to the items of current events or might evaluate items covered in the paper above referred to. The main address or paper of the evening would deal with some specific situations in Atlanta, Fulton County, or the State of Georgia, involving housing, health, recreation, education, or some condition or situation affecting the welfare status of the Negro in particular and the whole community in general. The club would come into possession of the type of factual information that would enable the organization to supply dependable leadership to the lay community.

In order to broaden the base of its exposure, the forum was organized and known as the "27 Club Forum." This group met on the fourth Sunday of each month and was open to the general public. There were usually two or more speakers giving the affirmative and negative side of the issue which formed the central theme of the discussion, following which the general public was given an opportunity to raise questions or make a contribution. At the alternate social meetings, some type of games or recreation in which the wives might participate characterized the program activity.

The business meetings were scheduled to begin at 8:27 P.M. and close at 11:27 P.M. The social meetings were less restricted in terms of either opening or closing hours, because there was no disposition to handle the wives with the same type of rigidity as was imposed upon the men. On December 27, during the Christmas holiday season, when that day did not occur on Saturday or Sunday, the Club held its annual Inaugural Dance. When the twenty-seventh occurred on Saturday or Sunday, Friday or Monday was usually chosen for the Inaugural Dance. The dance began at 10:27 P.M. and ended at 1:27 A.M. During the intermission, a brief installation program was held for the formal installation of the officers elected at the November business meeting, who were to be charged with the executive administration of the Club for the ensuing year. The "27 Club," has celebrated its twenty-fifth anniversary and is still a recognized influence in the "Gate City."

One Sunday morning in April, 1921, I was returning to Atlanta from New Orleans. I purchased the Atlanta *Constitution* from a newsboy and read an account of a bank being organized by Herman Perry, President of the Standard Life Insurance Company, to be named the Citizens Trust Company. On the following Monday morning I went down and opened an account in the bank, being the thirty-ninth person to make a deposit. From that day to this day, there has not been one minute that I have not had some money on deposit at the Citizens Trust Company, and I have never had a check turned down because of insufficient funds. My account remains No. 39. In addition to becoming a depositor, I purchased five shares of stock at two hundred dollars a share. The bank was a subsidiary of the Standard Life Insurance Company, so that when the Standard Life became involved adversely, the bank was threatened with insolvency. The banking department insisted that the stockholders should either put up the equivalent of the face value of their stock in cash or surrender their stock in order to save the bank. The stockholders surrendered their stock and the bank was saved.

In the early 1920s, the Atlanta *Journal* established a broadcasting station system (WSB) with a studio on the tenth floor of the Atlanta Biltmore Hotel. The Southern Field Director of the National Urban League became the first colored person to speak over the radio station in the City of Atlanta. The Atlanta *Independent* and the Atlanta *Constitution* gave wide publicity to this coming event, so that the Negro community was alerted with respect to this innovation. Every person who had an earphone, which was the media employed by air-minded citizens who had radios at the time was channeled to Station WSB. A peculiar circumstance gave added significance to the occasion. When I arrived at the hotel and approached the elevator, the pilot, with outstretched arms, informed me that I could not ascend on the passenger elevator. He instructed me to take the freight elevator. I refused to do so and went to the house telephone and called up Mr. Kay, who was the MC, and informed him that I was in the lobby of the hotel and had been refused permission by the pilot to ride on the passenger elevator, and that I would not take the freight elevator. Under these circumstances, Mr. Kay advised the listening audience, advising them that there would be a momentary delay and asking them to stand by, he descended on the passenger elevator and invited me to join him on the same elevator whose pilot had refused to take me up "on my own steam." This momentary anxiety increased the emphasis of what I had to say in the ten minutes allotted.

XI

Organizing the Atlanta School of Social Work

The major function of the office of the Southern Field Secretary was to organize local branches of the National Urban League and to secure trained personnel to man these local units. From the very beginning the difficulty of finding trained social workers emphasized the absence of trained Negro social workers in that area.

In 1919–1920 there was not a colored person who had received training at an accredited school of social work south of Washington or east of St. Louis. A few Negroes had gone out of the South for the purpose of securing training—to either the Chicago School of Social Administration or the New York School of Social Work—prior to 1920. When they completed their training, however, because the demand was so much greater than the supply, they could find in the community of schools employment which would pay higher salaries than they could receive in a corresponding position in the South, and the conditions under which they worked would impose fewer restrictions and limitations. These facts made it obvious that if the South was to be able to utilize the skills of trained social workers, it had to provide some means of training them in that section.

In the month of April, 1920, Mr. Eugene Kinkle Jones, Executive Secretary of the National Urban League, was scheduled to speak on the program of the National Conference of Social Work in New Orleans. Since Atlanta was closer to New Orleans than New York was, and since the national organization had an official representative in Atlanta, as an economy measure Mr. Jones asked me to take his place on the program. He suggested that I might include in my address any reference to the Southern situation as, in my judgment, would prove educational and helpful and focus the attention of the social workers in attendance upon some of the inescapable needs, in terms of both personnel and finance. It occurred to me that this was a good opportunity to call attention to the members of the National Conference of Social Work to the need of establishing a training center in the South where Negroes might receive scientific training in the field of social service.

At the meeting of the section before which I spoke, held on the morning of April 20, the seating arrangement had excluded colored people from the ground floor and had accommodated them in the gallery. Dr. Hoffman, Statistician of the Prudential Life Insurance Company of New Jersey, preceded me on the program. The presiding officer was a white person by the name of Dr. Bolton, from Baltimore, Maryland, as I recall. I was unable to give full attention to Dr. Hoffman's message because I was very much concerned about the seating arrangement of the delegates and I spent most of the time during his discussion trying to decide what to do or say about this seating differential when it came my turn to speak. About a minute or two before Dr. Hoffman completed his address, it occurred to me what I would do. I leaned over and whispered in the ear of the presiding officer and requested that, when he presented me to the audience, he state that I would speak from the gallery. He was very much embarrassed and nonplussed, and he sought to assure me that the National Conference was not responsible for the seating arrangement, that the Conference was in the hands of the local community. I still insisted on speaking from the gallery.

When Dr. Bolton rose to introduce me, he advised the audience that, because colored people were not seated on the ground floor, the next speaker had refused to speak from the platform and insisted on speaking from the gallery. He apologized for the situation but said that the local community was responsible for the seating arrangement, not the National Conference. At this point, a Mrs. Sears, a white person from Chicago who was connected with the Cook County Department of Public Welfare and whom I did not know then but came to know well later, arose and addressed the chair and stated that the Chicago and Cook County delegates would go with the speaker to the gallery. This precipitated a brief conference of members of the Conference and the presiding officer, and resulted in the colored people being invited to take seats on the ground floor.

The accounting of this experience is pertinent in relation to the organization of the Atlanta School of Social Work only to the extent to which that episode undoubtedly gave meaning to what was said with reference to the need of establishing a training center in the South, because it was obvious as I faced the audience that the unaccustomed or unorthodox behavior of the next speaker somewhat sharpened the anticipation as to what he would say.

At the conclusion of my remarks many people—white and colored—came to the platform to express their appreciation and commendation for the position I had taken. After I had become disentangled from the mob of people who came up to congratulate me, I came down from the platform and found a group of executive secretaries of Family Welfare Societies across the South waiting to get a more detailed concept of when the school could be established and where. After the matter had been discussed for a brief while, they expressed interest in the establishment of such a training school for Negro social workers and suggested that I ascertain the city in the South that afforded the best fieldwork possibilities. They agreed to attempt to secure authority from their respective agencies to pledge financial support to cover the cost of sending a colored person from their communities to the school at the expense of their agencies.

Upon my return to Atlanta I wrote to social welfare organizations in the cities of Jacksonville, Birmingham, Montgomery, Nashville, Memphis, Savannah, and New Orleans. When all the replies were assembled and questionnaires answered, it developed that Atlanta afforded the best fieldwork opportunities and also had the largest number of educational institutions from which we could hope to draw students. After it developed that Atlanta offered better fieldwork possibilities than any other city in the South, the question arose as to what school in Atlanta this enterprise should be affiliated with. At that time Atlanta University (which was then an undergraduate school) was the only Negro school that had a building devoted to library purposes. I approached President Adams of Atlanta University in the interest of having the Atlanta school of social work become affiliated with Atlanta University. President Adams seemed interested, but stated that he would have to bring the matter to the attention of his Board, which would not meet until June of that year, before any action could be taken. This did not prove a satisfactory arrangement, because it was our hope that the matter of establishing the school and its potential existence could be given to the members of the student bodies of the several institutions before the end of the school year.

The late Dr. John Hope, President of Morehouse College, had expressed keen interest in the project and offered the services of Gary Moore, who was the head of the Department of Sociology and Economics, to direct the school without any financial obligation to the school, and also offered to make available classroom space in Sales Hall as Morehouse's contribution toward this significant experiment. It seemed altogether logical and expedient to accept Dr. Hope's offer. Subsequent steps in the organization of the school are described in the minutes, the constitution, and the by-laws, which follow:

Atlanta, Georgia
May 12, 1920

On May 12 a group of citizens met at 23 Cain Street in the office of the Tuberculosis Association at the request of Mr. Jesse O. Thomas. The meeting, was called to order by Mr. Thomas, who outlined the purpose of the meeting, which was to consider the establishment of a School of Social Work.

Included among those present were Rev. Russell Brown, Lemuel Foster, Dr. and Mrs. John Hope, Prof. Gary Moore, Miss Rose Lowe, Miss Mary Dickerson, Mr. John W. Logan, Mrs. Hattie Green, Miss Mae Maxwell, Dr. M.W. Martin of Gammon Theological Seminary, President J.H. Lewis of Morris Brown College, Mr. Robert Dexter of the Family Welfare Society, and President W.W. Adams of Atlanta University. A letter of regret was read from President King of Clark University.

Mr. Thomas stated that at the request of Mr. Eugene Kinkle Jones, Executive Secretary of the National Urban League, who had been scheduled to speak at the National Conference in New Orleans on April 14, he had become a substitute. In Mr. Jones' communication he stated that Mr. Thomas, representing the Urban League in the southern territory, might include in his remarks any information pertinent to the work of that section. At that time, Mr. Thomas was having some difficulty in finding a trained social worker to become the executive secretary. Under these circumstances, he decided to point out the need for a training center for Negro social workers in the

South. He further stated that at the conclusion of his address in New Orleans, thirteen executive secretaries of Family Welfare Societies across the South invited him to remain for a few minutes and go into further detail about the organization of a school.

At the conclusion of the conference with the executive secretaries he was requested to canvass the large cities of the South in an attempt to determine in which city there was the best field-work possibilities. When that fact was determined, if he would organize the school, they would each see that a colored person was sent to the school at the expense of their agencies. Mr. Thomas stated that he had written to New Orleans, Jacksonville, Memphis, Nashville, and Birmingham, and when the information concerning the field-work possibilities in those cities were compared with the situation in Atlanta, by all odds Atlanta provided the best possibilities.

He suggested that in order for the matter which he had brought to present to the committee to be properly considered, the group form a temporary organization. On motion of Mr. Lemuel Foster, seconded by Mr. Robert Dexter, it was agreed that the group would form a temporary organization with Mr. Thomas serving as temporary chairman. The temporary chairman suggested that it would be his hope that the organization from the beginning would be interracial, and suggested that one of the white members of the committee be designated as temporary secretary. On motion of Dr. Russell Brown, seconded by Mr. Logan, Miss Mary Dickerson was designated a temporary secretary.

Mr. Thomas stated that inasmuch as Atlanta University had the best library facilities, he had had a conference with President Adams with respect to organizing the school in connection with Atlanta University, and that while President

Adams expressed keen interest in the enterprise, he advised Mr. Thomas that he could not take any action until the matter was presented to his Board, which did not meet until June of that year. He then stated that Dr. Hope had offered the use of Prof. Gary Moore as director of the school and classroom space in Sales Hall. In view of the fact that it was desirable to have the decision made before the colleges closed for the year, so that the information concerning the organization of the school could be given to the members of the graduating classes of the various colleges before they left the campuses, it would be advantageous to make a decision before the meeting of the Atlanta University Trustee Board in June.

He therefore recommended that Dr. Hope's offer be accepted, which was agreed upon by common consent. In anticipation of favorable reaction to the proposal, Mr. Thomas had written a constitution, a copy of which is herewith attached. The reference in the original Constitution referring to qualifications for admission was amended. The original draft said that the qualifications for admission should be graduation from an accredited high school. It was the opinion of Miss Dickerson that that qualification was too high, and she suggested that it be amended to read, "High School or the equivalent." The amendment was adopted and became a part of the original by-laws. Professor Moore, Dr. Hope, and Mr. Thomas were appointed as a committee to get out a bulletin announcing the opening of the school and to select a volunteer faculty.

Upon motion of Mr. Robert Dexter, seconded by Dr. Hope, the temporary officers were made permanent and other participating members gave their assent to become permanent members of the Board of Directors of the newly established School of Social Work.

There being no further business, the meeting adjourned to be called by the chairman when the need arose for another meeting.

JESSE O. THOMAS, *Acting Chairman*
MARY DICKERSON, *Acting Secretary*
Atlanta, Georgia
September 15, 1920

The Board of Directors of the Atlanta School of Social Work met at 23 E. Cain Street, at the call of the chairman. Present were Dr. Hope, Dr. Lewis, Dr. Martin, Miss Maxwell, Miss Lowe, Miss Dickerson, Mr. Dexter, Mr. Foster, Rev. Russell Brown, and Gary Moore.

Mr. Moore reported for his committee, stating that publicity had been given to the Negro press and bulletins sent to the Negro schools throughout the South announcing the opening of the Atlanta School of Social Work concurrent with Morehouse College. He also stated that none of the thirteen persons, representing the Family Welfare Societies, had reported or applied for admission. There was only one nonresident student in attendance, whose name was Miss Arabella DeCoursey from Jacksonville, Florida. Other students in attendance were Miss Virginia Belle Rodgers, Mrs. Louise Toliver, and Mrs. Ida Hill. Mr. Ira DeA. Reid and Mr. Howard Thurman were taking some subjects.

A voluntary faculty, composed of Dr. A.D. Jones, who was teaching medical school problems, Miss Rosa Lowe and Miss Dickerson, teaching case work, Mr. Thomas, and Mr. Dexter, Community Organization, and Prof. Moore, Director and also teaching some of all the classes when any member of this volunteer staff did not report.

It was also recommended that it would be desirable to add to the Board membership outstanding citizens with national reputations. In support of this idea, Prof. Monroe Work of Tuskegee Institute was elected a member of the Board, and Mr. Walter Hill, State Supervisor of Negro Education for the State of Georgia.

Dr. Hope and Mr. Thomas were appointed as a committee to contact Mr. L. Hollingsworth Wood of the National Urban League at the annual meeting to be held in Detroit, Michigan, in an effort to secure some financial support from some foundation or philanthropic individuals. Mention was made of the fact that the American Red Cross had given some generous assistance to Peabody College, Nashville, Tennessee, for the purpose of training social workers, and it was thought that it might be possible to secure a grant or some financial support from the American Red Cross.

This committee was instructed to explore all avenues, which offered any possible hope of financial assistance. There being no further business, the meeting adjourned.

JESSE O. THOMAS, *Chairman*
MARY DICKERSON, *Secretary*

In the early part of September 1921, I wrote a letter to Mr. John Glenn, Director of the Russell Sage Foundation, in the name of the late Dr. R.R. Moton, who was then President of Tuskegee Institute, describing the need for establishing the school and asking for a grant from the Russell Sage Foundation. In the course of a few weeks, Dr. Moton received a letter from Mr. Glenn advising that the Board of Directors of the Foundation had by unanimous vote approved a grant of five thousand dollars as an unconditional gift to the school. The grant was subsequently matched by the Laura

Spelman Foundation and formed the financial basis upon which the school developed as an institution of Class-A rank in the field of Social Service.

During the same year, we received a subsidy from the American Red Cross for the salaries of a supervisor of fieldwork. The person secured for the job was Miss Helen Pendleton, a graduate of Johns Hopkins University.

Gary Moore died the summer of 1922 and was succeeded by Dr. E. Franklin Frazier, who served as the executive director of the school from 1922 to 1927. In that interim, we had organized sufficient financial resources to move the school from Morehouse College to the Hendon Office Building on Auburn Avenue and assumed the full responsibility for the salaries and operating expenses of the institution.

In 1927 Dr. Forrester B. Washington was employed as Director to succeed Dr. Frazier. The school experienced its greatest expansion and growth under the directorship of Dr. Washington.

XII

Negro Participation
in the Texas Centennial

The history of Texas dates back to the early part of the sixteenth century. Texas has the distinction of having paid allegiance to six different flags. Texas is 760 miles long and 620 miles wide, giving it an area of 265,896 square miles. This is approximately eighty thousand miles larger than the country of Germany. At the time of the Texas Centennial its population was roughly distributed among 4,284,000 whites, 855,000 Negroes, and 684,000 Mexicans and Indians.

The Centennial commemorated the one hundred years of independence of Texas from Mexico. In contemplation of this historical event, the State of Texas appropriated three million dollars to finance it. There were a number of cities in the state whose citizens felt that because of the peculiar relationship that these particular cities sustained to the historical development of the state, this Centennial should have been held in each of them. Dallas, being the oil capital of the Southeast, was thus able to outbid any of her sister cities. In order that the function of the different departments of the federal government might be demonstrated in connection with this exposition, the federal government appropriated three million dollars; the state of Texas appropriated three million dollars and the city of Dallas four million, making a grand total of ten million dollars. For the purpose of comparative evaluations given by visitors who saw the total Centennial exhibit, for our purpose we would hope that the reader would keep in mind that the over-all expenditure was ten million dollars minus one hundred thousand dollars, which was allocated for the Negro to place in evidence of his contribution to American culture.

The exposition occupied some one hundred and eighty-six acres of land in Dallas in the community of the Dallas County Fair Grounds. For housing the exhibits there were some one hundred fifty buildings, including the Texas Hall of State, which was a memorial to those pioneers who, in 1836, won Texas' independence and carved an empire out of the great wilderness; an Agriculture Building which housed the agriculture exhibits; and the Esplanade of States, which was erected in the center of the grounds and contained a reflecting basin with fountains which brilliantly illuminated the grounds at night from oscillating colored lights. It was located midway between the Hall of Travel, the Transportation Building, and the Varied Industries Building; the Hall of Horticulture; the Administration Building, which housed the management's headquarters; the Band Shell and Amphitheatre, with a seating capacity of five thousand and a stage which accommodated three hundred actors and musicians; the Hall of Natural History; the Hall of Fine Arts; the City of China; the Ford Motor Company's Exposition Building; the Hall of Religion; the Federal Exhibits Building; the Black Forest, a picturesque German Village; the Live Stock Building; the Gulf Radio Broadcasting Studio; the replica of the Alamo, a shrine of Texas liberty; the Old Globe Theatre; the Texas Rangers' Cabin; the Chrysler Corporation and Exhibits Building; the Federal Building; the General Motors Exhibit Building; the Hall of Negro Life; the Cotton Bowl; and many other smaller and less important buildings housing various concessions and amusements.

The lighting system alone cost half a million dollars. The twenty-four 36-inch searchlights were as powerful as the giants that flash from the dreadnaughts of the Navy: they literally turned night into day. Each searchlight had a candlepower of sixty million, which was operated by a three hundred fifty thousand-watt generator. In addition to the above, there were more than three thousand floodlights, which sent their penetrating rays to every foot of space throughout the Exposition Grounds as well as into the exhibit buildings. There was also a battery of searchlights brought from Fort Crockett six feet in diameter and capable of producing candlepower of one and one-half billion.

Notwithstanding the fact that there are approximately nine hundred thousand Negroes in the State of Texas and there are approximately forty-eight thousand in the City of Dallas, neither the State of Texas nor the City of Dallas appropriated a single dime to cover Negro participation in the Texas Centennial. The Negroes of Texas made a number of unsuccessful attempts to secure an appropriation whereby they might organize evidences of their contribution to the development of the State and place them on exhibit. A group of Negroes appeared before the Appropriations Committee of the State Legislature. Other Negroes wrote letters and memorialized the State itself. To all of these the Legislature turned a deaf ear. The Negro group met the same fate upon their approach to the members of the City Council and the Board of Aldermen of the City of Dallas.

Perhaps the most romantic story of a Negro explorer is that of Stephen Dorantes, or, as he is usually called, "Estevanico." As the slave of a Spaniard, Dorantes guided and rescued the three white survivors of the Narvaez Expedition of 1527 and led the expedition on the first overland journey from Florida to Mexico, passing through what is now the State of Texas. In Mexico, Estevanico became the servant of the Viceroy of Mexico and was sent on a journey to the Northwest to discover the seven cities of Cibola. He entered what is now Arizona in 1539 and was eventually killed by the Indians. He was thus the first person from the Old World to set foot on the Southwestern part of the United States.

When the Negroes of Dallas learned that the federal government had appropriated three million dollars in order that the
various departments of the government might be able to demonstrate their function, a petition was sent to the members of the
Commission appointed to supervise the expenditure of this
three million. This Commission was composed of Vice-President
Garner, Chairman; and Secretaries Hull, Wallace, and Roper of
the Department of State, Agriculture, and Commerce. The petition asked for an appropriation from the federal government of
seventy-five thousand dollars. Secretary Roper secured the consent
of the Commission not to vote on the application until he had
had an opportunity of conferring with Eugene Kinkle Jones, who
occupied the position of Advisor on the Affairs of Negroes in the
Department of Commerce. Mr. Jones submitted a memorandum
asking an allocation of one hundred thousand dollars instead of
the seventy-five thousand.

The Commission set aside one hundred thousand of the three
million dollars to be spent roughly as follows: fifty thousand dollars for the erection of an Exhibits Building and fifty thousand
dollars for the collecting, assembling, and transporting of exhibits
and administrative overhead.

The Hall of Negro Life was 106 by 102 feet outside measure-
ments and contained approximately fourteen thousand square feet
of wall space for exhibit purposes. Paradoxically enough, the Hall
of Negro Life was the first building completed on the Centennial
Grounds. The contractor painted the building without instructions or consultation with the General Manager or members of
the Advisory Committee, with reference to the color scheme to
be followed. He used two colors for the interior: deep green and
red. When he was called into question as to the reason for painting
the building without official advise or authority, he stated that in
the first place he knew that Negroes could not assemble enough
exhibits to fill the building; in the second place, he understood

that Negroes like loud colors, and he thought when visitors came they ought to have something pretty to look at.

When he was called upon to paint the building according to the color scheme submitted by the General Manager and approved by the Director of Exhibits, he submitted a proposed statement to the effect that he would re-paint the building according to the color scheme approved for $1,289 extra. After much controversy back and forth, with the government refusing to pay any additional amount for the building being painted in accordance with the color scheme agreed upon, the contractor saw that he could not win, and he proceeded to re-paint the interior of the building. This was not the only misunderstanding we had with the contractor.

The specifications called for a fire hose in the walls of the building for protection. The contractor disregarded that part of the specification and put fire extinguishers in the walls. On June 6, when the Exposition formally opened, controversy was ensuing between the contractor and the representatives of the federal government concerning fire hose versus fire extinguishers. The government was insisting that specifications be followed; the contractor protested on the grounds that the fire extinguishers would offer adequate protection. The contractor was advised that each day he kept us out of the building on account of refusing to comply with the specifications, it would cost a forfeiture of one hundred dollars. It took him eight days under these circumstances to make up his mind that even in erecting a building to be occupied by Negroes, if paid for by the federal government, the letter of the law had to be complied with. In all of his experience in the past, undoubtedly he had always been able to disregard the law when the interest and welfare of Negroes came up for consideration. Anyone who is acquainted with the section of the country in which this contractor lived and the application of public policy to the Negro element of our population will not find this attitude on the part of the contractor at all strange or unusual.

158 MY STORY IN BLACK AND WHITE

The Hall of Negro Life was situated between the General Motors Exhibit Building and the Museum of Fine Arts. It was about three minutes' walk from the main entrance and slightly behind the Globe Theater. The building was one story in height and somewhat "L" shaped. The building was flanked with well-selected shrubbery, in the midst of which were planted floodlights, which cast their indirect rays against a background of bright color. In the front of the building, in large letters of wood twelve inches high with a bronze finish, appeared "The Hall of Negro Life." Just beneath this designation was a sculptured plaster model, bronze in color, which typified the Negro's contribution to the various phases of American culture.

The lobby in the interior of the building was octagonal in shape; in the center of it was a large information desk, occupied by two members of the intelligence personnel. In addition, the lobby was decorated with four murals done by a Negro, Aaron Douglas, an artist of New York City. These murals portrayed the chronological transition of Negroes from the days of slavery up to the present time.

Perhaps the greatest builder of public opinion in a democratic society is the public press. This fact makes the following comments of the metropolitan daily and weekly publications of Texas and the nation appear significant. From the Dallas *Morning News*, of September 4, 1936, comes the following editorial:

> The Negro Building at the Texas Central Centennial has given many white visitors, as well as Negroes, a clearer view of the achievement, which the black man has attained in America. The various exhibits lend weight to the statement of Harvey Allen that "no race has shown itself more capable of assimilating Western civilization than the Negro."

The Dallas *Evening Journal*, August 8, 1936, had this to say:

> The exhibit of Negroes at the Centennial continues to improve. A number of extremely interesting items have been added since the opening of the building devoted to Negro life and progress. If you have not visited the exhibit recently, it will pay you to go again; if you have not seen it at all, you have missed something which is instructive and inspiring. While the whites of the South are aware of the handicaps under which the blacks labor, it is not always that the white man fully appreciates the extent of the handicap. However, in the display prepared by Texas Negroes are individual examples of the triumph of man over very great difficulties. The fact that the victor is a man of African blood—and, in one or two instances, of meager schooling—really makes the victory all the more impressive.
>
> Notably in art and in mechanics, what can be done by an individual Negro, using what is at hand as material, is amazing. The work of such a distinguished scientist as George Washington Carver is inadequately displayed. (Dr. Carver is the man who found hundreds of commercial uses for the humble peanut and sweet potato and from the common clays of Alabama.) But, as if to make up for this, the possibilities that lie within the power of humble unknowns really challenge the beholder, whether he be white or black.

On July 31, 1947, this statement was carried in the Houston *Press*.

> In some ways the Negro building is more interesting than any similar exhibit at the fair, for it offers nothing that is old or traditional. It arises out of the ferment of the moment, and its implications are all of the future.

In the Dallas *Dispatch* the following comment appeared:

> Undoubtedly, many have not looked inside the Negro Life Building, where has been established as excellent and as interesting an exhibit as can be found anywhere within the grounds.

The Chicago *Daily News* said this:

> The Hall of Negro Life is the first of its kind at any major American Exposition.

The Texas *Weekly*, Saturday, July 18, 1936, had this to say:

> The Hall of Negro life gives a vivid and revealing picture of the amazing progress made by the colored race in the seventy-five years which have passed since emancipation. It is indeed good to know that throughout the Union the race is responding so eagerly to the efforts being made for its advancement and is also doing so much for itself. And it is especially gratifying to note that in this movement the State of Texas is taking a leading part.

The following editorial appeared in the Dallas *Express*, August 10, 1936:

DALLAS WELCOMES MACBETH

For the first time in the history of the legitimate theater, a Negro production of Shakespeare's immortal Macbeth is touring the United States and will show in Dallas, Thursday night, August 13th, in the amphitheatre of the Texas Centennial.

The following article appeared in the October, 1936, issue of the *Opportunity Magazine*:

THE TEXAS CENTENNIAL

It was perfectly natural for a great many people to feel a bit apprehensive about the participation of Negroes in the Texas Centenary Exposition which is now being held at Dallas, the metropolis of that state. Texas is South and Southeast.

There the traditions of race relations which characterize the South are vigorously maintained. There interracial cooperation has been slow in gathering momentum and bitter antipathy has sometimes found expression in outbreaks of mob violence.

The appropriation of $100,000 by the Federal government did not wholly allay the fears which were everywhere expressed as to the outcome of this venture to present on the Exposition grounds a panoramic record of Negro progress. And not until the building of the Hall of Negro Life had actually been completed was there any considerable interest on the part of the great majority of Negroes who reside outside the State of Texas.

From all reports Negro participation has been a great success. The Hall of Negro Life has proved to be a dynamic force in the education of citizens of both races as to the achievements, actual and potential, of the Negro. Up to this time nearly three hundred thousand people evenly divided between black and white have visited the Negro exhibit. Already there can be observed vast and significant changes in the attitude of whites toward Negroes in the state. Unbelievable improvements in transportation facilities have taken place in the last three months. For the first time in the history of Texas, and perhaps the South, a track meet in which individuals of both races participated was held during the summer.

The daily press has been kind to the Negro and the Negroes have been urged not only to visit the Negro exhibit but all the great educational and scientific displays on the Exposition grounds.

The excellence of the Negro exhibit, which has received universal praise, can be ascribed to the work of the Advisory Committee on Negro participation, which collected, organized, and assembled the great number of artistic and scientific objects which are on display in the Hall of Negro Life. The successful management and administration of the exhibit must be credited to Jesse O. Thomas, and his assistants, who in the face of great difficulties, have achieved what many believed would be the impossible.

We record below a sample of statements taken at random from people of different walks of life who paused at the information desk on leaving the building after having inspected the exhibits, who registered their impressions or wrote personal letters or statements for publication.

"The exhibits in the Hall of Negro Life are well arranged and representative of the Negro's contribution to American culture. They show very vividly the integration of the Federal Government into the life of a hopeful and ambitious race."— Hatton W. Summers, Congressman from the Fifth Judicial District, Dallas, Texas.

"No one can come into this building and inspect these exhibits without having his appreciation of the Negro's artistic ability heightened and his sympathy for the Negro's struggle for his rightful place in the sun broadened."—Joseph B. Shannon, Congressman from Missouri.

"Your exhibits are carefully arranged and tell a wonderful story. Your art and music sections are simply captivating."—Maury Maverick, Congressman, Twentieth Judicial District, San Antonio, Texas.

"I have been delighted with my visit to the Hall of Negro Life. I want to congratulate the management on the way your exhibits are displayed. They reflect credit upon the Negro race."
—Winthrop Rockefeller

"The Hall of Negro Life through its exhibits and the pamphlets given out at the information desk has done more to improve race relations in Texas than anything else during my lifetime."
—Mrs. Bell, Representative of the M.E. Church

"The progress that the Negro race has made in this country in the past seventy years and which has been accelerated in the past quarter of a century is little less than miraculous. His artistic appreciation, his intellectual advancement, his mechanical and agricultural productivity, his social advancement and his unquestioned patriotism have made for him a place in American culture that is unique."—Joseph F. Cuffey, Senator from Pennsylvania.

"The Texas Negro Educational Day held at the Texas Centennial brought together the largest number of Negroes I have ever seen gathered in one place at one time. They were orderly, interested, and unquestionably conscious of what this movement means in the development of their group in Texas and in the nation."—E.K. Jones, Department of Commerce, Washington, D.C.

"The presence of 65,000 Negro people at the Texas Centennial Exposition on October 19 indicates a remarkable spirit of race consciousness. Back of such a response to a day set aside for Negro participation lies the kind of race pride upon which assemblage arises as faith and hope in what the race can accomplish in the future. From such an orderly, well groomed, intelligent group of Negroes must come the kind of respect which is the basis for improved racial relations."—Dr. Sadie T. Alexander, Assistant Solicitor, Philadelphia, Pennsylvania.

R.L. Marshall of St. Andrews, Scotland, visited the Texas Centennial and was generous in his appraisal of the Negro's contribution to Southwestern civilization. The following is his impression:

"I have crossed the half of Scotland, the whole of the Atlantic and the states and even Fifth Avenue, New York before reaching Fort Worth. Surely this was the Texas Rangers in their very weakest moments—a naïve people's nightmare.

"Dallas offered more serious without flamboyancy, natural and without pretense; a genuine folk dream.

"At the end of an afternoon, the Hall of Negro Life was perhaps credited with the strongest impression. The entrance hall was perfect—and the murals the most interesting exhibit yet seen. The pattern of the exhibits was good, the composition well adjusted—and may I say, the personnel well chosen. My final impression was of an exhibition thoughtfully conceived and possessed of an earnest purpose. The result was worthy of the aim."

"The exhibits in the Negro building at Dallas are easily far beyond anything ever before assembled of African descent. It is a credit to the intelligence, and industry of those who had part in assembling it."—Bishop Beverly C. Ransom, Wilberforce University, Ohio.

The following communication was received from Edinburgh, Scotland.

Dear Sirs:

I am, and many of my associates are, intensely interested in the progress of Negro education and culture in U.S.A. If you have a catalogue of your exhibition or any literature on the subject of Negro culture I should appreciate your sending it to us.

Thanking you in advance, I am

Sincerely yours,
[s]Walter Prichard
21 St. Bernard Crescent
Edinburgh, Scotland

As General Manager of Negro Participation in the Texas Centennial, I succeeded in collecting and assembling the largest exhibit of Negro Art that has ever been brought together in any one place at any one time in the history of the United States. This was true not only for painting and sculpture, but also for mechanical and industrial art exhibits.

In addition, we had in our Book Exhibit more books by or about Negroes than had ever been assembled before at any one time. The Hall of Negro Life was dedicated on June 19, which is colloquially known in the State of Texas as Juneteenth. While the Emancipation Proclamation was issued as of January 1, yet because of the difficulty of transportation and poor facilities for communication, the information did not reach Texas until June 19. June 19, therefore, is a "National Holiday" in Texas.

The Hon. Cullen F. Thomas, Commissioner General of the United States Centennial Commission, made the presentation speech.

My friends of the Negro Race,

It gives me pleasure and a source of heartfelt gratitude to pay my respects to a race whose progress up from Slavery has outstretched the imagination of the most extravagant prophet. With this symbol of authority invested in me as Commissioner General of the United States Texas Centennial Commission, I present this building and all that it represents to the many millions of glad souls who rejoice in their freedom and look forward to a better day. Today marks a historical milestone in our forward march to better understanding and better living.

An acceptance and dedicatory speech was made by Eugene Kinkle Jones, Advisor on Negro Affairs of the Department of Commerce. Mr. Jones said in part:

We are assembled today to observe the anniversary of the freedom of the Negro in America following two hundred fifty years of bondage. We also take this occasion to dedicate a building at the Texas Centennial Central Exposition—a building devoted to an exhibit of the Negro's progress in education, in health, in aesthetics, in mechanical arts, in agriculture, in business—in fact, all lines of human endeavor which characterize civilized man and render him master of his environment and add to the sum total of his higher pleasures.

Negroes of this state own thirty per cent of the homes in which they reside. For the country as a whole, the percentage is approximately twenty-four per cent. In 1890, just forty-six years ago, the Negro's illiteracy in Texas was fifty-one and a half per cent. Today, it is much less than thirteen per cent. In one city, San Antonio, there is only five per cent Negro illiteracy.

With such a record, seventy-one years after the Negro shed the fetters of physical slavery, it is befitting, yea, it is almost pathetic, that Texas should be the location for an exhibit of progress Negroes have made in our great country. In America, we have developed right before our very eyes and under our nose one of the greatest phenomena of history. Here we have the Negro race—seventy years ago only four million in number, now more than twelve millions—partaking of customs, embracing modes of living, measuring up to every standard laid down by the dominant majority, confounding and challenging as to their capabilities and as to their ability to meet the demands of the new civilization into which they have been thrust. In fact, whenever the opportunity has been presented, actually producing individual geniuses who surpass their former masters in many feats of skill, in physical and mental processes.

October 19 was celebrated as Negro Achievement Day. This event did not in any way affect or discourage the attendance of the general public. It did, however, attract the largest number of colored people to the exhibit grounds that had ever come together at any one time or place in the history of America. More than sixty-eight thousand Negroes entered the exhibit grounds between 8:00 A.M. in the morning and 11:00 P.M. in the evening.

The main feature of attraction was the nationally publicized football classic with Wiley and Prairie View Colleges vying with each other for national championship honors. We also had the first interracial track meet ever held in the State of Texas. Participating in this feat were students from the Booker Washington and Woodrow Wilson High Schools of Dallas, students from Prairie

View, Wiley and Bishop Colleges, Southern Christian College, Texas University, and Baylor University, with Ed Tolan and Ralph Metcalf as stars.

In addition, we invited a number of organizations across the South to hold either annual, monthly, or special meetings in Dallas on the nineteenth. Included among those organizations were the Longshoremen's Association, Regional Conferences of the Omega Psi Phi and the Kappa Alpha Psi Fraternities, the Alpha Kappa Alpha Sorority, Texas Medical Association, Woodmen of the World Grand Lodge, Women's Federated Clubs of Texas, Undertakers' Convention, Young Men's Christian Association, Texas Postal Alliance, Texas Negro Press Association, Sunday School and B.Y.P.U. Congress, Texas Colored Teacher's Association, Southwest Colored Policemen's Association, Knights of Pythias State Grand Lodge, Excelsior Life Insurance Company, Church Ushers' Association, Texas Commission on Interracial Cooperation, Athletic Coaches of Southwest Association, and Church of God in Christ.

In addition to the members and official representatives of these organizations from local communities and distant points in the State of Texas, there was a large number of citizens—representatives of the federal government—and those connected with various national organizations who came from distances as far away as Philadelphia, Pennsylvania, the District of Columbia, Pittsburgh, Chicago, Illinois and Los Angeles, California.

The only other day when attendance was larger, than on this special event, was the day the Exposition opened. The fact that at no other time or place in history had that many colored people come together to witness any event, it was no overstatement on the part of every person who was called upon or who volunteered to give his appraisal of the occasion to say that "I have never seen this many people of color before anywhere, at any time."

Educational Tour Through
the Hall of Negro Life
(By Alonzo J. Aden, Curator of Exhibitions)

The Hall of Negro Life at the Texas Centennial Central Exposition in Dallas is a Federal Project for which one million dollars was granted, half of this being devoted to the building and the other half to the exhibitions. This beautiful building of pleasing bright and modern architectural design has for public view exhibitions which depict the story of the Negro and the contribution which he is making to American civilization.

On the Centennial Grounds just east of the auditorium, which houses the exhibits of General Motors and next door to the Shakespeare Globe Theatre, one approaches this inviting structure where some of the most interesting displays of the Exhibition are to be found. The only decoration on the exterior of the building, with the exception of color and shrubbery, is the huge circular seal, sculptured plaster model, which is strengthened by the bronze color of the central figure, the Negro in American life.

As the visitor enters an octagonal lobby, he is impressed with the beautiful effect of the rising sun, which gives the suggestion that a new day is dawning for the Negro. The rich golden light serves as a background for four mural paintings of well-blended complementary purple shades, which become a part of the upper wall. These paintings, of interesting designs, which show the influence of African motifs were done by Aaron Douglas, a Negro artist of New York City. They possess the qualities of masterly technique in mural painting. In one of the panels there is a scene from the life of Estevanico, the Negro who was the first member of Cabeza de Vaca's party to set foot on Texas soil. In the three other murals the dramatic story is told of the Negro from the time of his transportation from Africa to his present period of progress. In the first of these, the Negro is being brought in chains to America where he was forced into servitude. The second larger mural shows the "Negro's Gift to America." Here, "Human Labor" is the holder of the key to a true understanding of the Negro in a new world. Music, Art and Religion are all a part of the contribution. The agricultural workers on the left and the industrialists on the right bring their gifts to "Labor." The woman in the center of the composition with the babe in outstretched arms symbolizes a plea for equal recognition. Heretofore, in all submerged social elements, the Negro woman has occupied the lowest position. Here, she is given a place of honor. The child is a sort of banner, a pledge of Negro determination to carry on and share the burden of humanity in its struggle toward truth and light. The cabin, in the midst of the towers, is the symbol of Negro evolution from a crude primitive pioneer life to the complicated existence in the great urban centers. The star in the design is the "Lone Star of Texas." The final panel shows three figures, which represent Negro aspiration. They have risen above other Negroes who apparently are still in chains. As they are released from the machine-like state which has been the role of the Negro, it is less difficult for them to enter fields where mentality is a dominant factor.

The names below the murals on a horizontal curvature serve both as decoration and as a reminder of Negroes who started the ball of racial progress rolling. They are: Paul Lawrence Dunbar, the great American Negro poet; Benjamin Banneker, the inventor of the clock which strikes the hour and the Negro who had a part in laying out plans for the city of Washington, D.C.; Colonel Charles Young, the first Negro graduate from West Point Military Academy; Sojourner Truth, an anti-slavery lecturer; Frederick Douglass, a nationally known abolitionist; Harriet Tubman, a promoter of the Underground Railway; Wright Cuney, a Texas politician and statesman; Richard Allen, founder of the African Methodist Episcopal Church; Booker T. Washington, a founder of

Tuskegee Institute, Alabama; Dr. Daniel H. Williams, a famous surgeon of Chicago and Crispus Attucks, the first person to shed blood for American Independence during the Revolutionary War.

In the spacious lobby of this building is an array of modern blue furniture with chromium frames, which provides comfort and rest and forms a semicircle around a triangular-shaped information desk from which literature describing Negro progress is distributed.

From the lobby to the right the visitor is directed to the Hall of Education where he is greeted by the display of the United States Office of Education. The exhibition points out the advantages which this department makes available to Negroes throughout the country. In the next exhibition are seventy scenes from Howard University in Washington, D.C., which are viewed from a balopticon machine. Here, the life of the famous institution is shown from its beginning in 1866 under General O. O. Howard, the founder, through the various stages of its development to its present period of prosperity in educational achievement under the first Negro president, Dr. Mordecai W. Johnson. Continuing, one comes to the display from Hampton Institute in Virginia, the school from which Booker T. Washington was graduated. Prairie View State Normal and Industrial College, the largest college for Negroes in Texas, is represented by a dioramic miniature model which shows the one building, Kirby Hall, in 1876, from which developed a two-million dollar institution comprising 1,435 acres of land, with a seventy-acre campus. The modern plant, which is a small city, consists of thirty-four fireproof buildings and fifty-five cottages for teachers. Moving along the aisle, one comes to the well-known Fisk University in Nashville, Tennessee. Early in the history of this school the possibilities for the American–Negro spiritual were realized. It was in this institution that John W. Work, one of the early directors of the Fisk Jubilee Singers, had a great part in causing these songs to become more appreciated by music lovers all around the world. One of the best-known graduates from Fisk University in the music world is Roland Hayes. Progressing along the aisle, one finds other displays from well-known Negro schools, colleges, and universities, some of which have been the outgrowth of governmental appropriations, educational foundations, private endowment, individual effort, and various religious organizations. These exhibits illustrate the educational progress of Negroes during the past century.

At the end of this Hall there is an unusual collection of books by and about Negroes. In this library there are approximately five hundred volumes under the subject divisions: history, poetry, biography, drama, fiction, science, oratory, theology, and texts both of a secular and a religious nature. Outstanding among this collection are: "The Negro in the American Social Order," by Horace Mann Bond, "Black Reconstruction," by W. E. B. Du Bois, and "What the Negro Thinks," by Dr. R. R. Moton.

Continuing to the Hall of Fine Arts, one finds a seventy-five-thousand-dollar collection of Negro painting, sculpture, and graphic art, which was assembled by the Harmon Foundation of New York City. The best known of this group are: Archibald J. Motley, Jr., painter; Richard Barthe and Sargent Johnson, sculptors; and James L. Wells and Hale Woodruff, graphic artists and painters. The paintings, which have been the popular choice, of the collection are: "My Guitar," by Samuel Countee of Houston, Texas and "Portrait of Anne Washington Derry," by Laura Wheeler Waring, of Cheyney, Pennsylvania. Mrs. Waring is one of the most outstanding of the Negro woman painters. Several other artists represented in this art collection worked under the Public Works of Art Project, which was the first successful effort on the part of the United States government to give financial backing to the Fine Arts. This project has had, probably more than any other, a great part in arousing mass appreciation of art among Americans and in presenting to public view artists who could have become recognized in no other manner. As a result, several of the Negro artists have exhibited and made sales, and their works have become a part of the permanent collections of some of the largest art galleries and museums in the world. Included in this division are: the works in jewelry making, textile design, and wood block printing by children of the public schools and community houses which are exceptionally well done and do reflect honor on these institutions.

On entering the division containing the Music Collection, *one remembers that America's greatest contribution to culture is the Negro spiritual.* There are well-arranged charts with photographs of many of the foremost Negro musicians and composers. It has been interesting to persons of other races to note the beauty, depth, and harmony of the Negro in song, very often in the absence of training. Nevertheless, it is the consensus of opinion that art and music are among his rarest gifts. These songs have come about as an outlet or means of expressing the deep emotions of the soul. There seems to be a song suited to every mood. There are many Negro musicians in this collection who had made a definite contribution. Of these, Roland Hayes, Marian Anderson, Lillian Evanti, Paul Robeson, William Dawson, and R. Nathaniel Dett are among the most famous. There are included also compositions and arrangements, many of which have been frequently heard by persons who were unaware that they had been written by the pen of a Negro. Along with the music display is an R. C. A. radio-victrola on which recordings of Negro music may be heard. The greatest number of requests have come for the Victor record on which Marian Anderson sings three Negro spirituals arranged by Roland Hayes, H. T. Burleigh, and Hall Johnson, the Director of the "Green Pastures Choir."

From the Fine Arts Division, one passes into the booth of Art Crafts, where there are various displays of interest in the home. Many contributions in this collection have come from Texas as well as other states. Most interesting of these are the quilts, two of which are "Lone Star" designs. Other specimens which receive much attention are the table top made from eighty thousand pieces of wood, an exquisite example of inlaying, by R. A. Johnson, of Richmond, Virginia, and the colorful screen which has been designed by Miss Hallie Queen of Washington, D. C. It is made of pictures and prints from exclusive magazines, which include autographed pictures of Joe Louis, Jesse Owens, and the designer herself.

One now turns the attention of the visitor to the Hall of Health, the importance of which is universally recognized. In this division are charts with special statistical material, which have been prepared by the National Tuberculosis Association of New York City. These charts convey the newer knowledge of health and disease. They show also the cooperation of the Health Departments in teaching sanitation to parents and children of preschool age in the homes, to persons in prenatal clinics and this training as it is continued to children in schools. There are included in this division displays of Public Health Services, Schools of Medicine, Hospitals, and individual contributions which have been made for the insurance of health throughout the country. Most outstanding of these persons is Dr. Daniel Hale Williams, the first surgeon reported in medical literature to have performed a successful operation on the heart and pericardium. This was done in 1893 at Provident Hospital, in Chicago, which he founded, and is referred to in some of the leading texts on surgery. One booth alone exhibits the health work, which is being conducted in Texas.

Continuing through the corridor where the daily broadcasts are made from this building over the Gulf Network on the Centennial grounds, one may stop to view the open-air theatre, where there are radio hook-ups and sound equipment.

For the evening's entertainment the Harmon Foundation of New York City has loaned motion picture films and equipment for the showing of the "Contribution which the Negro Artist is making to American Culture."

Next, in the Hall of Agriculture, as one passes to the first booth, he sees well-planned miniature models showing the improvements of rural farm life in Texas. The inspiration for these models came about as a result of improvements, which have been made on a farm through the cooperation of farm demonstration agents. The model depicting farm conditions in 1863 was constructed as a result of information received from the owner who acquired it three years before Emancipation. He had received his freedom as a result of service in the Confederate Army. In 1918, the son of the original owner came into full possession of the property, and the resulting changes, which are shown in the model dated 1935 were begun.

Many pictures were taken and an extensive study was made with an effort to locate conditions, which would depict an average progress in rural life. This farm was selected after a thorough study was made by thirty-eight Negro county agents who work in a section of Texas that is thickly populated by Negroes, because it illustrated more completely the development in rural life from the slavery period to the present.

As one moves through this hall, he sees to the left a display of saddles and harnesses made by J. H. White, of Navasota, Texas, who has been one of the country's best saddle-makers for the past thirty years.

Directly across from this booth on the right is a collection, which shows a transition of agricultural implements. In this group is a farm tractor made by Henry Border, a farmer at Longview, Texas. This machine is made from discarded automobile parts. It has six forward and two reverse gears with two sets of brakes. It will pull all types of farm implements and possesses a highway speed of thirty-five miles per hour.

In the next booth, the exhibition of Creative Research and Experiment Station Work has created a vast amount of interest because of the eminence of the nationally known agricultural chemist, Dr. George W. Carver, who heads the work at Tuskegee Institute, Alabama. In this field he is recognized as one of the greatest scientists of the world. In the center of the booth are steps, on the sides of which are sketches showing the development of the South into an industrial center, which has been advocated by Dr. Carver since his arrival at Tuskegee in 1896. One will note that these steps increase in width as they ascend, showing in a very limited degree the scope and breadth of the scientist's work.

On the first step there is a plot of earth showing the condition of the soil in 1896 where only grass would grow. The second step shows cotton, which has until recently been the most staple crop of the South. The third step shows the growth of cotton, peanuts, and sweet potatoes, indicating a trend toward diversified farming, another method of his avocation. The fourth step shows cotton, peanuts, sweet potatoes, and pasture lands, a continuation of diversified farming and the development of the South into a livestock center. On the top step are examples of Dr. Carver's products: A cotton block, illustrating the use of cotton in road construction; sweet potato products from which starch flour, bran, and stock feed have been extracted; cattle grazing on Southern pasture land; and four of the ten peanut oils used to relieve residual effects of infantile paralysis. There are three dolls which show the stages of development in health before, during, and after treatment with these oils.

On the semicircular stands are seeds of Southern products, sweet potato products, clays of Alabama, and home-grown stock feeds. Dr. Carver has developed more than a hundred products from the sweet potato, approximately one hundred and fifty uses for the peanut, nearly sixty articles from the pecan, and has extracted many useful dyes from the clay of Southern soils.

There is a miniature model of a modern cooperative plant, which further illustrates Dr. Carver's theory of Negro self-help.

Leaving this exhibit, one enters the Hall of Mechanic Arts, where Tuskegee Institute of Alabama occupies a very important space, showing the fine quality of work produced in this famous institution. Three miniature models show a transition in home building. The first is a replica of the home in which Booker T. Washington was born and is typical of the slavery period. The second type was used by Negroes immediately after slavery and during the period of reconstruction. The third model home is typical of those used by many of the better-class Negroes of today. The various displays, the results of what the student is being taught, as well as the practical application, which is certainly very significant, demonstrating the modern trend in education that both theory and practice are essential. The wood carving display, in which there are candlesticks, card tables, and magazine racks, shows skillful craftsmanship. There are specimens demonstrating methods used in the development of plumbing, sheet metal, electrical processes, shoemaking, tailoring, and photography. Both Tuskegee and Hampton Institutes are famous for the quality of workmanship being done in their trade schools.

In the following booth is the display of miniature models of locomotives and very worthwhile inventions patented by Negroes. These are not listed as having been produced by Negroes, because they were not patented according to race. Many of the youngsters are greatly inspired by the small automobile with knee action, which has been constructed by a boy of eighteen years. The architectural problems, both renderings and actual models by students of the Booker T. Washington High School of Houston, Texas, are praiseworthy. Finally, of chief interest in this group is the collection of models by Stanley Lounds, a twenty-two-year-old high school graduate of Oklahoma City. In this group is an oil well with all the mechanical equipment necessary to make this contrivance go through the process of drilling and releasing water from the oil by a specially constructed slush pit. The other models are: a locomotive with tender and base, a reproduction of the marriage and coronation coach of Napoleon Bonaparte, and, suspended over these, as if in flight, is an airplane. The excellent craftsmanship which is apparent in each of these skillfully executed works attracts the attention of every visitor. As one finds himself in the Hall of Business and Industry, there is on the right an exhibit showing the evolution and development of Negro newspapers and publications assembled by the Associated Negro Press. This collection of the Negro fourth estate includes a hundred and twenty-six Negro weekly newspapers and the one daily published in Atlanta, Georgia. Desks and newspaper racks are provided for ready reference of the visitor to his hometown newspaper.

Continuing, there are pictures of Negro business institutions showing the vast amount of progress made in this field. In the center wing are two graphic balopticons with center maps showing the activities of Negroes in the Farm Credit Administration. On the left in this hall is a progression of photographs and diagrams illustrating the progress made by Negroes in the field of Social Service, including the works of Forrester B. Washington, Director of the Atlanta School of Social Work at Atlanta, Georgia.

In the next booth is the exhibit where one sees charts, graphs, and statistical information concerning the value, expenditures, growth, and development of the Negro churches of the United States and Texas.

Following this is the group of pictures which show the work which is being done with adult education by the Federal Government.

One must admire the exquisite architectural renderings and photographs of Paul R. Williams, one of the leading architects of the country. He has designed homes for Corinne Griffith, Lon

Chaney, and the plan for the residence of Yehudi Menuhin, the famous boy violinist, is included in this collection.

Before leaving the corridors of the exhibits to return to our starting point, one must pause at the Bureau of Census, where a very comprehensive collection has been sent down from Washington, D. C., by the Department of Commerce. In this booth, which is beautifully equipped with office furniture, one is able to view an interesting array of attractively colored maps all relating statistical facts concerning the Negro. Among the four largest of these, is one showing Texas Negro illiteracy, another, Texas home ownership, a third, showing Texas land and buildings owned by Negro farmers in 1935, and Texas change in acreage, colored farm operators in 1930–1935. There is housed in this department a library of the fifteenth census of the United States, which covers the complete span of American Negro life.

The final unit of the Hall of Negro Life is the office where the administrative duties are performed under the direction of General Manager Jesse O. Thomas and A. Maceo Smith, Assistant General Manager. The other members of the staff are: Alonzo J. Aden, Curator of Exhibitions; Charles E. Hall, Specialist in Negro Statistics; Robert H. Holly, Specialist in Legal Research; C. P. Johnson, Assistant to the Specialist in Negro Statistics; Margaret O. Burrell, Secretary to the General Manager; Bernice B. Calloway, Secretary to the Assistant General Manager; Earline Carson, in charge of the Negro library collection; and Ethel Scott Maynard, Bureau of Information.

These collections were assembled under the direction of a National Advisory Committee under the specific authority of the United States Department of Commerce and the United States Texas Centennial Commission. The members of this commit-tee were chosen by residential location and special fitness for the task. They are: Eugene Kinkle Jones, Chairman; Sadie T. M. Alexander, M. O. Bousfield, W. R. Banks, F. D. Patterson, Garnet C. Wilkinson, and Robert L. Vann. The exhibits in the Hall of Negro Life were assembled and installed under the supervision of this Negro–Advisory Committee. This is the first time in American history that Negroes have been given an opportunity to present this type and degree of evidence of their contribution to American culture.

XIII

Senior Promotional Specialist, United States Treasury

In the spring of 1941 I came through Washington on my way from New York to Atlanta and stopped by the United States Treasury to see my friends, Dr. Pickens and L. D. Milton. Mr. Milton was doing a part-time job in setting up the mechanics in connection with the office procedure in the War Bonds Division of the Treasury as relates to activities among Negroes. While in the office I met and received an introduction to Mr. James L. Houghteling, who was an executive assistant to Mr. Morgenthau and Director of the War Bonds Division of the United States Treasury.

In the brief conversation I had with him, Mr. Houghteling expressed himself as being interested in having someone plan a more organized approach to the Negro community which would make possible a more sustained means of channeling the sale of bonds to the Negro buying public. I told him that I would be interested in such a project, but would like to give it more mature thought than the time allotted would make possible. He suggested that if, after the matter had been given thorough consideration, I found myself still interested, I file a formal application for a position as Senior Promotional Specialist. In due course I filled out the famous "Form 57" and returned it to him. Within a reasonable length of time I received a letter from Mr. Houghteling stating that my application had been properly channelized and requesting that I come to Washington as soon as practical to be sworn in and to assume the duties and responsibilities of the assignment.

In October 1941 I secured a leave of absence from the National Urban League as Southern Field Director to accept the position with the Treasury. Before leaving Atlanta, I wrote a job analysis of the new position giving a detailed description of the way I felt the job should be done. The second day after my arrival, Mr. Houghteling called in the administrative staff and read to them my job analysis. When he had finished, he said to the members of the staff, "So far as I'm concerned, this is it." From that day until I resigned from the Treasury to accept a position with the American Red Cross in May, 1943, it never became necessary for Mr. Houghteling or anyone else to add anything to the diagram of activities, which I submitted upon becoming a member of the staff. As a matter of fact, if I had remained with the United States Treasury until the present time, I could have still been working with the framework of my original job outline.

When I had been with the Treasury for about three months, I recommended that we add two more people to the staff: one man to work with labor groups, and a woman to give her major concern to women's organizations. John Whitten, who had been on the staff of WPA and who was well acquainted with government procedure, was the man employed; and Mrs. Nell Hunter, who had been associated with Mrs. Bethune as a member of the National Youth Administration staff, was the woman added. Whitten gave most of his time to organizing labor and management committees in industry. It became my responsibility to plan and somewhat supervise the work of these two additional staff members, as well as to make field trips, fill engagements as guest speaker before various local, state, and national organizations, and plan for large mass meetings.

Upon my return from one of my field trips I had a conference with Mr. Houghteling, during which I told him that Negroes across the country were "squawking" because there were no Negroes connected officially with any of the State War Bond staffs. As a matter of fact, I said to him that Negroes were given more jobs with the NYA, WPA, and other alphabetical governmental agencies than they were with the United States Treasury. In a sense, the former organizations represented a relief type of agency in that they were set up primarily to create jobs for the unemployed. In the case of the United States Treasury, Negroes were called upon to invest and were responding enthusiastically in the support of the War Bond effect to the extent that their buying power would permit. Under these circumstances it was their feeling that they ought to be given some employment consideration for the positions that their money in a direct way was helping to make possible. Mr. Houghteling was very much impressed with the account I gave of the Negro's reaction and my analysis of the Negro's relationship to the War Bond enterprise. He asked if I would like to tell Mr. Morgenthau the same story. My answer was in the affirmative.

He immediately got in touch with Mr. Morgenthau and a conference was arranged for that afternoon. Mr. Morgenthau seemed likewise appreciative of the Negro's reaction. After some discussion of approaches that might be made to change the picture, Mr. Morgenthau asked if I would be in the city the following day. I told him that I would not because I had made an engagement to speak at Natchez, Mississippi, to the State Teacher's Association and had made reservations to leave Washington that particular night. He suggested to Mr. Houghteling that he clear with transportation with a view to securing a plane reservation for me so that I could leave the following afternoon and still arrive in Natchez in time to keep the appointment. Mr. Morgenthau said he wanted to think the matter over during the night. The next morning, around ten o'clock, Mr. Morgenthau's Executive Assistant, Ted Gamble, called me on the telephone and informed me that Mr. Morgenthau had requested that I cancel all out-of-town engagements and stand by. He further stated that Mr. Morgenthau had already called by long distance the State Administrators of Illinois, Michigan,

New York, and Pennsylvania and had requested them to come to Washington for a conference the following day. Around four o'clock that afternoon Dr. Pickens and I received a telephone call from Mr. Gamble to come over to Mr. Morgenthau's office for a conference at 4:30. When we arrived, we found the administrators from the states above referred to in Mr. Morgenthau's office, where they had spent most of the day discussing the ways and means, and so forth. They gave us the benefit of their discussion and the conclusion reached was a decision to stage some mass War Bond rallies among colored people in the cities of Chicago, New York, Detroit, and Philadelphia. They asked us for our opinion of what they had in contemplation. Dr. Pickens gave his reaction, and I told them that colored people did not want any Negro War Bond rallies; that they would be interested in participating in a rally of interested citizens—comprising the communities in which they lived—and in the second place, that they would want at such a rally an announcement to the effect that some colored person had been appointed Associate State Administrator on a per diem basis and another colored person as Deputy Administrator on full salary. Obviously, these state administrators had not planned to go that far, because when Mr. Morgenthau asked them their opinion of my submission they replied that they had not contemplated doing the kind of thing that was being suggested. However, when Mr. Morgenthau took the position that the speaker knew the thinking of the Negro community and that the Treasury Department was prepared to stand behind such an undertaking, all of the state administrators acquiesced. It was agreed that the first citizen's War Bond Rally should be scheduled for Chicago on May 27, the one for Detroit on May 30, and the one for New York on June 3. The following day Ted Gamble called me over for a follow-up conference and said to me, "We are going to give you a blank check on the United States Treasury so that you can secure whatever talent you and your promotional committees may decide upon as participants for the rallies at each one of the four cities to be covered."

The local people in each community would have the choice of the main speaker. The musical numbers and other participating talent would be secured and supplied by the United States Treasury through its official representative. In the rally in Chicago, which was held in the Amphitheater, there were some ten thousand people roughly distributed racially as follows: fifty-one hundred colored and forty-nine hundred white. As the guest artists we had for this occasion Richard Crooks and Marian Anderson, together with a hundred-voice chorus directed by J. Wesley Jones, Director of Music of the Community Church in Chicago, with Herbert Agar as our guest speaker. James Weldon Johnson's poem, "Fifty Years of Freedom," was read by Olivia DeHavilland from Hollywood. Immediately preceding the adjournment of the meeting, the State Administrator, who was the presiding officer, announced that he was adding to his staff Reverend H. H. Horace, President of the Negro Baptist Convention of Illinois, as Associate State Administrator, and Major C. Odell Turpin as Deputy Administrator.

At the meeting in Detroit, which was held in the Olympia, with a seating capacity of eighteen thousand, it is estimated that more than twenty-two thousand persons were in attendance, as standing room was at a premium. The guest artists on this occasion were Marian Anderson and Paul Robeson. The guest speaker was the late Associate Justice Murphy, former Governor of Michigan. Other participants were the late Bill Bojangle Robinson and World Heavy Weight Champion Joe Louis. When Louis's name was suggested as one of the persons to be on the speaker's platform, I said to the State Administrator that there ought to be some way that Louis could be associated with some type of activity rather than simply sitting on the platform. It was decided, therefore, to have the men in the Ford Plant, where Louis was formerly employed, present

Louis with a plaque. This plaque was presented to Louis by Bill Robinson. Associate Justice Murphy spoke for forty-five minutes, giving a rather historical review of the relationship of the United States Treasury to every department of the federal government and the extent to which the War effort depended upon resources provided by the Treasury. The War Bond enterprise was one of the chief sources of intake through which the Treasury was assisting in financing our military campaign. On the basis of this factual information, he urged the members of the audience to invest to their limit in the purchasing of War Bonds. When Joe Louis, was presented the plaque by Bill Robinson, the audience demanded through their applause that he make a speech. He bowed politely and took his seat. The audience would not be denied a speech. The applause became thunderous. Joe rose again and bowed and took his seat. The audience became more persistent and insistent. Joe finally came to the mike and said, as if responding to Associate Justice Murphy, "Yes, we are going to buy bonds. What we want is to be given some jobs so we can make some money with which to buy bonds," and sat down. The Detroit *Free Press*, the following morning, said that "while Associate Justice Murphy took forty-five minutes in which to make his address, which was a classical appeal on behalf of the United States Treasury, Joe Louis made the speech of the afternoon in thirty seconds." Olivia DeHavilland was also among the program participants at the Detroit Rally. The dramatic manner in which she read Johnson's poem was electrifying. Somehow it seemed to pull the audience up out of their seats. At the Detroit meeting Attorney Charles Mahoney, President of the Great Lakes Life Insurance Company, was appointed Associate State Administrator and Edward Baker was appointed Deputy Administrator.

On June 3 at Lewisohn Stadium in New York there were approximately eighteen thousand people about sixty per cent of whom were colored and the remaining forty per cent were white.

The chairman of the interracial sponsoring committee for the New York meeting was Dr. Channing H. Tobias. An effort was made to secure the services of the late Wendell Willkie as the principal guest speaker. When it was revealed that Mr. Willkie had made previous commitments, the committee sought and secured the services of Hon. Thomas E. Dewey, who was the then District Attorney for New York County. When the committee's selection became known to the Treasury Department in Washington, there was a great deal of apprehension expressed concerning the possibility that Mr. Dewey would not make an appeal on behalf of War Bonds but, on the contrary, would make a political speech of a Republican flavor. Effort was made to dissuade the committee from following through its commitments to Mr. Dewey, but Dr. Tobias took the position that his word had been given and he would not repudiate the agreement. It developed that the anxiety of the executive officers of the Treasury staff was well-founded. Mr. Dewey used that meeting to make what was regarded as his nomination speech for Governor of New York. As I recall, he did not make a single reference to the organization under whose auspices he was speaking or to any justification or reason why the members of the audience should buy bonds. He made an attack on the industries and business enterprises that discriminated against Negroes in the matter of employment. He excoriated the nondemocratic procedure of differentiating in employment consideration based on race, creed, color, or national origin. The New York dailies headlined the account of the meeting with Dewey's attack. There was very little in any one of the daily papers about the War Bond campaign. Dewey was subsequently nominated and elected Governor of the State of New York. State Administrator Ford related to him the position, which Dr. Tobias had taken when the suggestion came from Washington to strike his name from the program.

In recognition of the importance of this occasion, from a political point of view, Mr. Dewey, after being elected Governor, sent for Dr. Tobias and offered him a job, which Dr. Tobias declined on the ground that he was not interested in or candidate for a political job. He did, however, suggest to Governor Dewey that the latter would enhance his reputation among Negro voters if he would appoint Francis E. Rovers to a judgeship that had recently been vacated by the death of its incumbent. The Governor followed Dr. Tobias' recommendation in this respect. By coincidence, therefore, Judge Rivers' appointment was tied up with the War Bond mass meeting for which Dr. Tobias had a large part in selecting the participants and over which he presided.

Other speakers on the program were Dr. Marshall Shepherd, Pearl Buck, and Bill Bojangle Robinson. The guest artists comprised Erskin Hawkins' band, Marian Anderson, and Paul Robeson. Olivia DeHavilland was on hand to perform in the unique fashion, which the reading of Johnson's poem made possible for her. We brought her from and returned her to Hollywood by plane three times in ten days. Administrator Nevil Ford appointed Dr. Tobias Associate State Administrator and Robert Braddicks Deputy Administrator.

With the impact of these large interracial mass meetings, momentum was registered which resulted in the appointment of fourteen colored men as Deputy Administrators and eighteen as Associate State Administrators. When I resigned from the Treasury in 1943, Negroes were identified with the State Administrative staffs as Associate and Deputy Administrators from Michigan to Florida and from New York to Texas.

Few positions I have held afforded a greater opportunity for the exercise of creative imagination, or in which I enjoyed a more cooperative relationship with my immediate supervisors as well as the head of the department, than was true of my working experience with the United States Treasury. When my resignation was submitted, the expressions coming from top-ranking officials on Mr. Morgenthau's staff, as well as one from the chief himself, support my thesis. If I thought further evidence was necessary, I would refer to the fact that after my resignation had been accepted I was retained on the staff of the Treasury with the title of "Expert Consultant" for three years.

THE SECRETARY OF THE TREASURY

WASHINGTON

May 3, 1943

My DEAR Mr. Thomas:

It is a matter of great regret to me to have you leave the Treasury Department after more than a year of valuable service on the War Savings Staff. But I fully appreciate the importance of the work which you are assuming with the American Red Cross.

This letter carries to you my sincere thanks and good wishes for the future. Your work in the Inter-Racial Section of the War Savings Staff has carried the message of the War Savings Program very effectively to the Negro population of this country, as our record of War Bond sales amply shows.

I hope that you will always look back on this part of your war service with satisfaction, since you are, in my opinion, fully entitled to do so.

With best wishes,
Yours sincerely,
[s]H. MORGENTHAU, JR.

Mr. Jesse O. Thomas,
Associate Chief
Inter-Racial Section,
War Savings Staff,
Washington, D.C.

TREASURY DEPARTMENT

WASHINGTON

April 30, 1943

Jesse O. Thomas, Esq.,
Associate Chief,
Inter-Racial Section,
War Savings Staff,
Washington, D.C.

MY DEAR MR. THOMAS:

As the time approaches for you leaving the War Savings Staff I am more and more filled with regret at the prospect. You have done a superb job for the Treasury Department, and deserve its highest thanks. You have been instrumental in bringing large sums of money into the Treasury for the national unity among a large section of our population. The work which we have undertaken in our Inter-Racial Section has been unique and without precedent. I have had to rely on you and Dr. Pickens to analyze entirely new problems and devise practical methods of solving them. In this we have had to rely on your judgment, persistence and fidelity in a field which includes the whole United States. The results have shown that the work has been wisely conceived and thoroughly done.

We are deeply sorry to have you leave us, but wish you success and happiness in your new and important work with the American Red Cross.

Yours sincerely,
[s]JAMES L. HOUGHTELING,
Director,
National Organizations Division

TREASURY DEPARTMENT

WASHINGTON

January 25, 1943

DEAR MR. THOMAS:

Your letter of January 23 brings me news of your resignation and I learn of it with genuine regret.

The War Savings Staff will feel your loss very much, and I, personally, am sorry to have you leave. However, I am sure your decision is a wise one, and the American Red Cross is very fortunate in obtaining your services.

I hope you will find the enclosed letter useful if you should ever need it.

With every good wish to you in your new work, I am

Cordially yours,

[s]TED R. GAMBLE

Assistant to the Secretary

Mr. Jesse O. Thomas,
National Organizations Division
War Savings Staff
Treasury Department
Washington, D.C.

Before leaving Atlanta, I wrote what I regarded as a job description in the light of the interview that I had with Mr. Houghteling. The second day after I had been sworn in, Mr. Houghteling assembled his entire staff and read to them my job analysis and said, "Gentlemen, this is it."

For chronological sequence, that job description and my final summary when I severed my connection with the Treasury Department will end this chapter.

October 21, 1941

A SUGGESTED MEMORANDUM FOR
STAFF DISCUSSION

In successfully promoting the sale of Defense Savings
Stamps and Bonds among colored people in the United States,
there are a number of factors which should be included in the
long-range plan and program:

(1) The opportunity for the average colored citizen
to be intelligent with respect to what is being done by the
Government and what resources and facilities the Government
controls or manipulates for the benefit of its citizens are not
equal to what is true of other race elements.

(2) The approach now being made and in contemplation is the first such approach made on behalf of the Federal
Government to the rank and file of colored people.

(3) Because of the limited staff personnel and the desire to
reduce the cost of this educational and promotional program
to the minimum, it will be necessary to utilize to the fullest
extent possible resources of existing organizations and established agencies.

(4) In order not to invite unfavorable comment by the
Negro Press and stimulate antisocial attitude on the part of
Negro leadership, inasmuch, as the enterprise is Federally
sponsored and controlled, it should take on the complexion
of an integrated movement rather than an isolated one, as far
as it is found feasible and practicable.

(5) Inasmuch as State Committees have already been or
are in the process of becoming organized in most of the states
among the white people, it is of primary importance that

colored leaders be added to the State Committees as rapidly as possible. In order that the best possible results might be obtained, it would be advisable that a staff representative go into a state and collaborate with leaders in the selection of the most desirable persons and submit them to the Governor of the State or the State Administrator, who would officially, with the authority of the State and representing the Defense Savings Staff, assemble these persons as members of the State Defense Savings Staff. A letter from the Assistant Secretary or the Secretary of the Treasury would be written to the State Administrator of the respective State advising him of the proposed visit of our field representative from this office, so that he would be intelligent regarding this visit by the field representative and in a receptive attitude.

(6) The most democratic and effective way that this might be done would be to have these prospective appointees assemble at the State Capitol and at the same time invite Negro newspaper representatives, where these semi-formal induction ceremonies would take place. These ceremonies could be followed by a brief discussion on the part of the State Administrator and white and colored field representatives of the Treasury Department. This would give the impression that the colored citizens are an integral part of the movement and would stimulate very helpful publicity.

The selection of the colored representatives of the State Committee would take in consideration their organizational contact, their group influence, and their leadership status in the community where they live.

As the field representatives would go into these local communities in which the different committees resided, they would build up local organizational and educational programs around these appointees who had been honored by their membership on the State Committee. This plan, if carefully and intelligently developed, could operate both in the North and in the South without difficulty.

(7) There are certain organizations with physical facilities and staff personnel which might be used to good advantage as educational centers through which information would be disseminated to the general public. There are some forty-odd branches of the National Urban League with trained staff personnel and are housed in buildings which could be used with a voluntary staff of intelligent housewives as centers where the general public could be invited to come for information on how to buy stamps and bonds and what benefits might be derived both to the Government and to the individual purchaser. In most of these cities there are local branches of the Y.M.C.A. and Y.W.C.A. which have a full-time staff of employees, and also organizations with voluntary staffs: the N.A.A.C.P., Federation of Women's Clubs, Parent–Teacher Associations, etc.

(8) Parent–Teacher Association and local chapters of the National Federation of Colored Women's Clubs, as well as various organizations connected with churches, the Greek–letter fraternities and sororities are other avenues through which information might be intelligently presented to the average citizen.

As another means of national publicity, the Elks Lodge, which conducts an essay or oratorical contest every year among the Negro high schools of the United States, might be persuaded to make the Defense Savings Bond Campaign as its subject. The exact phraseology of the subject is not import in this connection.

(9) If the Grand Exalted Ruler and the head of the Education Department could be persuaded to accept this proposition, then in every high school aspirants for the Elks'

Scholarship prize would be writing about the Campaign. In the state elimination contest those in attendance would hear about the campaign. In the district elimination contest the same would be true, and at the grand annual conclave where twenty-five thousand or more people assemble each year, the grand scholarship prize, which amounts to a thousand dollars, would be awarded. If the plan is regarded as workable by the Elk officials, then every prize, the state, the district, and the grand prize, could all be awarded in the form of a Defense Savings Bond.

(10) As a matter of the division of labor it is being suggested that for the consideration of the Secretary and Doctor Pickens and Mr. Milton, the practicality of having Doctor Pickens to direct his major activities toward the assembly type of meetings that he has been so successfully and effectively speaking before. The writer would give his attention to the convention type of meetings among Negro people. Of course, if this plan is agreed upon, it will be sufficiently flexible for overlapping wherever it would be considered desirable by Doctor Pickens and myself.

(11) The convention type of meeting that would be in session one or more days could be used as a concentrative educational opportunity. A small portable booth, a detailed description of which I shall be glad to give, could be constructed which could be conveniently and conspicuously placed in a convention hall or near the door of the convention, where literature could be distributed by an intelligent and attractive person who would sit inside of the booth. On all four sides of the booth on the outside there would either be pictures of soldiers or men working in defense industries, or women knitting sweaters, etc., and appropriate sentences describing the contribution these several groups were making

toward National Defense with a statement of admonition to the nonmilitary citizenship for its support through the purchase of Defense Savings Bonds and Stamps, etc.

(12) I suggest that we consider the advisability of having a sound moving picture film that will show activities in defense industries in the training centers, including the ground aviation school at Tuskegee and Negro pilots flying. The narrator will, of course, indicate appropriately that these activities of the Government are very largely made possible through the sale of Defense Savings Bonds and Stamps. These pictures would be shown for thirty minutes at schools, conventions, etc., as a part of the educational and publicity program.

(13) In order to more systematically and constantly promote the payroll allotment plan, a visit should be made to and conference had with the executive officers of Negro insurance companies, presidents of Negro colleges and universities, and the executive officers of business enterprises that employ a large number of Negroes, such as the Tennessee Iron and Coal Company of Birmingham, Alabama, the United States Bethlehem Steel Company, the owners of laundries in all parts of the country, as well as other types of business enterprises in which large numbers of colored people are employed.

Through the bishops, moderators and presiding elders, and other federal and state officials of the various church organizations, an effective approach to the local memberships of various churches could be intelligently and cooperatively worked out.

(14) There are some 464 Jean's Fund Supervisors who operate in the counties of thirteen Southern states. These Jean's Fund Supervisors make daily visits to the schools in the counties and once a month they hold a county teachers' meeting with all the Negro teachers in the county. The county superintendent pays the salaries of the Negro teachers in the county

through the Jean's Fund Supervisor. The salaries are paid at the monthly county meetings. It is reasonably supposed that a payroll allotment plan could easily be stimulated and encouraged by the Jean's Fund Supervisors. I am sure Dr. Arthur Wright, Executive Director of the Jean's Fund, would be glad to cooperate by sending out a letter from his office to each Jean's Fund Supervisor requesting them to assist our office in facilitating the sale of Defense Savings Bonds to the teachers and students under their supervision. I suggest that this be done with regard to the Negro Farm Demonstration Agents, Home Economics workers, and Smith–Hughes teachers in every county where there is a considerable number of colored people. All of these persons could be used to advantage as points of important contacts in reaching the rural population, as well as those in smaller cities and industrial communities.

No attempt has been made to give a detailed description of how these ideas might be translated into concrete action because too much space would be required. We have simply attempted to give the idea of a long-range program and suggest some of the mechanics to be employed to reach our objective. Many other avenues will reveal themselves as we go on from day to day.

If I were to give an opinion as to what I thought would be the first step, I would suggest the organization of State Committees in all the states where there are considerable numbers of Negroes in order to avoid the unfavorable publicity that will come to any movement if it becomes known that white committees are being set up in various states and in most instances Negroes are not included.

Since there is no salary to be paid and no financial obligation assumed, the size of the committee should be determined entirely upon the basis of securing adequate representation for all of the important groups, including religion, labor, business, and the various professions.

* * *

It is conceivable that as much as herein suggested has already been considered, but I have simply jotted down some of those things that occurred to me as being essential in setting up a long-range program for the activity of this office. In order to have something concrete to discuss in the conference with Dr. Pickens, Mr. Milton, and yourself, I have drawn up this statement, a copy of which is on both Mr. Milton's and Dr. Pickens' desks.

Our primary concern is to sell or promote the sale of Defense Savings Bonds and Stamps. An important by-product, however, should be the democratization of every segment of our population and thereby increase each individual's sense of joint ownership in his government.

[s] Jesse O. Thomas
Staff Assistant
Defense Savings Staff

To: *Mr. James Houghteling*   February 22, 1943
From: *Jesse O. Thomas*

In severing my official connection with the National Organizations Division of the War Savings Staff, United States Treasury, I wish to submit a brief summary of my activities for the approximate eighteen months, which represents the period of my connection with your staff. A more detailed account of all of these activities has been given in my weekly reports, of course. I am submitting this statement to somewhat indicate what progress has been made toward certain objectives, what mechanics were employed, as well as what projects are unfinished.

In our original interview, before becoming a member of the staff, you called attention to your desire to have a person on your staff who would give his major concern toward discovering and developing agencies and avenues through which our Negro population could be encouraged to purchase War Bonds and Stamps on a sustained basis. In consideration of the above, while I have given considerable time to pubic forums and have made a number of speeches in the interest of wider participation on the part of Negroes, I have devoted my major concern toward discovering and organizing channels through which there would be a constant flow of money from Negroes into the coffers of the United States Treasury through the purchasing of War Bonds and Stamps. It was also evident at the time that there was a good deal of unrest among the colored people on account of the lack of recognition and consideration on the part of local and state administrators, when it came to the question of official identification with their local and state War Bond Committees. For example: There was not in October, 1941, a single colored person in the United States forming a part of the official staff of a state administrator. My first task, therefore, was to set in motion some influence and mechanics which would stimulate the building of morale among the Negro population. We immediately began conferences and correspondence with state administrators with reference to the appointment of Negroes as associate state administrators on their staff. These associate state administrators were to serve as dollar-a-year men. Their responsibility was to organize the Negro population of the state, give them certain administrative supervision as was found necessary, and encourage the chairman of the local Negro War Bond Committee in counties and municipalities to enlist the cooperation of Negro leadership in keeping the importance of Negro participation in the War Bond campaign constantly before the total Negro population.

It will be recalled that, at that time and for some weeks after-wards, almost daily—certainly no week passed—that some letter was not received at the Office of the secretary which ultimately found its way to your desk coming from some col-ored person complaining about the extent to which the Negro population was ignored or neglected. Through the coopera-tion of the state administrators, we were successful in securing the appointment of Negroes as associate administrators in the following states: New York, Maryland, Virginia, two in North Carolina, Tennessee, West Virginia, Alabama, Florida, Mississippi, Oklahoma, and Ohio. We are expecting momen-tarily to receive word that Dr. P. P. Creuzot has been appointed Associate State Administrator of Louisiana. In the States of Georgia, Missouri, Illinois, and Louisiana, Negroes have been appointed as chairmen of Negro activities but with no official status. Colonel Cheatham, Deputy Administrator of Georgia, is committed to the appointment of a Negro as associate state administrator in the State of Georgia. We have not been suc-cessful in getting a commitment from Administrator Allen of that State, however. You may be interested in observing the caliber of men who are represented as associate admin-istrators of these several states: In Alabama, Dr. Patterson of Tuskegee Institute; in Florida, we have President J. R. E. Lee of Florida State College; in Tennessee, we have President W. J. Hale of the A. & I. State College; in Virginia P. B. Young, Jr., Manager–Editor of the Norfolk Journal & Guide, one of the most widely known Negro newspapers in the nation; in North Carolina, we have President Bluford of A. & T. College, and President Spaulding of the North Carolina Mutual Life Insurance Company, which is the largest insurance company owned and operated by Negroes in the United States; in West Virginia, we have President John W. Davis of West Virginia State College; in Mississippi we have W. W. Blackburn, who is Executive Secretary of the State Teacher's Association of that State; in Oklahoma, Dr. J. W. Stanford, former President of Langston University, and an outstanding educator of the State of Oklahoma, who was recently appointed; in Maryland, Willard W. Allen, Grand Master of Masons for the State of Maryland; and in New York, we have Dr. Channing H. Tobias, who is the Senior Secretary of the Negro Division of the Y.M.C.A.

In addition to the above we have been able to get deputy administrators on salary appointed in the States of New York, Missouri, Illinois, Texas, Virginia, and North Carolina. Not only have these representatives, in the capacities indicated, greatly facilitated the sale of Bonds and Stamps among colored people but they greatly reduced to the minimum complaints registered against local and state administrators, on the one hand; on the other hand, they have made an effective contribution toward the building of wholesome morale among colored people. For the past eight or ten months there has not come a single letter of criticism from any part of the United States, so far as I know, representing unfavorable reaction among colored people toward the War Savings Staff, either on a local, state or national level.

As another contributing factor in morale building, I might refer to the interracially sponsored War Bond Rallies, which were held during the months of May and June 1942, in the cities of Chicago, Detroit, and New York—later in Cleveland. A decision to hold these rallies grew out of some observations I made, you recall, following my return from a visit to Tuskegee on April 27. After a conference held in Mr. Gamble's office, Administrator Collins of Illinois, Isbey of Michigan, and Patterson of New York were invited to Washington. In this conference a decision was reached to hold mammoth interracial War Bond Rallies in the cities represented. The writer was

asked to go to these cities and assist the local people in organizing these rallies in keeping with the decision that they should
not take on a racial complexion either in terms of attendance or
program participants. The degree in which we were successful
in organizing these rallies might be suggested in pointing out
that in the Amphitheater in Chicago we had forty-one hundred
white people and fifty-nine hundred colored, which represents
the capacity of the audience; in the Olympia in Detroit we
had twenty thousand people and, the number representing
each racial group was not obtainable. In both Chicago and
Detroit other thousands were turned away for lack of seating
accommodation. Suffice it to say, the attendance represented
the most patriotic element of the white and colored citizens of
that community. In New York in the Lewishon Stadium, we
had fifteen thousand white and colored citizens. According to
the New Times of June 4 they were equally divided between
the two races. In Cleveland, we had thirty-five hundred white
and colored citizens. At least six per cent was white. In each
instance, the sponsoring committees were composed of white
and colored. This was also true of the participants, including
both guest speakers and artists.

As a means of encouraging sustained buying of Bonds
and Stamps on the part of colored wage earners, shortly after
our appointment we worked out with your approval a Payroll
Savings Plan for Negro schools. This plan was adopted and
became operative among the faculty members and other
employees of 112 Negro colleges and 1,741 high schools. With
some modification, we used the same plan for Negro insurance companies. The thirty-eight member companies of the
National Insurance Association accepted the plan. These companies operate in twenty-nine States and have more than three
million policyholders.

It was upon our recommendation that two additional persons were added to the staff in the latter part of 1942: a man, who was to give the major part of his time toward organizing and stimulating labor-management committees, comprising Negro wage-earners in defense industries, and the woman was to give her time primarily to work among women's organizations. You, as head of our division, instructed me to supervise and plan the work of these two people. Through correspondence and telephonic conversations with state administrators, I have been able to arrange for these two people assignments in the different states and enjoy the cooperation of local and state administrators in making daily contacts with women's organizations and laboring organizations, both organized and unorganized.

You also instructed me to coordinate the secretarial force in the office. As a result, the work of each member of the secretarial staff was so clearly outlined that their unit production was greatly increased and the interoffice morale was greatly improved.

We have given time in counseling with representatives of organized groups who wanted to launch community and nationwide War Bond Campaigns. We made a special trip to Durham, North Carolina, to confer with the president of the National Negro Insurance Association and the members of his War Bond Committee in laying plans for the nationwide War Bond Campaign under the sponsorship of this National Negro Insurance Association.

We initiated and are giving supervision to a nationwide War Bond Campaign under the sponsorship of Negro youth. This campaign was launched on February 12, the birthday of Abraham Lincoln, and is scheduled to terminate on April 6, the birthday of Booker T. Washington. All of the Negro colleges through their Student Councils are participating in the campaign, and five thousand high schools and elementary schools. In addition, there are such out-of-school groups as the NYA, Boy and Girl Scouts, New Farmers of America, 4-H Club, and the different youth organizations, such as the Southern Youth Congress and the Youth Section of the N.A.A.C.P., the Junior Auxiliaries of the different religious denominations, such as the B.Y.P.U., etc., who are actively participating in the nationwide patriotic enterprise. In connection therewith, we secured through the originator and director of "Wings Over Jordan" an opportunity for a member of the youth group to speak on behalf of this campaign over a nationwide hook-up through the courtesy of the Columbia Broadcasting Company March 7. Inasmuch as this campaign will continue until April 6, it represents an incomplete project as of this date.

Upon our recommendation, Tom Campbell of the Agricultural Extension Service was made Special Consultant. Through his contacts we were able to organize the Home Economic and Farm Demonstration Agents in several Southern States, over which he has jurisdiction, actively behind our War Bond Campaign. In addition, Mr. Campbell was successful in securing a sixty-four-piece band from the Army Flying School at Tuskegee, which traveled with us for three days over the State of Alabama in an intensive War Bond Drive. It happens that at the end of each day we were near enough to an army base for these soldiers to be housed and fed under Government supervision—Craig Field in Selma, Alabama, and Maxwell Field in Montgomery. This meant that the local committee was free from the responsibility of feeding and housing the members of the band. The parading of this band through the main streets of these cities attracted to the Court House, where these meetings were held, a large number of colored and white citizens. Participating on the program in each instance were representative white citizens. In the case of the Montgomery meeting, His Excellency, Governor Sparks, was among the speakers on the program. This would make it appear that the appointment of Campbell has already been justified.

There are some four hundred seventy-five Jean's Supervisors, which correspond in function to Assistant County Superintendents, who have the administrative supervision over the teachers of five hundred counties. In each of these five hundred counties there are from twenty-five to one hundred teachers in the rural schools over which these Supervisors have jurisdiction. We were successful in organizing these Jean's Supervisors into a campaign unit behind our War Bond Campaign. The County Superintendents pay the county teachers through the Jean's Supervisors. The Supervisors have a monthly meeting of their teachers—at which time their checks are delivered. This relationship puts the Jean's Supervisors in a position to constantly call the attention of the teachers to the importance of investing in War Bonds and Stamps. In one county, on account of the activity of the Jean's Supervisor, every Negro teacher and student in the county purchased Stamps or Bonds during the school year 1941 and 1942.

All of these agencies should be followed up with constant reminders so that their participation may continue to represent the type of sustained support, which has characterized them up to this point.

Since dictating this statement, I have had a visit with the State Administrator of Arkansas, Mr. Roy G. Paschal. It will be recalled that Mr. Paschal was one of the few administrators who expressed no sympathy at all with our attempt in getting Negroes officially identified with his State program. I made a courtesy call on him while in Little Rock. Our discussion naturally drifted toward more effective participation on the part of Negroes. He kept me in conference for more than an hour. At the conclusion of our discussion he reserved the position and promised to appoint a colored person as Associate State Administrator after he had had an opportunity to confer with Mr. Ed McCuistion, State Agent of Negro Schools for the State of Arkansas. In the light of the almost dogmatic position, which Mr. Paschal had maintained on this subject, I regard the latter result as a distinct achievement.

Supplementary–April 26, 1943

With reference to the type of men appointed as Associate State Administrators, I am quoting from a letter just received from Acting State Administrator E. R. Mowbray of West Virginia, written under date of April 20:

Dr. John W. Davis, President of West Virginia State College has been serving on the West Virginia War Savings Committee for many months. Dr. Davis is one of the most prominent and outstanding Negro citizens in West Virginia, and he has agreed to take the time necessary to organize Negro committees throughout the state and to visit various communities in the interest of the War Savings Program.

The West Virginia Committee of One Hundred has just been reorganized by Dr. Davis, and a copy of this complete committee list is attached for your information. Should any of these committee members call upon you for suggestions, material, literature or assistance of any kind for the promotion of War Bond sales, I will greatly appreciate your giving them every cooperation and consideration.

In checking with the Personnel Department, I was informed today that Mr. R. C. Childress, Assistant State Supervisor of Negro Education and Director of Field Work for the A. M. & N. College of Arkansas, has received Civil Service clearance and is now an official member of the staff of Mr. Paschal.

A letter has just been received by the Personnel Department also from Mr. MacRay Clement, Deputy Administrator of Alabama, enclosing form #57, which has been properly executed by Mr. Harry Sims and recommending Mr. Sims for the appointment of Deputy Administrator on his staff in Alabama.

Administrator Allen of Georgia has expressed the willingness to appoint a Negro Deputy for his State. He referred us to Mr. Adams to ascertain the possibility of adding another member to his staff. We have complied with his request and have been informed by Mr. Adams as to the procedure, which we are following. We expect in the near future to have a Negro Deputy on the staff of Mr. Allen in Georgia.

Letters have gone out to Presidents of Colleges and Principals of Schools, requesting that they report on the results of the nationwide War Bond Rally conducted under the sponsorship of the in-and-out-of-school Negro youth, directed by this office. Until we have heard from these institutions we will not know how many Bonds and Stamps were purchased and sold by teachers and students, as well as other citizens in these various school communities.

We have two samples that may indicate the manner in which this youth element of the Negro population has evidenced a desire to assume its full responsibility in support of our all-out war effort.

A report has come from Tennessee State College that a partial report of the campaign activities in the State of Tennessee has netted thirty-five thousand dollars.

At the annual meeting of the New Farmers of America, an organization which takes into its membership Negro youth living on the farms and attending for the most part rural elementary and high schools, held in Greensboro, North Carolina, where the writer was a guest speaker, more than fifty-eight thousand dollars was reported as representing the amount of Bonds and Stamps sold and purchased by this group. This report, of course, does not include the activities of the young people in the public schools of the cities and the colleges. Obviously, the per capita investment on the part of these young people, most of them being gainfully employed, necessarily was small but the aggregate will, I am sure, represent a considerable sum of money. In addition to the inculcation of habits of thrift and frugality, we feel sure that the participation on the part of these young people in this nationwide patriotic enterprise has increased their sense of citizenship responsibility. The morale-building possibility of the campaign cannot be overestimated.

Mr. Willard W. Allen, Associate Administrator of Maryland, has been appointed as my successor to the War Saving Staff. Mr. Allen is Grand Master of Masons of Maryland, executive officer in both the National Negro Business League and the National Negro Insurance Association, as well as thirty-third degree Most Puissant Sovereign Grand Commander of Masons of the Southern Jurisdiction. I am sure that Mr. Allen will call upon the executive secretary of the National Negro Business League to supply him with the names of the Regional Vice Presidents, the Presidents of the local Negro Chambers of Commerce, Boards of Trade, and Business Leagues, which are affiliated with the national organizations. The President of the National Negro Insurance Company, I imagine, will be requested to send in the names of the Presidents of all Insurance Companies, and the District Manager of these companies and the Grand Master of Masons in the different states will be called upon, I am sure, to supply the names of executive officers of local lodges.

A letter from Mr. Allen will go, I am sure, to each one of these important individuals who occupies a position of leadership responsibility, outlining in some detail how and in what measure these men may accelerate the sale of Bonds and Stamps among the people they are in a position to serve daily.

At the request of Mr. Allen, the writer has secured the services of a Mrs. Goldman, who is to become his secretary. We are giving Mr. Allen and Mrs. Goldman the benefit of our experience and such information as we have accumulated in connection with our War Bond campaigns.

At the request of a large number of citizens, white and colored, you were kind enough to arrange for the writer to sustain a dollar-a-year consultant to the War Bond Staff.

In our position as consultant we have pledged to you, as chief of this division and to the staff of our interracial section, our continued cooperation in any capacity where our services may be helpful.

At the request of Mrs. Hunter and Mr. Whitten, we have agreed to cooperate with our successor in planning their work and arranging for them opportunities to go into different states where they have not already worked. It is the expressed opinion of my successor that the wide acquaintance of the writer with the administrators of the different states and the leading Negro citizenship will enable us to serve as an important point of contact in this zone of public relations.

As we assume our new duties with the American Red Cross, we shall serve as close to the War Bond Staff as our telephone.

cc's: Messrs. Coyne, Sloane, Graves, Morgenthau, Gamble, Pickens, Allen.

XIV

Employed by the American Red Cross

Of all the positions I have held, my employment with the Red Cross was the most interesting in many respects and the most difficult and challenging. All previous positions that I had held had placed me either at a distance from my immediate supervisors or employers or the program pattern followed had discouraged or eliminated immediate supervision. My work with the Red Cross called for far more creative imagination and organizational responsibility than any of my previous positions. Not only had the Red Cross never employed colored persons in administrative positions professionally in the sixty years of its existence on the national level, it had never employed them in professional categories on area and chapter levels. This is even more significant—as you think of the traditional Red Cross as a volunteer movement, that the skills of Negroes were not utilized to any appreciable degree as members of the staff or personnel of any of the Volunteer Services.

Historically, the Red Cross represented a "closed shop" so far as Negroes were concerned. It should be said, however, from a point of view of giving relief to refugees, evacuees, and other victims of floods, fires and other disasters, that the Red Cross more nearly than any other institution or organization, not excluding the federal government, gave relief on the basis of need without regard to the racial identity of the beneficiary. In many of the disasters, such as floods or tornadoes, the Negro represented a disproportionate number or percentage of the victims. The Negro has usually lived near the riverbanks and the houses in which he lived were less fireproof or durable and thus less able to resist fire or wind pressure than the houses in which the more favored element of the population lived.

When you add to the Red Cross' record of nonemployment of Negroes and its failure to utilize their skills in its Volunteer Services, you have a discriminatory policy that provoked the mass reaction of Negroes toward the Red Cross. In response to its appeal for funds, they gave sparingly if at all, with a hope that they would never have to call on the Red Cross for financial or any other humane consideration, in spite of the fact that they receive a disproportionate amount of aid in times of disaster. Because the disaster casualties were to fall so heavily on that segment of the population, it is reasonable to suppose that special consideration would have been given to its members in terms of first aid training, home nursing, and the like.

When the Blood Donor program was first established, all Negro blood was rejected, in spite of the fact that a Negro, Dr. Charles Drew, was given the responsibility of developing the Blood Bank program for the American Army. This undemocratic procedure invited universal disapproval. After months of adverse criticism by the public press, scientific organizations, and influential individuals in business and private life, the policy was amended to accept Negro blood but on a differential basis. Of all the ethnic groups in the United States, the Negro donor represented the only prospect whose racial identity made it possible to separate his blood from the main stream. While this new policy served as an appeasement to certain reactionary individuals and groups and organizations, it did not change the position of the majority of medical associations, scientific magazines, labor unions, or metropolitan dailies, as well as a countless number of other types of organizations and individuals.

FOLLOWING IS THE POSITION OF THE AMERICAN NATIONAL RED CROSS REGARDING THE ORIGIN OF BLOOD COLLECTED AND MADE AVAILABLE FOR USE IN THE ORGANIZATION'S NATIONAL BLOOD PROGRAM.

The American National Red Cross has taken a clear-cut position on this question, which heretofore has not been contested. The organization's policy states:

Inasmuch as on the basis of recorded scientific and medical opinion there is no difference in the blood of humans based upon race or color, the plan does not require the segregation of blood; however, whenever necessary to insure the success of the plan, which is to make available blood and blood derivatives to all the people of the United States regardless of race or color, chapters will collect and hold blood in such a manner as to give the physician and the patient the right of selection at the time of administration.

This means that the origin of the blood will be made available upon the request of attending physicians at the time of administration of the blood, but will not be made available under any other circumstances.

July 22, 1948

This resolution of change of policy was indecisive and accepted by the majority of the people as so much "double talk" on the part of the Red Cross. A more comprehensive evaluation of the Negro communities' relationship to the Red Cross can be obtained through a sort of chronological review.

In 1927 the Honorable Herbert Hoover, who was then Secretary of Commerce, appointed a committee which was designated the Hoover Advisory Committee to work with officials of the

American Red Cross in evacuating and rehabilitating Negro refugees and victims of the Mississippi Flood Disaster. This Committee was composed of some ten or twelve prominently known colored people with the late Dr. R. R. Moton, former President of Tuskegee Institute, as its Chairman. The Red Cross reimbursed the committee for such expenses as were incurred incident to its travel and other living expenses in connection with its official conduct.

At the termination of its work, the committee prepared a factual statement describing in some detail the many different types of experiences it encountered in its work with Negro refugees, landowners, public officials—including officers of the law—and many private citizens in the States of Tennessee, Arkansas, Mississippi and Louisiana. The report also included some recommendations as to how the American National Red Cross might increase its efficiency and more adequately serve the total population if the skills of all segments of the population were utilized on a parity. The attention of the administration was called to the conspicuous absence of Negroes from its payroll in professional and administrative categories.

In 1937, Negro citizens at-large were then again called upon to cooperate with the American Red Cross in its effort at evacuating and rehabilitating Negro refugees and victims of the 1937 Flood in the States of Ohio, Kentucky, Missouri, Illinois, Arkansas, and Tennessee. At the conclusion of this cooperative enterprise, Negro leaders met again with the Red Cross officials at Washington and again called their attention to the extent to which the organization had not availed itself of the professional skills of the Negro. Some impression of the attitude of the administration at that time toward the employing of a colored person or colored persons on the national level might be gained from a statement contained in a letter from one of the executive officers of the American Red Cross to one of the officials who was not present at this meeting. Among other things, this officer stated that some of the more radical

Negroes insisted that the Red Cross employ a colored person on its administrative staff at headquarters, but that the answer given by Red Cross officials in his judgment was of such a nature that that question would never come up again.

In 1942, at the invitation of Mr. James L. Fieser, Vice-Chairman of Domestic Operations, a cross-section of Negro leadership consisting of some twenty-five representatives of various national organizations, including the National Medical Association, National Urban League, National Association for the Advancement of Colored People, National Council of Negro Women, National Association of Negro Nurses, the Alpha Kappa Alpha Sorority, the National Council of the Young Men's Christian Association, and departments of governments met in Washington for two conferences with Red Cross officials. In each instance, morning and afternoon sessions were held at headquarters and a critical review and analysis was given of the Negro's experience with the Red Cross in all parts of the United States.

In addition to the questions raised and the matters discussed in the two previous conferences of Negro leaders with Red Cross officials, the blood plasma controversy supplied most of the heat and perhaps less light for the discussion. At the conclusion of the two-day session, a committee of five, with Dr. F. D. Patterson, President of Tuskegee Institute, as chairman, was appointed to make specific recommendations to the American Red Cross as to how it might improve its position in Negro culture. It is no secret that by 1942, as a result very largely of the manner in which the Red Cross was identified with the blood plasma enterprise, the total Negro press and a large percentage of the Negro clergy and leaders in all phases of Negro life were united in the nationwide repudiation of the American Red Cross. It was difficult to get any favorable comment on Red Cross activities in the Negro newspapers. Coincidentally, while the Negro leaders were in conference with Red Cross officials a statement from the Army was presented requesting the Red Cross to establish Negro and white Red Cross clubs on the Continent of Europe to provide recreation and entertainment for members of the Armed Forces.

The advice of Negroes was sought in this connection. It was the unanimous opinion of Negro leadership that it would be most unfortunate and fraught with international complications if the American Red Cross should go on foreign soil carrying a program of segregation in parts of the world where legal segregation did not obtain. It was at this meeting that a decision was reached providing for the staff of clubs located near the concentration of white soldiers to be manned with white Red Cross personnel, and for those located near the concentration of Negro soldiers to be manned with Negro personnel. All clubs, regardless of the racial identity of those in managerial control, were to extend their facilities and services to any and all persons in American uniform regardless of race or sex. The Committee, of which Dr. Patterson was chairman, made the following report:

BLOOD PLASMA PROJECT

In justice to what we know to be the practically unanimous sentiment among Negroes in America, we affirm the need for alteration of the segregated blood plasma policy announced by the American Red Cross for its blood bank in keeping with the directive, which it received from the Army and Navy. We believe failure to alter this policy will continue to have a depressing effect upon Negro morale because such a policy is an insult to the Negro race. It would, in our opinion, be wise to change this policy in the interest of the war effort, both from the point of view of improved morale of the American Negro and in terms of goodwill of the colored people among our allies in the struggle for democracy and human freedom. This policy in the name of these interests and for the sake of the high standing and integrity of the American Red Cross should be repudiated and abolished.

With a changing of the charter upon the recommendation of a committee appointed by President Basil O'Connor, the Red Cross became one of the most democratic organizations in the world from a point of view of administrative structure. After constant needling and conferences with appropriate administrative officers at local, area and national levels, and repeated discussion (roundtable) with delegates of the National Convention plus outside pressure from newspapers, labor unions, medical associations, scientific magazines, professional organizations and lay citizens, in 1948 a resolution was passed at the National Convention which restrained local chapters from employing any differential, mechanical or otherwise, for the handling of blood of Negro donors.

Since the passing of this sweeping resolution insofar as the administrative policy of the American Red Cross in concerned, all blood is red.

RECREATIONAL CLUBS STAFFED BY RED CROSS

It was the opinion of the invited groups assembled on September 1, and to which the Committee affirms, that a wise distribution of Negro staff members should be made in clubs serving white and Negro soldiers abroad. It is felt that those clubs patronized largely by Negro soldiers should have a predominantly Negro staff. Both white and Negro personnel should be appointed for all clubs and American soldiers of all races should be welcomed at all clubs. It is significant that efforts to encourage practices of segregation in the relations of the British people with white and Negro soldiers has been mentioned in Parliament and has been denounced by the British people themselves.

The recommendations which we made as to staff are ably supported in the press of today in a statement by Brigadier General B. O. Davis, a member of the Red Cross Group, which appointed this committee. General Davis, as a result of his on-the-scene observation of conditions among Negro troops in England and the Isles denounced the emphasis on color he found in the American Army and encouraged the British people to stand firm in their fair treatment of Negro troops based upon ideals of democracy and freedom. It is hoped that wise handling of the overseas clubs will obviate further criticism in this important relationship.

We believe it to be in the interest of a more effective attitude of Negroes in the American Red Cross to accord this group membership at its several levels of participating. It is, therefore, suggested that provision be made for the inclusion of Negroes on (a) The Central Committee; (b) Regional or Area Committees; (c) Local or County Committees. We are grateful for such steps as have been taken to date to achieve this result.

In like manner, it is recommended that all possible steps be taken to encourage Negro nurses to enroll, at the completion of their training, in the Red Cross Nursing Corps.

Since membership in the Red Cross is based on the expression of a humane interest in the relief of the distressed and suffering, and upon the payment of a membership fee of one dollar, it is felt that Negroes should be encouraged to participate on a basis of equality with all other citizens in the program and work of the local Red Cross chapters.

There should, the committee felt, be adequate Negro representation in all categories of the national and local Red Cross staffs. This would include positions of social service workers, staff and administrative assistants, nurses, instructors in the several branches, such as First Aid and Water Safety, field supervisors and army camp directors and supervisors. The committee is aware that some of these positions are now filled by Negroes. It wishes by this recommendation to encourage and strengthen the practice.

In the reports given to the group meetings to which this report refers, statements relative to the conduct of the program of the Junior Red Cross seemed exemplary in terms of the opportunity for participation and the treatment accorded Negro youth. We commend this as the type of integration, which will develop the appreciation and encourage the full cooperation of Negro citizens. We feel greater publicity should be given to this phase of the Red Cross program.

In concluding this brief report, the committee wishes to indicate clearly that such criticisms as it has registered have been stated in the spirit of helpfulness. We express our unqualified appreciation for the broad program of human service, which the American Red Cross renders; and our sincere esteem for the present leadership exhibited by its national officials. Such recommendations as have been made were made with the belief that their institution will align the Negro people of America squarely behind its efforts in terms of their enthusiastic moral support, their services and their funds.

Respectfully submitted,
Claude A. Barnett
Mrs. Mary McLeod Bethune
Channing Tobias
Walter White
F. D. Patterson, *Chairman*

Immediately upon receipt of this committee's report negotiations were entered into with the writer, who was then employed as Senior Promotional Specialist of the United States Treasury, to become the assistant to Mr. Fieser. Because of the reluctance of Mr. Morgenthau to release me, it was May 1943, before I could report for duty with the American Red Cross. In that interim, Mr. Fieser had been replaced by Mr. DeWitt Smith. Mr. Fieser became Vice-Chairman-at-Large.

This change in administrative personnel seriously affected the program envisioned by Mr. Fieser for the integration of Negroes in the various departments of the Red Cross at head-quarters and complicated the situation because no previous understanding had been entered into between the new Vice-Chairman of Domestic Operations and the person originally employed to assist Mr. Fieser in developing a program concern-ing which there had been considerable discussion. Mr. Fieser had been more closely in touch with Negro leadership and, therefore, was more sensitive concerning its reaction to Red Cross activities than anyone else on the national staff.

Upon my arrival and finding his change of status, I was momentarily frustrated because I had not had an opportunity of discussing with my new chief the duties and responsibilities I would assume or any of the final objectives, which he had decided upon toward which we should direct our major interest and con-cern. I, therefore, became a "Joseph not known to Pharaoh." As assistant to the Vice-President of Domestic Services I was to have as my immediate supervisor a Mr. Walter Davidson, who, I believe, was Welsh by birth. I am not sure how long he had lived in the United States. I am sure he did not know a score of Negroes either by name or by reputation. He was more limited in his knowledge of Negro culture or Negro thought. The most he could do, therefore, was to struggle to keep me in channels. I was constantly, even intentionally, getting out of channels.

One gets the impression there are certain people employed by the American Red Cross who, at the end of each day, are able to say to their Lord, "Lord, I am happy to again affirm that all day long I have kept in channels," and with compassionate benediction I can imagine their Lord replying, "Blessed be thy name, what else have you done?" To this searching and even penetrating inquiry the answer had to be, "Nothing, Lord, it took me all day to stay in channels." Now, I know you have to have rules and regulations and established procedures to follow, but I think about channels and rules and regulations as Jesus Christ thought about the Sabbath. Channels ought to be made for men and not men for channels.

I recall vividly the first time I saw Mr. Davidson. He came out to the Cardoza High School to a meeting of the Tri-State Social Workers Conference. The membership of this conference was composed of social workers in Virginia, Maryland, and the District of Columbia. Mr. Davidson was the Red Cross representative on a panel. I do not recall the central theme of the panel, but I do remember that questions in rapid-fire order began to be fired at Mr. Davidson concerning the policy program of the Red Cross as it related to the subject under discussion, and I never saw a speaker so helpless and humiliated as was the Red Cross representative on this occasion. A rather peculiar thing happened, which had nothing to do with his mental behavior, but coincidentally, while he was trying to grope his way out of the haze of confusion, one of his sock supports released his sock and the sock descended to the top of his shoe, and there he stood with one sock up and the other sock down vainly trying to defend the undemocratic practice of his agency. I shall never forget that picture.

The reputation, which the Red Cross had earned among colored people made the position of a liaison representative anything but easy or tranquil. Whether with the Red Cross or any other organization or institution, a person who occupies an interpretive position and attempts to serve with dignity and self-respect two interests, which are frequently brought into sharp conflict is called, I believe, a social engineer. Sometimes he finds himself compelled to serve not only as engineer, but as fireman, brakeman, switchman, and conductor. He is always going too far for one group or too slow for another. When he is moving in a snail-like pace in the evaluation of one group, he is sailing like a non-stop constellation in the conception of the other group. In spite of this fact, my work with the Red Cross was most intriguing and the obvious results have been surprisingly satisfying on all levels.

During the period when the writer was being considered for the position to which he was subsequently assigned, he had a conference with the late Mr. Norman Davis, then Chairman of the American Red Cross. When he asked Mr. Davis what were the duties of the office in question, Mr. Davis referred him to Mr. Fieser. The impression gained in that conference concerning the lack of administrative clarification as to what the American Red Cross had definitely decided to do so far as integration of Negroes was concerned had been confirmed. For an example, different administrative officials at headquarters held different points of view as to what, if anything, should be done toward employing colored people in professional categories, and the absence of any centralized authority to give specific and final direction not only seemed to have supplied the pattern for domestic activities but also represented the lack of an established policy in dealing with Negroes on foreign soil. In each theater the Commissioner very largely determined how the Negro staff personnel was to be handled as well as in some degree where Negro-staffed clubs were to be located and what soldiers were to be admitted to which club. Club and field supervisors in different theatres of operations were permitted to make decisions in the light of their own background or attitude with respect to where Negro Red Cross staffs should be employed and the positions they were to occupy.

At the death of Mr. Norman Davis in the latter part of 1943, the late President Roosevelt appointed as his successor the Honorable Basil O'Connor, a former law partner of President Roosevelt and President of the Infantile Paralysis Foundation and of the Trustee Board of Tuskegee Institute. Mr. O'Connor remained President until September 1949. During that period he effected significant changes in the administrative structure, which made it possible for the democratic process to gain some foothold on the top administrative level and penetrate down to the grass roots. He supplied the leadership with the support of a committee of twenty-seven persons, which he appointed, composed of six from the Central Committee, six from the Board of Incorporations, and fifteen from the public-at-large, upon whose recommendation the Charter that was granted by the Congress in 1905 was replaced by a new Charter in 1946. This new Charter abolished the self-perpetuated Board of Incorporators and in lieu thereof created a Board of Governors of fifteen persons, one-third of which would retire every year and no member of which would serve more than three years. Eight of the members of the Board were appointed by the President of the United States, who was ex-officio Chairman; thirty were elected by the chapters and twelve were selected from the citizens-at-large in order that every segment of the population would be represented, every religious denomination, every section of the nation, and every size of chapter.

This same Charter requirement extends down to the directorate of each local chapter. The committee also recommended that there should be only one class of membership instead of the five classes, which were then operative. The person who gives five dollars as a member is in the same classification as one who gives five hundred dollars as a member. It was recommended and became part of the new Charter that if and when in the collective judgment of twenty-five members of a local chapter the business or affairs of that chapter were not being conducted on a democratic basis, if these twenty-five members would submit in writing to the Board of Governors evidence in support of their thesis the Board of Governors would examine the administrative conduct of the chapter in question. This radical change in administrative structure brought the wrath of indignation down upon the Chairman's head from reactionary quarters on all levels. That was understandable when one considered the social prominence and financial prestige which characterized persons in the leadership of chapters across the nation, many of whom had been at the headship of chapters for five, ten, fifteen, twenty and some thirty years. This system of self-perpetuation made it possible for and encouraged persons to feel that the Red Cross belonged to them.

I am confident that if Basil O'Connor had been Chairman when the agreement was reached to formulate the program for the handling of American soldiers and American Red Cross personnel overseas, definite instructions and a clear-cut statement as to policy would have been enunciated which would have kept the policy-making aspect of the organization centralized at Washington rather than decentralized and placed in the hands of each Commissioner and finally left to each individual club or field supervisor. We quote below a copy of a letter received from Commissioner Cleverley, describing the success he had with an integrated staff and the concurrence of Commissioner General John C.H. Lee:

Mr. James T. Nicholson, Vice Chairman
Insular and Foreign Operations
American Red Cross
National Headquarters
Washington 13, D.C.

DEAR MR. NICHOLSON:

Enclosed is a copy of the report of the Negro Newspaper Publishers Association to the Secretary of War. Perhaps you or Jesse Thomas have already seen this report.

However, in fairness to the American Red Cross, I should like to bring to your attention Paragraph "K". The situation mentioned in that paragraph may be true in the European Theatre of Operations, but it is definitely not true in this theatre. As you know, we have operated and are still operating with integrated staffs in clubs in areas where there are both Negro and white soldiers. Ever since we instituted this policy of operation there had been complete integration in all the activities of these clubs, and this includes dances. This policy has proved most successful and, to date, we have no reports from any one of our clubs that would indicate that we are wrong in our belief that "it can be done". This policy has been completely concurred in by the Commanding General, John C. H. Lee, who has been favorably mentioned in this report.

I am writing this with the idea that you may wish to bring this to the attention of the Secretary of War to both supplement as well as to contradict statements made in the above mentioned paragraph of the report.

Very truly yours,
[s] F. T. Cleverley
Commissioner to Italy

A few days thereafter, however, a letter was written by an assistant to the Vice-President in charge of Insular and Foreign Services to Mr. Robert C. Lewis, Commissioner of the Southwest Pacific Theatre, from which the following quotation would seem not to give official sanction to the innovation which Commissioner Cleverley's letter so graphically and convincingly described:

There are many delicate aspects in situations of this kind which require very careful handling and precautions must be taken to avoid possibilities of misinterpretation of reasons for removal and transfer of staff. I am wondering whether there may not have been a questionable decision originally when she was assigned to this club and whether the later decision to place her in another club was as tactfully handled as it should have been.

I also particularly wish to bring to your attention another phase of her allegations with reference to terminology used in the designation of some of our clubs. As you may know, all Red Cross clubs are open to all American service men and we at all times must carefully refrain from the designation of any club other than as an American Red Cross club and should not designate them as "white" or "negro",etc. You will further note her comment with reference to one of your publications, the ARC weekly bulletin for the area, which it is stated referred to a club as being "for colored G.I.'s". On the Personnel Service rating submitted by Miss Esther Haskins and approved by Miss McClellan, the terminology is again used that there would be better working relations "if she were in a colored club" and the further recommendation that "she be transferred to a colored club". I know that you will agree that we must in all of our official documents and in our day by day supervision of our services refrain from terminology which will only lead to problems. We should refer to clubs predominantly serving colored troops and where Negroes are on duty for the American Red Cross as being "negro staffed" and not as "negro clubs". This is not a small problem and careful adherence to some of the fundamentals will save us a lot of grief in public relations.

At least we would have reason to suppose that the statement above quoted would more nearly represent the official position of the organization than the communication from the Commissioner of the M.T.O. Theatre. No other conclusion could be reached by Mr. Lewis, after reading this letter, than that the American National Red Cross questions the wisdom of integrating staffs on an intercultural basis in Red Cross clubs. This lack of administrative clarity and double interpretation of policy has been most confusing and complicated as we have attempted to identify Negroes with the various activities and services of the American Red Cross on both domestic and foreign soil in respect to numbers of persons employed as against the number of soldiers in a given locality with regard to different professional categories and administrative responsibilities.

Many unsuccessful attempts were made from this office over a period of months to ascertain on what basis we would determine the number of Red Cross workers required for the staffing of a club in a given location in relationship to the soldier population, and why the number of Negro Red Cross employees represented relatively a percentage considerably smaller than the ratio of the Negro soldier population to the total soldier population.

For an example, in the China–Burma–India Theatre there were a total of 175,143 white servicemen and 28,892 Negro servicemen. In that theatre there were 497 white Red Cross staff personnel and only 40 Negro Red Cross staff personnel. In the Great Britain and Western Europe Theatre of Operation, there was a total of 2,883,885 white servicemen and 181,620 Negro servicemen. The white Red Cross staff personnel for that theatre numbered 2,349, whereas the Negro Red Cross staff personnel numbered only 113. In the Mediterranean Theatre of Operation, the white soldier population was 698,953 and the Negro soldier population was 43,747. The white Red Cross staff numbered 541 and the Negro staff, 130. In the Pacific Ocean and Southeast Pacific Theatres, there were 1,345,791 white servicemen and 206,512 Negro servicemen. White Red Cross staff in that theatre numbered 746; the Negro staff numbered 90. In every instance there was a smaller number of Negro staff per thousand Negro servicemen.

I quote from a letter written by Mr. Robert E. Bondy, Administrator, Services to the Armed Forces, to Mr. Don Smith, and a letter from the writer to Mr. Bondy, which substantiates the statement made above concerning our effort to get at the basis of the differential:

Will you please assign some staff members to make a thoroughgoing review of our overseas services to colored members of the armed forces and our staff of that service both by white and colored staff. It may be that Colonel Prosser can get some confidential information for us on colored military strength overseas its distribution among the theaters and its distribution among the branches of service. The review should also include the careful listing of Red Cross facilities with Negro staffs including on-post clubs, if any, off-post clubs and clubmobiles.

The distribution by theatre of the colored staff by classification should be shown. There should be some conclusions drawn as to the adequacy of the staff and the classifications in which there may be deficiencies. Other aspects of the question may arise as the study continues.

One point that should be checked is the determination as to whether or not Negro staff overseas are in the proper classifications. Mr. Thomas on several occasions lately has questioned whether assignments given for bigger responsibility have resulted in changing classifications. I attach one such observation he makes in his memorandum of March 15 regarding Miss McDougald. You will also see his remarks in his memo of March 17th to Mr. Allen.

I should like to have this study completed by April 8 when I should like to discuss it with you and whoever has gotten the material together, which should be in final report form by that date.

Robert E. Bondy
Administrator
Services to the Armed Forces

Mr. Robert E. Bondy
Administrator
Services to the Armed Forces
American National Red Cross
Washington, D.C.

MY DEAR MR. BONDY:

There are two questions that this story in the Courier raises which I cannot answer and, therefore, I am turning to you.

One is whether the statement, as made here by the representative of the Courier, is an accurate description of the situation as obtaining.

Second, is the need sufficiently acute in our judgment that we feel something ought to be done to meet it?

The attached Progress Report from Mr. Walsh also inspires some apprehension in the light of the newspaper story referred to above. We seem to be getting no demand for Negro Club Directors, Program Directors, Assistant Program Directors, Field Directors, Assistant Field Directors or Able-bodied Recreation Workers.

In Mr. Walsh's August 27 report, he indicates that there is immediate need for 800 Assistant Field Directors. For several months past, the only request for Negro staff has been for Staff Assistant and that number has been, as indicated, very small. It happens that the Staff Assistant position falls in the lowest salary bracket of any position in our club setup, which somewhat intensifies my confusion.

The response to our appeal for a thousand Field Directors in the daily papers further complicates our situation when we have no acceptable answer.

Very truly yours,
[s] JESSE O. THOMAS
Assistant to the Vice Chairman
Domestic Services

The same discrepancy was revealed to the clubmobile distribution with respect to soldier population on a racial basis. The total number of clubmobiles in all of the theatres manned by white staff was 282, or ninety-eight per cent. The number manned by Negro staff was seven, or two per cent. This was true in spite of the fact that Negro soldiers represented approximately ten per cent of the soldiers. There was no Negro clubmobile personnel in the China–Burma–India Theatre, African Middle East Theatre, or the Pacific Ocean Theatre. In Hospital Services there were employed by Red Cross in all the theatres 1,856 white persons and three Negroes. There were no Negro hospital workers employed in Great Britain, Western Europe, or the Mediterranean, China–Burma–India, or African Middle East Theatres. I have been unable to secure a reason why no Negro hospital workers were employed at all in the theatres mentioned above, and only three in the Southwest Pacific Theatre.

This same pattern was followed in the matter of upgrading Negro personnel to supervisory or administrative positions. There was one Negro in the Commissioner's office in Great Britain serving as a liaison officer and one Negro given a similar status in the Southwest Pacific. Neither of these designations carried any official status recognized by either the Negro personnel or the administrative staff. They were apparently regarded by the administration as token employees and by the Negro staff as plainclothes detectives. There was one person on the accounting staff in the Great Britain Theatre who was employed by accident. He was invited to Washington for an interview when it was thought he was a white person. On the strength of the implied contractual information in his possession the writer was able to follow through, and on the basis of the person's qualifications as revealed in the interviews, and after satisfying our medical department of his physical fitness, he was employed. Any reference to the fact that we had a qualified Negro accountant on our accounting field staff should include the fact that it was purely an accident and did not represent any change of policy so far as qualified Negro accountants are concerned.

During the months of October, November, and December the writer made an inspection tour of Red Cross installations on the

Continent and discovered that, in addition to a comparatively small number of Negro Red Cross personnel in relation to the number of Negro soldiers, various types of differentials were imposed in the location of the clubs staffed by Negro and white personnel and in the equipment and facilities in the clubs. There seems to have been a general understanding that the clubs to be staffed and occupied primarily by Negro Red Cross personnel and Negro soldiers should be located at a greater distance from the main arteries of transportation and recreational traffic, from the PX's, headquarters, and so forth, than was true of those to be primarily occupied by white Red Cross staffs and white servicemen.

We quote from a letter received from Mr. Marcus H. Ray, who was Civilian Aide to the Secretary of War at that time, which calls attention to a serious international complication resulting from the Red Cross extending the American pattern into its occupied territory of Japan:

18 September 1946

Mr. Jesse O. Thomas
Assistant to the Chairman
American National Red Cross
Washington, D.C.

Dear Mr. Thomas:

I have just returned from a tour of the Pacific installations during which I visited Red Cross clubs staffed by Negro workers in Guam, Okinawa, Manila, and Yokohama. I thought you might be interested in my observations.

The interest and capabilities of the workers were reflected in the response of the military personnel and their full usage of the installations. Especially I should like to commend for his superior and outstanding performance of duty, Mr. Scott, who directs the Golden Dragon Club in Yokohama.

In Manila, where there is a USO club in addition to the two Red Cross installations, I was pleased to note that at least in the case of the USO Club the staff was integrated, possessing both white and colored workers. This is in keeping with the current War Department policy as enunciated in Circular 124, a copy of which I am enclosing. It is my thought that the Red Cross could aid in processing of this new and forward looking policy if club staffs were integrated, thus carrying into leisure time activities the policies now being implemented by the Army.

Many of the directors commissioned me to relay their regards and also the hopes that you will soon visit the Pacific Theatre.

Sincerely yours,
[s] MARCUS H. RAY
Civilian Aide to the
Secretary of War

While we were allegedly carrying the spirit and the theory of democracy to Japan, we were conveying it in a jim-crow vehicle characterized by the segregating of Negro installations instead of having an integrated staff in all the clubs located in metropolitan centers. We seemed to have been operating on the same differential basis as we would in Georgia or Mississippi. The uncertainty of administrative policy was not limited to its foreign application. One day the director of personnel at national headquarters found himself in an embarrassing situation and called my office for some suggestion as to how to wiggle out of it. Appeals were being made over the radio and through the press for Red Cross personnel, including persons with stenographic and secretarial skills. Many Negroes, hearing the appeal, responded and successfully passed our stenographic and typing examinations. What to do with these people, since there was apparently no policy to employ colored people in these categories in the different services at headquarters, was his headache. I think he compromised by employing one, and thus "buck-passed" the others out of existence.

The Red Cross of 1951 was as different from the Red Cross of 1942, so far as the Negro is concerned, as Mississippi is from Massachusetts in some aspects of their cultural pattern. Since Mr. O'Connor's retirement, the Red Cross has had two Presidents: General George C. Marshall, who served from September, 1949, to December, 1950, resigned to accept the position of Secretary of Defense. He was succeeded by Mr. E. Roland Harriman. However, the democratic process set in motion during the O'Connor administration slowly gained momentum in the bloodstream of the organization in spite of obstructing impurities.

Starting at zero in 1943, colored people were employed by local chapters of the American Red Cross by 1945 in professional categories in Miami, Florida; Savannah, Georgia; Birmingham, Alabama; New Orleans, Louisiana; Dallas, Texas; Denver, Colorado; Los Angeles, Oakland and San Francisco, California; Minneapolis and St. Paul, Minnesota; Milwaukee, Wisconsin; Chicago, Illinois; St. Louis and Kansas City, Missouri; Cleveland, Columbus, Cincinnati and Dayton, Ohio; Buffalo, New York City, and Brooklyn, New York; Boston, Massachusetts; Bayonne, New Jersey; Philadelphia and Pittsburgh, Pennsylvania; Baltimore, Maryland; the District of Columbia, and Louisville, Kentucky.

In addition to the above, colored persons were serving as members of chapter boards and committees in these and many other chapters across the nation. More than five hundred colored persons who were graduated from many of the outstanding colleges and universities of our country were included among the Red Cross employee personnel in its overseas recreation and entertainment program. The majority of these persons had their bachelor degrees, many were recipients of master's degrees, and several had their doctorates. On the national staff there are still persons employed as Field Directors on foreign and domestic soil, and as part of the clerical personnel, correspondents, and members of the Historical Section with a total salary of more than $1,940,000.

In spite of the fact that Negroes are serving as committee and board members of many chapters, large and small, the vibrations of their voices have not been felt to any considerable degree in the official policy-making circles. The three members who have been elected to membership on the Board of Governors, Dr. Frederick Douglas Patterson, President of Tuskegee Institute, the late Dr. M. O. Bousfield, former Medical Director of the Liberty Life Insurance Company, and Mr. Claude A. Barnett, Executive Director of the Negro Press, have had the opportunity of adding the weight of their influence to issues in the zone of their origin. At the November meeting of the Board of Governors, 1950, they passed a resolution calculated to completely eliminate all aspects of the racial identity of the donor.

Even though far-reaching changes, as indicated above, have characterized the organization's program and policies in the past few years, there were still "reactionary clippers" on the team.

To: *Mr. DeWitt Smith*   Date: December 5, 1945
From: *Mr. Mitchell*

As I have indicated in my memorandum of November 5, I think that any preparation for the scheduled meeting of the committee representing Negro leadership, of which Mr. Patterson is chairman, should include a preliminary discussion by the members of the staff principally concerned with the issues and problems confronting us in this field. The Negro leaders with whom we have dealt have not evolved any statement of objectives which can be expressed in specific action by the Red Cross and the Red Cross, on its part, has not formulated any statement of general policy for the guidance of Red Cross representatives in this field of race relationships. It is doubtful if such objectives can be stated by the Negro group or a significant statement of policy be formed by the Red Cross. The solution of the problem with which our Negro advisers are concerned is far beyond the scope of Red Cross authority, responsibility, or action, yet we seem to become involved in our discussions with expressions of propaganda or prejudice rather than the practical question—what should the American Red Cross do to serve the interests and meet the needs of our Negro population?

As I have studied the record of the previous meetings of Negro leaders and the report of the subcommittees of that group, it is apparent that the relatively defined issues that have thus far been presented are as follows:

(1) Negro leadership requested action to provide greater participation in the personal direction of the Red Cross through membership on the Central Committee, on regional and area committees, on chapter committees and by employment on the national staff in other than custodial positions.

(2) Negro leadership has vigorously protested the segregation of blood plasma.

(3) Negro leadership has at various times protested what has been described as a "Jim Crow" policy of the Red Cross in the maintenance of its clubs.

(4) Negro leadership has protested the failure of our armed forces to recruit a proportionate number of Negro nurses and has appeared to believe the Red Cross has been to some extent responsible.

The record of Red Cross action with reference to the last three issues has now been established for the better or for the worse and, while we worked during the war on these issues, there is little that we can do at this time other than to be prepared to discuss these activities again if called upon to do so.

The request for greater personal participation of Negroes in the direction of the Red Cross will continue to be a live issue and may become more acute in the years immediately ahead. No one can deny that in large areas and on certain levels of our organization Negroes have been practically excluded from active participation in the direction of Red Cross work. This situation cannot be attributed to any official action on the part of the national organization or on the part of the great majority of our chapters. I do not think that careful and objective consideration of the request for proportionate representation of Negroes on the governing bodies and staff of the Red Cross could lead to action satisfying to those who have made the request. If we accept the statement that Negroes should be employed on the national staff in all services and on all levels in order that the interests of Negroes may be adequately dealt with, we will at the same time by indirection endorse the principle of segregation, which is to say that only Negroes can represent Negroes or serve Negroes—that Negroes can serve or be served by the Red Cross only through Negroes in official positions. I do not think that the national organization should ever endorse such as assumption by its action. Nor do I think that the interest of our Negro population would be served by Red Cross acceptance of such a proposal.

The sound principle is that the Red Cross will, as a matter of policy, employ Negroes in any capacity and at any level of its organization, not because of the color of their skin, but because the individuals employed have qualifications, skills, and experience, which the Red Cross should utilize. For example, we might employ a Negro nurse because in addition to required professional qualifications she had unusual knowledge of public health problems in an area containing a large Negro population. We would not employ her if she could bring to the Red Cross only the questionable resource of an identifiable representative of the Negro race and we could employ more competent personnel to represent the Red Cross.

I feel quite sure that the real issue which will confront us in this field in the near future will be Negro representation in the direction of the Red Cross. We cannot deny any group of American citizens this privilege on social grounds. Negroes should be given opportunity to participate in the direction of the Red Cross, but such participation must be justified by their merits and performance as individuals rather than skill in propaganda in the interest of their race.

[s] L. M. MITCHELL
Administrator
General Services

LMM:1w

The record of the previous meeting and report of the special Negro committee is contained in exhibits 4–10 inclusive in Davidson's monograph attached.

To: *Mr. DeWitt Smith*
From: *Mr. Mitchell*

In response to the suggestion in your memorandum of October 29th that information be assembled in regard to the two meetings of Negro representatives held at national headquarters in anticipation of the meeting now scheduled in December, in accordance with the exchange of letters between Dr. Patterson and the Chairman, you will find attached the monograph on Negro relationships prepared by Mr. Davidson.

I think that most of the essential facts in regard to the action to date in this field are contained in Mr. Davidson's material together with certain other observations which are his own. I should think that our principal consideration prior to the December meeting should be directed toward the preparation of some agenda which would tend to direct the discussion along lines that are likely to lead to some practical Red Cross objective. Without waiting for the creation of an agenda by the initiative of the Negro representatives, we might present them with our suggestions for their approval.

This is a matter that should, I believe, engage the attention of the Vice Chairman in charge of Public Relations and the Vice Chairman in charge of Area Offices and Chapter service. A good number of persons on the staff have certain convictions about the Negro problem so far as the Red Cross is affected by it, but there does not seem to be any unanimity of opinion or any agreement as to the general course which the organization should pursue. I am sure that now that the war is over there will be a constantly increasing need to define the functions of Mr. Jesse Thomas. The original definition set up by the Administrative Committee at the time of Mr. Thomas' employment is in the right direction but it is stated in such general terms that it does not prove very useful in practice.

It occurs to me that you may wish to call a meeting of the Vice Chairman who would be particularly concerned with a view to assigning more specific responsibility for preparation of the meeting now scheduled in December.

[s] L. M. Mitchell
Administrator
General Services

To: *Howard Bonham*   September 12, 1945
From: *Jesse O. Thomas*

The attached memorandums from Mr. L. M. Mitchell, under dates of November 5 and December 5, to Mr. DeWitt Smith are self-explanatory. I have read and reread the contents, the observations and suggestions contained therein.

It would be somewhat amusing, if it were not of serious import, to see how complicated we make any consideration of Negro participation or inclusion. The easiest way to arrive at what would be satisfactory to Negro leaders is to decide what would be satisfactory to any leaders.

The Negro wants and expects in American culture on parity exactly what every other American citizen wants and expects, and that is his attitude toward the American Red Cross. When we make him a special social entity, a peculiar individual, it then becomes necessary for us to determine what peculiar and special consideration should he receive, and what contributes to our frustration.

If the American Constitution and Bill of Rights did not guarantee to every citizen equal opportunity, life, liberty and the pursuit of happiness, then representatives of minorities would have a right to strive to become equal in status with members of the majority group. By the same token, if the American Red Cross did not enunciate that its policy was non-discriminatory in its application to the welfare needs and job opportunities of all Americans, without regard to race, sex, creed or color, the Negro or members of any other minority group would have no reason to suppose that his skills would be as available to the Red Cross as the skills of other more favored members of our society.

I was interested in Mr. Mitchell's suggestion that the Administrative Committee should re-define my function in

JESSE O. THOMAS 239

the light of peacetime needs of the American Red Cross. This special consideration is at the foundation of all of our difficulties dealing with members of this largest minority in our population. I am entirely in agreement with Mr. Mitchell's statement that Negroes do not have to be served exclusively by Negroes or by Negroes at all. That statement, however, presupposes that a white person who would be called upon to work with Negroes would be prepared to accept the fact that Negroes can serve white people just as efficiently and are serving them just as acceptably as white people can and are serving Negroes. The attitude that the white person who is to serve Negroes assumes toward them will in a large measure determine the values and productivity of his services to them.

In 1944, Mr. Harry Boyte, who was a member of the Personnel Administration SAF, asked the writer to secure for him a competent secretary. A young woman who had served as secretary to the Registrar of a Negro college in Alabama was employed. In Mr. Boyte's evaluation of her he said, "She was the most competent secretary that he had ever had." That was not because she was colored. If she had been white, she would undoubtedly have been as competent. In spite of this fact, a member of Personnel came to me the other day very much distressed because while the organization was making appeals over the radio for persons with secretarial and stenographic skills Negro women were responding and successfully passing the examination, but because they required special consideration they were not accepted. This representative was in a quandary because he did not know what answer to give these people, nor where to begin with the administration to secure authority to employ them.

I was in a community a few days ago where the leading case work agency had a Negro woman as a supervisor and all of the people under her supervision were white. Before she became a supervisor, she was a caseworker and because she proved to be the best caseworker in the town she was made supervisor. Now, she was not the best caseworker because she was colored; she was the best caseworker because she had the most skills and applied herself most diligently to the job.

What I am trying to point out is that once we reach a collective mind that the Negro will be given no more consideration than anybody else, and no less, our approach to him and attitude toward him will be greatly simplified. He should not be employed or given representation on boards or committees or even given relief because he is a Negro. By the same token, he should not be denied any of these because he is colored.

I take kindly to Mr. Mitchell's suggestion that some preliminary discussion should take place involving members of the Administrative Committee, so as to reach a conclusion as to how far and in what direction the organization is prepared to go in terms of prudence and practicality toward increasing the participation of Negroes on the various levels and in varied categories.

Dr. Patterson is to be in town tomorrow and I know he will not be interested, as he has been each time I have seen him in the past year, in knowing when his committee is going to have a chance to meet with the Chairman. During the campaign I was able to explain that the Chairman was busy speaking in the Drive; after the campaign, I gave as a reason, the Chairman's trip abroad. This about exhausts my supply of logical reasons why the Chairman of the American Red Cross cannot meet with a group of Negro citizens any time during a calendar year. Both Dr. Bethune and Dr. Patterson got the impression from the Chairman's reply that he was anxious to meet with the Committee, and they have hopefully looked forward to this occasion. It seems a long time yet from becoming a reality.

With this approach to the problem, I am sure that the proposed meeting with Negro leaders which the Chairman has twice indicated that he should like to have will prove most helpful and we here at headquarters will discover, I believe, that the Negro is heir to all of the vices and virtues of the other members of the human family and should be dealt with exactly as we deal with other persons who come within the jurisdictional responsibility of the Red Cross. I am sure that this is the type of program approach to which Mr. Mitchell would subscribe.

This open-minded and receptive attitude will make it unnecessary for us to try to set down in specific, rhetorical or legalized terms what it is that the Negro wants from the American Red Cross as a reason for our being hesitant to meet with leaders of his group and familiarize them with our position and, at the same time, secure from them their interpretation of the best ways our services can be extended to that group and the most effective ways his resources can be made available to the Red Cross.

[s] Jesse O. Thomas
Assistant to the Vice Chairman
in Charge of Public Relations

As recently as April, 1951, from the top administrative level, the following invitation was sent out to the Area Managers:

March 30, 1951

Personal

Dear Harold:

When the area Directors of Personnel were in a meeting in March, the 17th, among other things, we discussed at some length the greater utilization of Negro personnel both in SAF field operations and in the area office. We agreed that there were field stations domestically and overseas, both in Camp and Hospital work, where we could place Negro Assistant Field Directors without creating any serious problem. We also agreed that we should gradually feed into our area office staffs some Negro personnel.

Will you please discuss this question thoroughly with those concerned in the area office and come prepared at the time of the Manager's Meeting, to discuss this question to a conclusion?

Sincerely yours,
[s] F. A. Winfrey

Mr. Harold B. Nearman
Vice President, Area Manager
Eastern Area
American National Red Cross
615 N. St. Asaph St.
Alexandria, Va.

This is concrete evidence of the fact that the sanctuary of reaction is still entrenched.

In the beginning of this chapter, reference was made to the leadership supplied by Mr. James L. Fieser in broadening the base of Red Cross activities. It would seem appropriate to close the chapter with a letter of evaluation from Mr. Fieser to President O'Connor.

AMERICAN RED CROSS
NATIONAL HEADQUARTERS
Washington, D.C.

August 31, 1945

To: *The Chairman*
From: *Mr. Fieser*
Subj: Negro Cooperation

Beginning even in my days with the Indianapolis school system, I realized the value of close cooperation and understanding with Negro leaders. In Columbus, as head of the Associated Charities beginning in 1912, I found occasion to employ two people on the staff: one Miss Eva D. Bowles and the other Mrs. Cordelle Wynn, both exceptionally able and well educated Negro women, each of whom, in due course, left Columbus for New York where they held responsible positions on the staff of the Y.M.C.A.

After coming to the Red Cross, I found—particularly in the field of Disaster Relief, frequent opportunity to call upon Negro leaders for assistance, notably in the bigger disasters of the South like the Mississippi Valley Flood of 1927. Many questions arose over the years, some of them very complicated. However, by coming to close grips with them from an interracial standpoint, it was possible to secure growing improvement. Soon after coming to Washington as Vice Chairman in Charge of Domestic Operations, I sought opportunities to discuss the Red Cross with even the extreme leaders like Dr. DuBois, then head of the American Association for the Advancement of Colored People. I recall one discussion with him running from 5 to 7:30 in the evening. In the big flood of 1927 a Negro Advisory Committee was created under the Chairmanship of Dr. Moton, then head of Tuskegee. It was an outstanding group of people including our Mr. Jesse O. Thomas. They met frequently with Mr. Herbert Hoover as Chairman of the President's Cabinet Committee helping the Red Cross and with myself. On occasion afterward, I met with these people separately or in groups from time to time. During the depression years I brought a similar group together. Gradually progress was made in the direction of understanding. This question improved in the big Ohio and Mississippi flood area of 1937.

In 1942, as part of our public relations contact preparatory to the war effort and necessary war fund campaigns, two meetings, each lasting an entire day, were held here in Washington under my chairmanship. Some twenty-five representatives of the leaders of the Negro race, men and women, attended each meeting. All outstanding national Negro organizations were represented by one or more persons. Some, like General Davis, topmost Negro officer in the Army, and Mrs. Bethune, attended from government groups. Full and frank discussion concerning the integration of the Negro into the various services of the Red Cross characterized these formal conferences which consumed the morning, luncheon and afternoon sessions. It was my privilege not only to sign the invitations for these meetings but to preside over them also, and to maintain certain correspondence and conference contact with individuals afterwards.

I very much hope that you and Mr. Poteat will have an opportunity—in fact, will make it–to read the report of a small Committee of which Dr. F. D. Patterson, of Tuskegee Institute, was Chairman, of which the following were members: Mr. Claude Barnett, head of the Negro Associated Press, Dr. Channing H. Tobias, outstanding Negro leader in the Y.M.C.A., Mr. Walter White, of the American Association for the Advancement of Colored People, and Dr. Mary McLeod

Bethune, representing the Negro Nursing group. Among other things, this Committee, after fullest deliberation, recommended that the Red Cross include Negroes more largely on its staff, locally and in areas, and nationally.

One result of these meetings and the recommendations of this Committee was the employment of Mr. Jesse O. Thomas on our national staff. He became the first member of his group in the history of the American Red Cross to be employed in a professional or administrative capacity. This was late in coming; in fact, twenty-five years or more after similar steps had been taken by the Y.M.C.A., Y.W.C.A., Family Welfare groups, and others who had not traditionally aired so extensively their freedom from limitations of race and otherwise.

It is my impression that relationships of the Red Cross to the Negro, community and group generally, have gradually improved since Mr. Thomas joined our staff. Employment opportunities of the Negro have likewise increased in chapters, areas and nationally, within the past two years. Much of this improvement can be traced directly to his efforts and recommendations because, almost single-handedly, he has had to carry this burden of fair play. There are still a number of other recommendations, which he made shortly after he had an opportunity for surveying the field and becoming familiar with our employment practices which have not yet been acted upon. Included in his first report to Mr. DeWitt Smith, and consistent with the intent of the report of Dr. Patterson's Committee, were recommendations that competent people be added to such services as Home Nursing, First Aid, Water Safety, Accident Prevention, Disaster Relief, Junior Red Cross and the College Unit Staffs. There is great alertness among leaders of the Negro race upon the subject of health. Properly implemented, great progress could be made in many of the

fields above mentioned. Negro educators dealing with schools—
elementary and high school groups and college groups—are
another field, which lies before us.

Since I was largely responsible for bringing together these
leaders and for many other steps connected with their interest
and those of the Red Cross, I have a sense of personal responsibility for passing along to you obligations for interest in the
future development of this democratic idea and for the continued success of Mr. Thomas, whose job has been a singularly
lonesome one. At the time his position was created, I was Vice
Chairman in Charge of Domestic Operations. He secured his
release from the United States Treasury Department and came
to us after some difficulty because Secretary Morgenthau and
other Treasury officials were most reluctant to release him. Mr.
Thomas would have been an Assistant to me in the over-all
domestic field had he arrived before the transition occurred
which changed my status to that of Vice Chairman at Large.
His usefulness to the organization and his group has depended
and, in large measure will continue to depend, upon what
progress he is able to make in accomplishing the objectives
enumerated in Dr. Patterson's Sub-Committee report above
referred to, and in representing the sentiment of this important
cross-section of Negro leadership.

In passing, I should like to add my confirmation of his
expressed desire to make an inspection trip of Negro club
activities on the Continent. I have believed, and believe now,
that he could render a service to the club personnel and the
Negro people including members of the Army of Occupation
and to the Red Cross if such an inspection trip could be
arranged. First-hand information to foreign correspondents
of Negro Weeklies concerning many of the newer and wider
opportunities now being given colored people by local chapters here at home, at National Headquarters and in the Areas,

would increase their knowledge of the over-all program of the Red Cross and the extent to which Negroes are rapidly integrated. Through these contacts there would be a toning down and a neutralization of the sharp criticisms of the Red Cross which appear periodically in some of the national Negro Weeklies.

Mr. Thomas and many of those of the original group which met with us and have continued their interest since, are abidingly devoted to the Red Cross as a great humanitarian agency. Some of them, like Mr. Thomas, have known us and worked with us for a long time. Indeed we could often have been helpless in the face of misunderstanding and criticism without their aid and counsel. I do not see how Mr. Thomas alone has done so much. I hope that this fund of knowledge may still be enriched by opportunity to observe and counsel on our situation abroad not merely as an offset to possible criticism but as a device for constructive steps in the future.

You have a deep interest in all of these questions I know and will give every detail the most careful consideration.

Again, in closing, may I express the hope that you may read Dr. Patterson's report and that support may be given further progress in mutual understanding and work between ourselves and the Negro leadership of America who, after all, are a part of our organization.

[s] JAMES L. FIESER
Vice Chairman at Large

Time and circumstance may suggest a procedure that may have potentiality. In support of my thesis I submit here below some personal experience with the American Red Cross on both domestic and foreign soil:

On the occasion I was talking with the Administrator and I called his attention to the fact that since I was the only colored person employed by the American Red Cross at the administrative level, there would be a tendency on the part of colored people, generally, to hold me responsible for areas of judgment reflected in employing colored people on the basis of comparative competence. I stated that under those circumstances it would seem reasonable to me to have an opportunity to examine the folder or file of every colored person whose application was processed before he was employed and every colored person whose services were being terminated involuntarily for any cause.

The Administrator found himself in complete agreement with my position and immediately thereupon dictated a memorandum to the heads of services that put the suggestion above referred to in effect. Thereafter no colored person came into the Red Cross or went out from the Red Cross without my having an opportunity to review this record or examine his folder.

Not long after that a colored club director by the name of John Harris was returned to Washington from North Africa with a sealed folder. The charges made against Mr. Harris were so convincing so far as the director of the personnel staff was concerned that his clearance was almost completed before the matter was brought to my attention. He was advised to come in the following day and his clearance would be completed and his service with the Red Cross would thereby come to an end. Just for the record, his folder was sent to my office so that I might be intelligent as to why his services were terminated. The following statement was in the folder, "We are returning Mr. John Harris to Continental United States with the recommendation that the Red Cross not continue him in its employment either on domestic or foreign soil. Mr. Harris is a troublemaker. He insists on the intermingling of the races. Signed: THOMAS IRVING." When the folder came to my desk I was preparing to leave for an engagement in Chicago. I dictated one sentence, included it in the folder and returned the folder to the Director of Personnel. That sentence contained the following statement: "I do not support Mr. Irving's conclusion. Signed: JESSE O. THOMAS." The following day when Mr. Harris came in to complete his clearance, he was informed that Mr. Thomas had held up completion of his clearance.

Some days afterward when I returned to headquarters I was called to meet with the administrative staff in the Executive Committee Room at a given hour. Upon my arrival at the appointed time at the place where the staff was assembled, the Administrator said to me, "Mr. Thomas, the members of the Administrative Staff are at a loss to understand the basis on which you take exception to Mr. Irving's recommendation." I replied, "I take exception on two points." In the first place, Mr. Irving had made a general statement. I did not know what he meant by "intermingling of the races." Second, I did not see why the Red Cross should have any policy with respect to intermingling of races on foreign soil. I had an idea what it meant, and the other members of the staff had an idea what it meant, but it was not in the record and I would have made it uncomfortable for anybody to inject it into the record. The Administrator then said to me, "We are seeing five thousand miles from Washington." We have to take the word of some one on the scene, and remember this is the recommendation of Mr. Thomas Irving, an executive officer of Red Cross, in charge of personnel in North Africa." I replied, "I am an executive of Red Cross and I do not agree with him." At this point one member of the Administrative Staff said, "I agree with Mr. Thomas, it is a general statement." Addressing the Administrator, he said, "Do you know what he means by 'intermingling of the races'?" The Administrator replied, "All I know is what is in the record." The same member then inquired of several other members of the Advisory Staff, all of whom knew, replied in the negative. The Administrator then turned to me and said, "What do you recommend Mr. Thomas?" My reply was that I could understand the possibility of there being a conflict of personality, that I would recommend that Mr. Harris not be returned to North Africa, but I did recommend reassign-ment. He was sent to the European Theatre of Operation, where there might be more intermingling of the races.

On another occasion a club director by the name of Dawson, in charge of a club in Southampton, married an English woman. At the time of the marriage, the Provost Marshal in that theater was the Officer in Command. He was subsequently replaced by a Provost Marshal from Texas. On September 12 of the year in question, Mr. Dawson received a telegram from headquarters in London to come to London at once for reassignment. At the end of the reassignment clause was added the instruction that he should bring all his belongings because it was not the intention of headquarters to return him to Southampton. When he reached headquarters he was advised to hand in his AGO Card, prepara-tory to returning to the United States. When Mr. Dawson inquired as to the reason for his being summarily discharged, he was told that serious charges had been made against him by the Military. Mr. Dawson insisted on knowing what the charges were, and was told that if he did not voluntarily return to the States he would be court-martialed. Through the "grapevine" the information reached my office at headquarters. I sent a memo to the office of the person in charge of Insular and Foreign Service, stating that I under-stood a Mr. Dawson and Mrs. Street had been suspended from the Directorship and Assistant Directorship of the Red Cross Club in Southampton, and that I understood the reason for their suspen-sion was that Mr. Dawson had married an English woman. The assistant to the Vice President, when my memo reached the office of his chief, informed me that no such information had reached the office of the Vice President but a cabled inquiry would be made at once. A few days thereafter the charges of the Provost Marshal were received at headquarters and sent to my office. He claimed (1) that the club was being operated below Red Cross standards; (2) that the hostesses were prostitutes; (3) that the venereal disease rate among Negro soldiers had accelerated since the club had been located there. I challenged the Provost to support these charges. I had been in the club. It was one of the few clubs on the Continent that had no sleeping accommodations, so that if a soldier had any physical contact with a female it would not be at the club. I knew that the hostesses had been secured by the members of the Red Cross staff through the Young Women's Institute, which compared in some degree with the Young Women's Christian Association, and certified by the Police Department. This challenge was returned to the Provost Marshal through London Headquarters. After some three or four weeks word came back that the Provost Marshal refused to substantiate his charges. It was February 14 when this final word was received from the Provost Marshal, while Mr. Dawson was standing by in London. I was asked if it was my desire that Mr. Dawson should come back on the payroll on the fifteenth of February, which was the beginning of the pay period. My answer was to the effect that if a higher court affirms the position of a lower court, the litigant has whatever character the lower gave him; whereas on the contrary, if the higher court invalidates the decision of the lower court, then the litigant has whatever character he had when he went into the court of equity. Under these circumstances, Mr. Dawson could go back on payroll as of September 12. I was advised that the matter would have to be passed on by the Red Cross' chief attorney, Mr. Hughes. When the matter was processed to Mr. Hughes, his reply was that "Mr. Thomas was eminently correct and Mr. Dawson would go back on the payroll in this retroactive fashion."

On one other occasion of a different nature, a supervisor on the personnel staff refused to supervise a unit because some colored correspondents had been added to the unit. I was asked to meet with the personnel staff and evaluate the position taken by this supervisor. She was called upon to state in my hearing what she had said to her supervisor with respect to the assignment. She gave her name and said she was from a certain city in Florida. She said she was unaccustomed to dealing with colored people on the basis of equality. She then made a threat, saying that she was sure that if her Chapter heard that the Red Cross insisted on her dealing with these colored people as her equals, the national organization would not receive any financial support from her Chapter. The only source of financial support that the national office receives comes from local chapters. The Administrator, addressing me, asked if I wanted some time to think over this person's submission or if I wanted to act momentarily. My reply was that I would act instantly. Referring to the statement made by the person under discussion, I said that her statement represented only her opinion, which might be at variance with the facts. I said that my opinion was that a great many people who did not at the time contribute to the Red Cross would begin to contribute to the Red Cross, and I wouldn't be surprised to find some of them in her chapter if they understood that we had a personnel practice which imposed no differential on account of accident of birth. I then stated that what the person in question was saying was substantially that we were calling upon her to do a job for which she had neither aptitude nor skills. My recommendation was that we give her a month's severance pay, in which event she might find employment with an agency where she could do the kind of job in which she had aptitude and skills.

There was a Mrs. Glenn, who was the granddaughter of a good friend, Hiram W. Sibley, of Rochester, New York, who was on the Red Cross personnel staff. She turned to the committee and said, "I take it that the committee supports Dr. Thomas' recommendation." She then turned to the person under discussion and said, "You must also have some annual leave. If you will come to my desk I will add your annual leave to the month's severance pay." Thus ended the incident.

As part of the interviewing staff in connection with the recruiting program for overseas personnel, there was one woman appointed by the Vice-President in Charge of Insular and Foreign Operations who had the exclusive right to pass judgment on any woman under twenty-five or over forty-five. With her approval we could employ persons as young as twenty-three if it appeared that their experience might have accelerated their maturity beyond their chronological age.

A young woman who would be twenty-three on her next birthday, which would be November 23, came into the office and applied for an overseas assignment in June preceding her twenty-third birthday. I was impressed with her skills and requested that Personnel should process her application. In the early part of November, I sent this processed application to a person, Mrs. B., whose approval was necessary to employ this under-aged prospect. I recommended that we bring in the young woman, interview her, and, if we agreed to employ her, we would employ her as of November 23 and thus save two weeks of the time that her services would be made available. She returned the application with the statement, "I do not recommend that we bring this young woman for interview at this time. Signed: Mrs. B."

I waited until the twenty-third and then requested Personnel to bring the young woman in for an interview. There were some six persons on the interviewing staff; all of them were favorably impressed with the young woman and all except Mrs. B. approved of her being employed. She vetoed the application with a statement, "The young woman's recreational skills are so sketchy." As a matter of fact, the young woman had extraordinary recreational skills, and obviously this was not the basis of her rejection. Mrs. B. was overheard by one of the members of the interviewing staff saying to the vice-president to whom she was directly responsible, "This young woman has no Negroid features at all."

It happened that I had gone to Chicago again to participate in a job clinic, and this member of the interviewing staff hot-footed it up to my office and told my secretary what she had heard, expressing a feeling that the matter should be brought to my attention before the young woman returned to Tuskegee, where she was then living. My secretary called me by long-distance telephone the following morning at the Grand Hotel in Chicago and advised me what had transpired. I suggested that she have the young woman stand by; that I was leaving Chicago that night and would be in Washington the following morning. Upon my arrival I called the same vice-president and asked for a conference, which was granted. I took the young woman's folder over and told him that I wanted to discuss the case of this young woman with him. I informed him that all of the members of the interviewing committee staff had approved her employment except Mrs. B., and that the impression was that Mrs. B. had turned her down because of her complexion. That statement evidently refreshed his mind concerning what he had been told by Mrs. B., because he did not look at the folder in which the girl's picture was enclosed. He asked me if the girl was fair in complexion. I replied that she was very fair, but I said, "I am not sure that we are interested in that. If we are, we are sixty years too late." He asked what I meant. I said, "This girl's grandfather, who did not believe in social equality in the daytime, went out in his backyard in Culpepper, Virginia, sixty-eight years ago to pay his cook, and we get the by-product." He then asked me, as a practical proposition, if I thought it was a good thing to employ a person concerning whose racial identity there should be a question. I said to him that if my answer was to formulate a policy for a great national humanitarian organization it should require and be given a great deal of thought and careful consideration. I told him, however, that I had two impressions right off the top of my head: (1) there was not a position in the Red Cross, not excluding the chairmanship, that I could not occupy with some measure of efficiency, but there were some positions I would never hold because I did not select my grandfather. Therefore, I could never be a party to the formulation of any program calculated to condition the welfare fortune of a prospective employee on account of accident of birth. Then, speaking as a white person, I said, "If we should adopt this as our employment policy, what we really would be saying is substantially this: this child looks so much like our other children we cannot tell them apart, and for fear, therefore, that we may make a mistake and treat this child like a first-class citizen, we should penalize her by not giving her a job." He said to me, "That is the best I have ever heard. I will never raise that question again—go ahead and give the girl a job."

After my resignation addressed to the President of the American Red Cross had been submitted and accepted, one of the vice-presidents, Ramon S. Eaton, asked me to give an over-all objective evaluation of the program against the background of its philosophy. A copy of that evaluation is submitted herewith:

To: *Mr. Ramon S. Eaton*   August 9, 1951
From: *Jesse O. Thomas*

Two of the assignments you gave me the other day have already been fulfilled (formalizing a proposed job description framework, and submitting the names with accompanying data on education and work history of three prospects). You also asked that I give the benefit of my experience with the Red Cross as relates to some areas in which immediate and prolonged concern should be directed for the good of the organization. Accordingly, I am setting down in a somewhat rambling sample fashion some experiences and impressions I have encountered and registered since being officially connected with the Red Cross.

Eight years ago, there seemed to have been more of a climate for growth, expansion and departure from the traditional procedure than now seems evident. I have somehow come to the conclusion that because of our training and experience, our concern with loyalty to the past, we have reached the saturation point in our creative imagination, spirit of adventure, and leadership pulling power.

As relates to intercultural development, we encounter still an additional handicap. Everybody I hear speak for the Red Cross, it does not matter what the occasion is, does not conclude his remarks without stating that Red Cross services are made available without regard to race, creed, color, etc. To the listening public this is accepted to mean that in every department of our culture, need and competence are the only prerequisites that determine the quality of service rendered. One can make a statement or hear it repeated so often that he will come to accept it as a fact, even though there is concrete evidence all around him to the contrary. I heard of a man who had repeatedly stated that he owned a horse so often and so long that he believed it himself and went to town and bought a saddle.

It is only when we have a spectacular situation, as the Memphis Chapter presents at the moment, that the general public has the opportunity of discovering the extent to which exceptions might be taken to our over-all nondiscriminatory declaration. I had two rather interesting experiences recently with persons formerly employed by the Red Cross. One was connected with the Department of Personnel, and the other with Medical Service. I was so enthusiastic about a copy of a memorandum, which one of the vice-presidents had written to the area managers concerning the employment of Negroes in the areas that I showed it to this former deputy of Employment

Service. He said to me: "As long as you have been with Red Cross you should not be that naïve to believe that any sincere attempt is being made to have areas employ colored people as a result of this memorandum." A few weeks later I received another copy of a memorandum emanating from the same source, but with a type of conciliatory approach calculated to crystallize or solidify discrimination rather than minimize or eliminate it. The physician said to me that there were four people on the medical staff who were being retained beyond their automatic retirement age in order to qualify for Social Security benefits, implying that more consideration was given the persons on the medical staff than I had received under the same circumstances. It is significant that both of these persons waited until they were no longer on the Red Cross payroll to express any disagreement with what they obviously regarded as unfair practice.

Some weeks ago, a director of a chapter in a city where the area office was located said to me that the manager of the area, instead of supplying leadership for the chapter in interracial relationships, was applying the emergency brake wherever the question of moving forward in this area was raised. When Mr. Harry Boyte became the manager of the Atlanta Chapter, he inherited a double-salary schedule, predicated upon race, which his predecessor had imposed. When he brought this matter to the attention of his Board, pointing out that all of his Negro case workers were graduates with master's degrees from the Atlanta University School of Social Work and that most of his white case workers did not have similar background training, the Board voted unanimously without a dissenting vote to remove the differential. This raised the question as to whether or not the general public, as represented by the local chapter communities, is not leading rather than following the national staff.

I raised the question with Mr. Keisker, who was then manager of the Midwestern Area, as to why no Negroes were employed in any professional categories on his staff. He felt that the community was not ready for that type of integration. I made a preliminary study the following day and discovered that there were a number of social welfare organizations, public and private, as well as some business enterprises, that had been for some time employing colored people in the above-mentioned categories. In Atlanta, Georgia on the regional staff of the Y.W.C.A., there are colored professional personnel housed in the same office with the other members of the regional staff. The same building houses the headquarters of the Council on Race Relations, which has an integrated staff. In these communities, at least, it would appear that the Red Cross in its employment policy on a regional level is lagging behind public opinion.

During the time when we were making a strenuous effort to meet the requisition demand of the overseas military theatres of operation for additional personnel, we utilized the daily press in a mass appeal. Many colored people, including some of our former employees, read the account of our acute need and immediately filed applications with the area offices having jurisdiction over the States in which they lived. Notwithstanding the fact that they had been employed by the Red Cross and given excellent evaluations, as soon as it was discovered that they were not white persons, they were given a "brush-off." I took the matter up with the Directors of Personnel in the Eastern and Southeastern Areas and with the Acting Director of Personnel at national headquarters. I was advised that unless the requisition from the theatre stipulated specifically that colored persons were desired, it was assumed that whites only would be accepted.

At national headquarters, I have been told over and over again by the Director of Personnel and other members of his staff that there are heads of Services who place requisitions for stenographic and secretarial personnel but who refuse to accept qualified colored people. I do not believe, in our history, that a colored person has been employed as a typist in the stenographic pool.

More than two weeks ago, I was moved from Room 305 in the 18th Street Building to the Basement of the 17th Street Building. I registered a complaint as to the method employed in the transfer and later discovered that the first information that Mr. Boochever and Miss Fee received concerning my being moved was when they received the memorandum of complaint. The penalty imposed, apparently, for the complaint is the failure to make telephone connection in the office I now occupy. Being without the use of a telephone for two weeks is not a pleasant experience to contemplate when many of the things one accomplishes administratively is by telephone communication. I cannot imagine that it is the customary procedure for Office Management to move a person from one office to another simply at the request of another employee who may want to occupy the space under consideration and without clearing with the departmental head on whose staff the transferred occupant is serving.

I should want to emphasize one thing that is important in connection with this incoherent summary, and that is the fact that it is not influenced by acute sensitiveness or a chip-on-the shoulder attitude. They may appear trivial and insignificant, but it is the accumulation of smaller things in the life of an individual, organization or a nation, which ultimately conditions his or its welfare fortune. With all the millions America is spending today through the Marshall Plan, or otherwise, and in spite of our "Know How," as long as a helpless and defenseless Negro is jim-crowed and segregated and the victim of disfranchisement and discrimination, America can never assume the position of moral leadership of the world.

I am more interested in the application of the democratic creed as relates to the whole community than I am in what happens to the Negro, because I well know that no organization can indulge very long in unfair treatment of any one group before this undemocratic practice will so enter the administrative bloodstream of the organization that all who are brought in daily contact with it will be affected in some degree more or less. There comes a time in the life of every individual, agency or organization when what he or it does then will not only in a large measure determine what he or it may do in all of the future, but it will to a remarkable degree re-evaluate all that it may have done in the past. It is my humble opinion that what the Red Cross does in the next ten years will determine to a significant degree the position it will occupy in the field of social welfare and human relations for the next half century.

Somehow, I think we can improve on our method of handling people whose services are terminated for one reason or another. While I realize it is always an unpleasant experience to be declared surplus or to have to become detached from an organization or agency under any circumstances involuntarily, I believe it is possible to handle this transfer in such a way as to have fewer people leave the Red Cross in an unsympathetic and unfriendly state of mind. In all of the organizations with which I have been connected, I have not seemed to recognize anything approximating the high percentage of people who found it necessary to sever their official connection who have done so with the degree of antisocial reaction as has characterized a large percentage of persons who leave the Red Cross.

I hasten to indicate that this has no reference to my own situation. I believe we are more vulnerable at this point than any other department in our departmental behavior. Too much concern from the administrative and policy-making level cannot be exercised as relates to this particular aspect of our human relationship, as well as to the other more detailed descriptive sampling of this memorandum.

Finally, one who has been employed by the Red Cross or identified with the program in a voluntary capacity for any length of time will be influenced to put the Red Cross in the category of the Baptist Creed: "Once in Christ, never out." Like the seven-year's itch, the Red Cross gets into your blood and does something to you. The writer is no exception to this general rule. I will never withhold from the Red Cross any resource at my command which it may call upon me to make available. The years spent on its staff as a part of its official family have been the most challenging of my whole career and have made it possible for me to become intimately associated with some of the finest spirits with which God has blessed this earth.

[s] JESSE O. THOMAS
Public Relations Consultant

cc: Mr. Harriman
    Mr. Nicholson
    Mr. Boochever

XV

Joining the Office
of Price Stabilization

When I reached the automatic retirement age with the Red Cross I accepted a position with the Office of Price Stabilization. Quoted below is an article from a release appearing in the *Washington Post* chronicling the transition and making brief reference to my work history, beginning with the Southern Field Assignment with the National Urban League:

JESSE O. THOMAS PUTS NEGRO IN BLOODSTREAM OF RED CROSS AND JOINS OFFICE OF PRICE STABILIZATION

Mr. Thomas joins Honorable Michael DiSalle's staff as Information Specialist in the Office of Price Stabilization. [Michael DiSalle was on leave as Mayor of the City of Toledo, Ohio; he later became Governor of the State of Ohio.]

It is a far cry from 1942 to 1951, so far as the Negro's employment relationship to the American National Red Cross is concerned. For the first sixty years of Red Cross history, prior to 1942, Negroes had been conspicuously absent from its payroll in professional categories and consistently denied the opportunity of making their skills available to the Red Cross either on local, area or national levels as bona fide professional or administrative employees. Any accepted policy or operative procedure that stretches out over a period of threescore years accumulates historical sanction. Any departure from or disposition to effect procedural changes will encounter stubborn opposition as an unwelcome innovation. This established policy of the Red Cross had earned for the organization an unenviable reputation among Negro America. It required a great deal of sagacity, persistence, and steadfastness of purpose on the part of the one colored person who occupied a position on a policy-making level to effect a change in the employment practice whereby Negroes might make available their professional and administrative skills.

Today, Negroes are employed by the Red Cross in professional categories by local chapters beginning in Miami, Florida and extending to St. Paul, Minnesota, and from Los Angeles, California to Boston, Massachusetts. Negroes have also been employed in the above-named categories on area and national levels. In addition to those employed domestically by the national organization, some 450 colored persons were sent overseas as a part of Red Cross recreational personnel and served in practically every military theatre of operation during World War II. Two Negroes have been appointed to membership on the Board of Governors, which is the highest administrative body of the organization.

Jesse O. Thomas is quoted as having said that, "Beginning at zero in 1942, by April, 1945, Negroes employed on domestic and foreign soil by chapters and the national organization were drawing in salaries alone approximately $1,940,000."

In August, 1945, Mr. James L. Fieser, former functional head of the Red Cross, wrote a letter to President Basil O'Connor concerning Mr. Thomas' activities in which he said: "It is my impression that the relationship of the Red Cross to the Negro community and the group generally has greatly improved since Mr. Thomas joined our staff. His job has been a singularly lonesome one. I do not see how Mr. Thomas alone has done so much." These results are characteristic of the professional or administrative behavior of Mr. Thomas in other positions he has occupied prior to entering the services of the Red Cross.

When he became Senior Promotional Specialist with the United States Treasury in 1941 there was only one other member of his race on the administrative staff, and no colored person identified officially with any State War Bond organization. Within eleven months there were two other colored people added to the administrative staff at National Headquarters, and fourteen members of his race employed as Deputy Administrators on salary at state level and eighteen as Associate State Administrators in a dollar-a-year category.

When he became Southern Field Director of the National Urban League, there was not a local League branch in the South employing a single colored person. When he took leave from the National Urban League to join the United States Treasury, Negroes were employed as administrative officers and associates in the cities of St. Petersburg, Tampa, and Jacksonville, Florida; Atlanta, Georgia; Richmond, Virginia; Louisville, Kentucky; New Orleans, Louisiana; Memphis, Tennessee; Little Rock, Arkansas; and Fort Worth, Texas. Perhaps the largest single contribution he has made to the field of social welfare was in the organization of the Atlanta School of Social Work.

During the latter part of 1950, Mr. Thomas was informed by one of his associates that the organization had not planned to employ anyone to succeed him. In order that his job assignment might have been continued, this information was relayed to some important Negro and white citizens which resulted in a meeting being arranged by a committee of citizens from across the nation with the President of the Red Cross and the Executive Vice President. This committee had little difficulty in having the President recognize this contemplated error in administration. To Mr. Thomas goes the credit for seeing that this door, which stands ajar, was not closed.

Before resigning from the Public Relations Consultant position with the Red Cross, he entered into an agreement with top management that the activities in the area in which he had functioned be continued and proffered his services, in cooperation with Personnel, in the selection of his successor. Surely his record with the Red Cross must be illustrative of what was meant by the Good Book, when it said, "One can chase a thousand, and two may put ten thousand to flight."

In his new assignment, he will share the responsibility of the other members of the administrative staff of the Office of Price Stabilization in making the consuming public conscious of its responsibility in employing this governmental device in order to either prevent inflation or minimize the effects of its onslaught.

The following schedule of assignments contained in a release given to the press by Mr. Max R. Hall, Director of the Office of Public Information of the Office of Price Stabilization, will give some impression of the job assignment coverage of the organization that was concerned with neutralizing the inflationary pressure through price-control media:

MARCH 14   The Annual Membership Dinner of the Y.W.C.A., Alexandria, Virginia

MARCH 16   An interracial mass meeting in the Beulah Baptist Church, Muskegon, Michigan

MARCH 17   The Muskegon High School, Muskegon, Michigan Participated in an interracial workshop in the auditorium of the Fairview Homes Housing Project, Muskegon, Michigan

MARCH 18   The Muskegon Junior College, Muskegon, Michigan
ABC Club noonday luncheon, Muskegon, Michigan
(All of the activities in Muskegon were under the
auspices of the Urban League of Greater Muskegon,
William W. Layton, Executive Secretary.)

MARCH 22   Served as Chairman of a workshop for the Maryland
League of Women's Clubs at Morgan State College,
Baltimore, Maryland. The subject of the discussion
was "What Is Happening to Your Dollar?" This
group is composed of members of various women's
organizations throughout the State of Maryland.

MARCH 26   The Pyramid Club, Philadelphia, Pennsylvania

MARCH 27   Afternoon session of the Pittsburgh Courier's Home
Show

MARCH 28   Cabinet Council of the Armstrong Association,
Philadelphia, Pennsylvania (The engagements in
Philadelphia were arranged by Wayne L. Hopkins,
Executive Secretary of the Armstrong Association
of Philadelphia.)

APRIL 2–3   Guest speaker, Florida State Negro Business League,
Tallahassee, Florida

APRIL 6   Symposium speaker and consultant, Annual State
PT–A Home and Family Life Program, Delaware
State College, Dover, Delaware

WEEK OF
APRIL 20   Meetings with neighborhood clubs and block units
in Cleveland, Ohio under the auspices of the Urban
League of Cleveland and the Phyllis Wheatley
Association

APRIL 27   Guest speaker at the Vespers Services of Wilberforce
University

April 28	Speak to the students of Central State College, Wilberforce, Ohio
Tentative	
April 30	Guest speaker, Annual Farmers and Homemakers Banquet, Maryland State College, Princess Anne, Maryland

* The Office of Price Stabilization was terminated at the end of the Truman administration.

XVI

Some Experiences on Trains, in Dining Cars, in Restaurants and on Boats

Some author once said, "I am a part of all that I feel, smell, and see, and a part of all that I do and all that is done to me."

Some years ago I was a passenger on a Seaboard and Airline train between Denmark, South Carolina, and Washington, D.C. The only space allocated to colored people on the train from Denmark to Washington was a half of a wooden day coach. The other half of this coach, which ordinarily would have been available to colored people, was occupied between Denmark and Columbia by white passengers. There being more colored passengers than there were seats, it became necessary for many of the passengers to stand in the aisle. The distance between Denmark and Columbia is approximately fifty-one miles. The white passengers in the rear half of the Negro coach either had reached their destination or transferred to another train when the train reached Columbia.

After standing that fifty-one miles under the circumstances described above, I was ill-tempered, if that is what one means when he is mad as a person could be without giving dangerous rise to his blood pressure.

On leaving Columbia I took the front seat in the Jim-Crow coach. It was the custom (and I think such custom still obtains in some parts of the South) on some trains for the conductor, brakeman, and flagman to occupy the two front seats in the Negro coach for their "Office." The conductor usually puts his little safety box containing his tickets and other records in one of these seats and he occupies the other as they face each other. The reason this "Office" is not established in the white coach is because white passengers would not stand while employees of the railroad utilize otherwise unoccupied space for an "Office."

I was the first passenger that the conductor approached as he entered the door when the train left Columbia. His introductory approach was, "All right, Jim, move to the seat on the other side of the aisle there." In the first place, my name is not "Jim"; his use of the term meant that his methodology did not reduce my blood pressure nor create a congenial climate for our future relationship. I asked why I should be moved to another seat. His reply was, "I want this particular seat for my office."

I rejoined, "If you have to have an office, you might find one in the next coach." That coach was occupied by white passengers.

It was a long train, running on an express schedule, and it did not stop at local stations. The station stops were something like fifty or seventy-five miles apart. The next station stop, as I recall, was Chero. It took the conductor most of the time between this station and Columbia to collect the tickets from all the passengers on the train, including those in the several white day coaches and those in the Pullman cars; so he did not return to his proposed "office" between Columbia and Chero.

Leaving Chero, he approached me first again, since I occupied the first seat, and said to me, "You did not understand me. I told you I wanted this seat for my office."

My reply was, "Yes, I understood you. I am at fault, because I did not make myself understood. I am going to remain in this seat."

The next stop was Camden which was equally as far from Chero as Camden was from Columbia. It took the conductor most of the time that the train was traveling from Chero to Camden to collect the tickets from the passengers who boarded the train at Chero. On leaving Camden he came, finding me still in the seat where he had planned to establish his "office," with a notebook in one hand and a pencil in the order, and he asked me my name. I realized that something was going to happen that might involve some publicity or legal action. My reply was, "J.O. Thompson." At that time I was employed by the Federal Government in the Department of Labor. Woodrow Wilson was President. I did not know what attitude the government would take toward an employee thus involved in litigation during the Wilson Administration—hence, "Thompson" instead of "Thomas." He wrote it down, and then I took out my notebook and pencil and asked his name. He first said, "I am not going to give you my name." I then asked the number of the train. On second thought, he gave me the number of the train and his name, which was Captain Gibson.

When the train reached Hamlet, North Carolina, the conductor got off and sent a telegram to the Police Department in Raleigh. When the train arrived in Raleigh, two officers came on the train, and, finding me still in the conductor's "office" seat, asked me if my name was Thompson. I replied in the affirmative. They then said, "You are under arrest. Get your bag."

I replied, "I am due in New York tomorrow morning, and if you detain me it will at the expense of the City of Raleigh."

"We will take care of that. Get your bag," was their answer to this.

When I came out of the train with my bag, the colored passengers in unison reflected that, "That is what I say. Some colored person is always trying to run the white man's business. He knew that was that white man's office." When I came down off the train's platform, the conductor stood there and beside him was a reporter of Josephus Daniel's paper, *The News and Observer.* He asked the conductor my name and was told the name of Dr. J.O. Thompson. He inquired the reason for the arrest, and was told by the conductor that I refused to move out of the seat he wanted for his office. The conductor then told the officer that if he was needed he would return to Raleigh the following morning from Richmond, where his run terminated on Train #1, and would get to Raleigh by nine o'clock in the morning. The officers took his address and informed him that if his personal appearance was demanded by the court he would receive a telegram.

On the following morning on the front page of the *Observer* an article appeared with the headline "DR. J.O. THOMPSON YANKED OFF THE BIRMINGHAM SPECIAL", and the article began by saying, "A rather smooth-looking Negro by the name of Dr. J. O. Thompson will have an interesting time in court this morning before Judge 'X' explaining why he refused to move out of the seat which Conductor Gibson wanted for his office," etc.

The railroads at the time were being operated by the federal government, which put the case in a federal court. I was taken by these two officers up to the Post Office Building and arraigned before a federal judge. Five lawyers spent about an hour and a half trying to find some language in their law books that would cover my behavior.

After an hour and a half, with frustrated impatience, I said to them, "If you would spend the time you are employing in perusal of your law library in finding a rope, it would be spent to some purpose."

One of the lawyers came over to me and said, "I do not think it is that bad."

I said, "That confirms my position. Any place an interstate passenger can be taken off a train without a charge made against him, he can be lynched. I recommend that you lynch me. If you do not, it is misapplied detention."

This brought everything to a standstill momentarily; then the Judge asked, "Do you know anybody in Raleigh?"

My reply was, "I know somebody in every respectable community in America." I named several people whom I knew in Raleigh; among them was Father Satterwhite. A messenger for the court was a member of Father Satterwhite's church and heard his name given. He informed the court that Father Satterwhite was the Rector of his church. A telephone request was made to Father Satterwhite and he was asked to come to the courthouse. When he arrived he was asked if he would sign a bond for three hundred dollars guaranteeing my appearance in court the following morning. He replied in the affirmative without hesitation. At this point, before affixing my own signature, I corrected the name of the defendant from J. O. Thompson to J. O. Thomas.

Having satisfied the bond requirement, Father Satterwhite and I went to the office of a law firm, which he recommended, and I engaged the senior member of the firm to represent me in court the following morning. We then visited a number of offices and places of business of professional businessmen and women, and he said to each of them that he would appreciate it if they would register their protest against that type of injustice by simply being present at the courthouse during the trial. Because I had given the name "Thompson," even though a news story concerning my arrest appeared on the front page of the daily paper, none of my friends in Raleigh associated me with the incident until they had been informed otherwise.

At the scheduled hour, the court convened and the conductor took the stand. To my surprise, he told exactly what happened as if he had taken it down in shorthand. I was sure that he was going to allege that I cursed him or threatened him or otherwise behaved in an unorthodox fashion. When he had finished his preliminary statement, my lawyer made the following observations and asked the following questions:

"Captain Gibson, whenever I get on a train I never give the conductor my ticket until he gives me a seat. I do not know whether I have any law on my side or not in so conducting myself. I want to ask you a question. Are there seats on the train for the conductor's office?"

Captain Gibson replied, "I have been running on this road twenty years and I always use that seat."

Attorney Clark said, "That does not answer my question. Have you the authorization of your Company to do so?"

Gibson replied, "I do not."

"One other question," said the lawyer. "Has a passenger the right to remain in the seat for which he has paid?"

Captain Gibson replied, "Well, you could say that he has."

"So this passenger was within his rights," continued the lawyer.

Captain Gibson replied, "Well, you could say that he was."

"You have police power, don't you, Captain?" asked the lawyer.

Captain Gibson replied, "Yes, I do."

"You had this passenger arrested as an agent for your Company?"

Then the conductor attempted to demur. "No, I had him arrested on my own hooks."

"That is rather unique—one passenger having another passenger arrested. In any event, Captain, your Company will have an opportunity to determine in what capacity you had this passenger arrested."

My lawyer then addressed the court. "Your Honor, I find we have no charge against my client."

The Judge replied, "No charge."

"Is the case dismissed?"

The Judge replied, "Yes, the case is dismissed."

The lawyer then said to the Judge, "If it pleases the court, I would like to make a statement for the record. You have been on the Bench, I believe, for twenty-six years and I have been practicing at the Bar for twenty-eight years. I dare say that you have witnessed something here this morning which you have not witnessed before to the same extent since you have been on the Bench. I am confident you have never seen as many colored people in this court, representing the class of people that are here this morning, since you have been on the Bench. This is the type of person we have embarrassed. I want the record to show that I stated that I am ashamed that this kind of thing should occur not only in the city of Raleigh, but that it should occur anywhere in the State of North Carolina. For your information, Captain Gibson, we go from this court to my office to complete papers for filing suit against your Company."

The case was dismissed without my having to make a single statement in court. We won the case against the Company and settled out of court for six hundred dollars. This experience established the fact, once and for all, that there are no seats on any train for the conductor's office. On the contrary, the seats are for passengers and not the employees of the Company.

Some years later, I had another experience on the Seaboard and Airline Railroad. This time it involved an encounter with the steward in the dining car. This was before the Supreme Court had invalidated the partition or curtain separation of Negro and white passengers in the dining car. It was customary for Negro passengers to be restricted to two tables behind a glass partition in the dining car or behind a curtain drawn in front of these two tables. If more white passengers came in than could be seated in the inside of the partition, they would spill over beyond the curtain or partition and fill up the entire dining car.

As I entered the dining car on this particular occasion, I discovered that white passengers were in the seats at the end of the dining car behind the partition. The only unoccupied seat was one in the middle of the dining car at a table with a seating capacity of four. I took this vacant seat. The steward came to me and inquired of me in a whisper if I would wait until the white persons behind the partition has finished and take my seat there. This was asked in a whisper in order that the other three persons at the table would not be aware of what was transpiring.

I asked him in a whisper, "Why should I wait?"

He replied, "we reserve those two tables for colored passengers."

I asked in a whisper, "What are those white people doing up there?"

He replied, still whispering, "They are technically violating the law."

My answer was, "I will technically violate it here."

At this point, a waiter called the steward and, when he went over to the waiter, he whispered something to him. The steward then came back and gave me a menu card. I ordered my breakfast and was served. The waiter who spoke to the steward was not the waiter who served me my breakfast. When I finished my breakfast, I sat for a while smoking a cigar. When the steward got down to the far end of the dining car, I asked the waiter who had served me my breakfast if he would inquire of the waiter who spoke to the steward what it was he said to him. He conveyed my message to the waiter in question, who came over to my table and said to me, "Mr. Thomas, you do not know me. I used to run on the Atlanta and West Point Railroad between Atlanta and Montgomery. I know how you make people treat you, and I told that steward, 'I know that man; he is not going to move; you might as well prepare to serve him at that table.'"

Three things stand out in my memory in connection with my experience with conductor Gibson and the court trial. Two of them are very pleasant to recall. One of them is somewhat depressing to contemplate. It was a very satisfying experience to observe that physicians, teachers, and businessmen left their places of business and offices to be present as a means of registering interest and concern and to protest in connection with an obvious injustice done one interstate passenger and an American citizen. It was most gratifying to me to recognize the readiness with which Father Satterwhite agreed to sign the bond without asking any questions as to the charge preferred or the allegation. It seemed clear in his mind that whatever happened had been provoked, and he was ready instantly to sign his name and give whatever collateral security that act implied in making himself responsible for the appearance of the defendant the following day for trial. He asked what the charge was after he had signed the bond and was told that he would have to wait until Captain Gibson returned the following morning before the nature of the charge could be stated.

The thing that was depressing was the reaction of the colored passengers in the coach. It emphasized what this whole program of segregation and discrimination does to its victims. Custom had made it a tradition in their appreciation for a conductor or any railroad employee to utilize such space as he may choose in the Negro coach, regardless of the number of Negro passengers inconvenienced or denied seating accommodation. This was a right that no colored person was expected to challenge, and if one was so reckless as to challenge it, he would invite the unsympathetic reaction akin to mass condemnation.

Most of my adult life and even before I became of age, somehow I was given the responsibility, or had to assume the responsibility, of adjudicating disputes, passing judgment or imposing penalties for injustice inflicted upon members of my own family or friends. This pattern of behavior to me seems well-nigh irresistible. As a result of this disciplinary conduct on my part, information gained wide currency to the effect that, if some member of my family or a friend were mistreated during my absence, the adjustment would be made upon my return to the scene where the cause of action arose.

Some months after I had established headquarters in Albany, New York, some friends of the family with which I was living reported that there was a restaurant on Washington Avenue, about two blocks from the State capitol, that refused to serve colored people unless they agreed to sit behind a screen. On the following day after I received this information, I went in to this restaurant, took my seat at a table, and waited to see what would happen.

After a few minutes of inattention on the part of the waitresses, the wife of the manager came over and said that the table at which I was sitting had been reserved for some expected guest. My reply to her was that I was just going to have a piece of pie and a glass of milk. At that time you could get a glass of milk and a piece of pie for ten cents. I told her that I would have finished my lunch before the guest came for whom the table was being reserved. She then said, "We cannot serve you unless you eat behind that screen," toward which she pointed.

As though I didn't understand what her purpose was, I replied, "I am not bashful and I do not mind people seeing me eat." This reply somewhat frustrated the wife of the manager; so she went over and reported to her husband what her experience had been.

The manager then came over and asked me if I could understand English. I told him that English was not my major, but I had not had much difficulty in making myself understood. He then repeated the injunction that had been given by his wife, "If you eat in this restaurant, you must eat behind that screen." I repeated the statement I had made to his wife and added that I was only going to spend ten cents for a piece of pie and a glass of milk. For that small amount of money, it would hardly justify his bringing over the screen and placing it around me, since I was not going to move.

With that statement, I left the restaurant and went straight to Judge Brady's Court and filed a complaint against the manager of the restaurant. The following morning he and I met in Judge Brady's Court, and I related to the Court what had happened the day before.

In his defense, the manager said, "Judge, I did not refuse to serve him. He is the only colored person who has objected to eating behind the screen. Lawyer Chew, of Troy, New York, comes in my restaurant with his lady friend and uncomplainingly eats behind the screen."

The Judge replied, "I would personally prefer being refused service than to be compelled to eat behind a screen."

The Court then asked the defendant if he knew the law on the subject. He replied, "Judge, I do not wish to plead ignorant of the law, but I have never read it." The judge then read the law to him, which said, "for such conduct of a proprietor of a facility offering service to the public to discriminate in the fashion described above, would be guilty of an offense, as a result of which the Court could impose a fine of five hundred dollars or five hundred days in jail, either or both at the discretion of the court."

He asked the defendant if he had five hundred dollars. The reply was in the negative. The Court thereupon directed the Bailiff to lock him up.

About a year or more after that, I was waiting for a streetcar at the corner of Dove Street and Delaware Avenue, and the defendant upon whom this sentence was imposed came up to me and said, "You did not treat me right. My old man…" When he got to that part of the sentence, the street car was approaching and I said to him, "I am sorry, but I am taking this car."

I have not seen or heard from him since, but I did eat in the restaurant several times afterward without being "screened" in. I think what he was going to say was, "My old man fought in the Civil War to free your people." That statement above the Smith and Western line falls in the same category as the "Black Mammy Identification."

During the month of August, 1941, Dr. and Mrs. Mays and my wife and I spent a vacation in Havana, Cuba. We set sail from Miami, Florida about seven-thirty in the evening. Approximately an hour after we had set sail, in response to a call to dinner, we went down to the dining room. We were met at the entrance to the dining room by both the first and the second stewards, who requested that we return to our staterooms and return to the dining room within an hour. We inquired as to the reason for this procedure and were told that they expected the white passengers to be finished with their dinner at that time. We insisted on being served instantly, either in the dining room or on the deck. It was much cooler and more pleasant on the deck than in the dining room.

They agreed to serve us on the deck and assigned a waiter to take care of the Thomas and Mays party. In the meantime these stewards argued that the boat was operating in accordance with the Florida Segregation Law. To which we replied that the State of Florida didn't own the ocean.

The other passengers, observing the deluxe services given the Thomas and Mays party, went to the management and protested against what they considered discrimination against the white passengers.

When we returned the following morning for breakfast and requested service on the deck, we were refused deck service and requested to come into the dining room. All other meals, going and coming from Cuba, were served and eaten in the regular dinning room along with the white passengers.

The following accounts appeared in the *Associated Negro Press* relating to the Thomas' and Mays' experiences in Havana.

MOREHOUSE PRESIDENT'S WIFE
OBSERVES BIRTHDAY IN CUBA

By Jesse O. Thomas

HAVANA (ANP)–Co-incident with the arrival of the Mays–Thomas party in Havana, Dr. B. E. Mays, with the cooperation of Dr. Mercer Cook, who is studying this summer at the University of Havana, arranged in one of the exclusive cafes a very unique birthday party in honor of Mrs. Mays, whose birthday falls on August 5.

Included as guests to the birthday dinner were Miss Dorothy Scott, who is also a student in the University of Havana, and a recent addition to Morehouse faculty as teacher of Spanish, Dr. Mercer Cook, Mr. and Mrs. Jesse O. Thomas. The birthday gifts were characteristic of Cuban life and products.

JESSE O. THOMAS AND MOREHOUSE PRESIDENT SEE EX-CUBAN CHIEF

ATLANTA (ANP)–The Thomas and Mays party has returned to the Gate-City from what they describe as a most pleasant and eventful visit to Havana. Jesse O. Thomas stated that among the most interesting experiences he and Dr. Mays, president of Morehouse, had while in this tropical metropolis was the forty-five minute informal conference with Gen. Mario G. Menocal, former president of the Cuban republic.

Incidentally, Gen. Menocal is a graduate of Cornel University, class of '88, and therefore has a ready vocabulary of English. He is seventy-four years old and has been intimately identified with the evolutionary and revolutionary developments in Cuba. He is thoroughly familiar with the political history of the states as well as with their commercial growth.

In this informal interview, he revealed the similarity of Cuba with the southern section of the United States during the period when it survived almost completely on the one-crop system. While sugar cane is the chief industry in Cuba, extensive cultivation of tobacco represents an industry of second importance. In later years, dairying and stock raising as well as the establishment of manufacturing enterprises forecast a more diversified economic culture for the people of that island in the future. Ex-President Menocal looks forward to seeing this transition occur during his lifetime.

Back in 1929 the State Social Workers held their annual meeting in Columbus, Georgia. The evening session was held in a white Baptist church. They had worked out an arrangement whereby the colored members would sit on the left side of the church and the white members and citizens would sit in the center of the church and on the right side beyond an aisle.

When I came in I took a seat in the center body of the church. Shortly after I had taken my seat, a young white usher came to me and in a whisper asked if I would move over to the other side of the aisle into the section occupied by the colored people. My reply was that the seat I was then occupying was very comfortable and I would like to remain in it.

He whispered to me, since there were other persons near me whom he did not want to hear what was being said: "We have reserved seats on that side for colored members of the Association."

I whispered back to him, "They did not know I was coming, so they could not make any reservation for me."

This confused the usher so that he went over and reported the incident to an older person who thought he could make the matter more explicit. He came over and went through very much the same procedure with exactly the same result. He evidently decided that I was either so dense that I could not understand what he was trying to implant, or that I must have been from "up North somewhere" and was totally ignorant of the Southern mores.

I heard no more from the white community, but there were reverberations among certain pseudo-Negro leaders who expressed themselves as feeling that I reflected a noncooperative attitude and one calculated to set the race back.

From my point of view, they were already "setting back."

During the period of my employment as public relations consultant with the American Red Cross, the transportation personnel never secured for me an upper berth. If there was no lower berth available, reservation in the drawing room was secured.

On one of my field trips from Washington to Austin, Texas, I had a stopover in Houston in order to make a side trip to Prairie View College, a distance of some forty miles. I spoke to the faculty and student body at Prairie View at noon and had planned to return to Houston sometime in the mid-afternoon, or before ten o'clock that evening, in order to occupy my reservation, which was a lower berth in the drawing room from Houston to Austin.

When President Evans of Prairie View learned of my plans, he was somewhat disturbed because the faculty had made plans to tender me a reception that evening, beginning around seven o'clock. The train on which I was scheduled to leave Houston did not stop at Prairie View but did stop some nine miles beyond Prairie View at Hemstead Station. President Evans suggested that I not disappoint the faculty, and that since the train did not leave Houston until 10:30, I could remain at the reception until ten o'clock, and he would have me taken to Hemstead by automobile. I was glad to accept this arrangement.

When I boarded the train at Hemstead and proceeded to the drawing room designated by my ticket, the pullman conductor informed me that since I had not claimed my reservation immediately upon the train leaving Houston, he had sold the space. I accepted his explanation at first in good faith, and since I observed some unoccupied lower berths, I suggested as an alternative that I would take a lower berth in the body of the car. The custom prevailing in that section was not to sell Negroes Pullman accommodation in the body of the car. I took my bags and went into the day coach and inquired of the train conductor as to whether or not he had any jurisdiction over the sale of berths in the Pullman car. I knew he didn't, but I wanted some collateral evidence to support a suit that I had decided to bring against the Pullman Company. I also asked the train conductor his name and address.

When I returned to Washington I engaged the legal service of Attorney Thurmond L. Dodson. He filed a suit against the

Pullman Company, and we made an out-of-court settlement for six hundred dollars.

The conductor did not deny that there was unoccupied space because the diagram would have been demanded by the court. He did claim that I refused to occupy a lower berth, which the court rejected, basing its ruling upon my testimony and employment record which my attorney submitted.

The court held that a person who had held the responsible position which the plaintiff had occupied had to be a person with some integrity in the judgment of the court. Based upon this conclusion the court made a decision and ordered the company to pay the damages.

The Most Embarrassing Experience of My Whole Life

Shortly after I became employed by the American Red Cross, Mrs. Franklin D. Roosevelt made an inspection trip of Red Cross installations and military bases of operation through India, Australia, and other Southwest Pacific communities. When she returned to Washington I sought a conference with her because I wanted to get some firsthand information on what her experiences were with Red Cross personnel in our clubs. I was concerned with what she saw or heard that would suggest the value of the services we were rendering soldiers, or how those services might be enhanced or improved.

Through her secretary, a conference was arranged. Thinking that the Red Cross officials would be delighted to know that a member of their staff had succeeded in securing an interview with the First Lady, I informed my immediate supervisor, whose name was Davidson, of the proposed conference. When I was telling him about my plan to see Mrs. Roosevelt that afternoon, he seemed impatient and he terminated the interview rather abruptly and disappeared. Within half an hour he returned to my desk and said he had just left the office of the vice-president, who instructed him to ask me to cancel my engagement with Mrs. Roosevelt on the theory that nobody below the status of vice-president was permitted to confer with anybody at the White House.

Under these circumstances, I had to humiliatingly call up Mrs. Thompson, Mrs. Roosevelt's secretary, in the best way I knew how and ask that the engagement be canceled, giving as the reason that I was below the official level of persons in the Red Cross who could officially discuss any matter touching upon Red Cross policies or services with any person with White House authority or official status.

I have never had anything that was quite as embarrassing, as humiliating, and, to me, as unreasonable as the request made to cancel this important engagement.

XVII

Organization of the Atlanta
Chapter of Frontiers of America

The Frontiers of America is a service organization somewhat comparable in the Negro community to the Rotary, Civitan, Kiwanis, Lions, and Optimist Clubs in the white community. It is the only organization of its type among colored people, and is international in its territorial jurisdiction.

The objective of the organization is to discover, expose, and appraise acute unmet needs in the Negro community and to make available such skills and other resources at its disposal toward meeting one or several of the needs falling in the category mentioned above.

In 1950, the Founder of the club, Nimrod Allen, of Columbus, Ohio, came to Atlanta to receive an honorary degree, which was conferred by Morris Brown College. While he was in Atlanta he discussed with the late President Lewis, of Morris Brown College, and some other Atlanta citizens, including Dr. L. D. Reddick, who was the Librarian at Atlanta University at the time, the possibility of organizing an Atlanta Chapter of Frontiers of America. His suggestion was received cordially, but no follow-up action was taken.

In 1953, when the writer returned to Atlanta in retirement status, Mr. Allen reopened the case with me. With the force of Mr. Allen's suggestion, a group of representative citizens was called to meet in the Reception Room of the Mary Triangle at Morris Brown College. After considerable discussion and appraising the need for and the functional possibility of such an organization, the group gave unanimous consent to establishing an Atlanta Chapter of Frontiers of America. The writer was elected President and M. R. Austell was elected Secretary. The writer served as president for five consecutive terms, at the end of which he declined to be re-elected and was elected President Emeritus.

At the annual Convention of the national organization held in Chicago early in 1953, the writer was appointed Deputy Organizer.

In the early spring of 1954, he organized the Augusta Chapter of Frontiers of America. In the collective judgment of the Augusta membership, the most acute unmet need in that general community was an institution for the training of mentally handicapped Negro children. There was located near Augusta, at Gracewood, an institution for the training of mentally handicapped white children which had existed for more than two decades with an appropriated budget of approximately eight hundred thousand dollars.

Representatives of the Augusta Chapter approached the judge of the Juvenile Court in Richmond County and secured his cooperation, by agreeing to write to every other judge occupying positions corresponding to his in the state for the purpose of ascertaining what, if anything, was being done in their respective counties by a tax-supported institution for the training of mentally handicapped Negro children. The universal reply was: nothing! The members of the chapter presented this factual information to Senator Carl Saunders, of Richmond County, and asked that he arrange an opportunity for the members to have a personal interview with the governor. The Senator agreed. An engagement was arranged and the committee representing the Augusta Chapter wired the president of the Atlanta Chapter to join them in the conference with the governor.

Carl Saunders not only arranged the conference, but he and the judge of the Juvenile Court and the Richmond County delegation presented the chapter's submission to the governor. The factualized statement was so compelling in its analysis of the need, on the one hand, and of the differential imposed by the state upon the Negro child of the state on the other hand, that after a sixteen-minute discussion, the governor terminated the conference by stating that he would present a bill to the legislature calling for the appropriation of five hundred thousand dollars for the establishment of an institution for the training of mentally handicapped Negro children. Such a bill was presented to the legislature. The legislature passed the bill, and the state appropriated a half million dollars. As a result of this appropriation, four buildings, including two dormitories, one for boys and one for girls, have been built contiguous to the institution that was already existing at Gracewood for white children.

The Negro citizens of the state are indebted to the Augusta Chapter of Frontiers of America for the opportunity now afforded the mentally handicapped Negro child to be trained at a tax-supported institution.

When the Atlanta Chapter was organized, there was not a school in Atlanta which accommodated blind Negro children. There was a resident school for the training of white children in the City of Atlanta. All blind Negro children as of that date in the City of Atlanta were sent to Macon to the State Institution for Training. This condition was outlined in the form of a statement to the Board of Education. The Board acknowledged the nonexistence of a training institute for blind Negro children and agreed to provide the equipment at one of the elementary schools and to send a Negro teacher to Minneapolis, Minnesota for special training, so that she would qualify as a teacher for the sightless children. A room was equipped at the Thomas Slater Elementary School. Then the question of transportation became a problem. The board of education has no more responsibility for transporting of sightless children than it has for the transporting of sighted children.

The founder of the Atlanta Chapter of Frontiers of America was a retired officer of the American Red Cross. He and the Executive

Director of the Atlanta Chapter of the American Red Cross had been members of the employee staff of the National Red Cross, and on the basis of this relationship, the Red Cross agreed to supply a station wagon and gas for the transportation of these blind Negro children, conditioned upon a member of the faculty of the Thomas Slater Elementary School taking the Red Cross driving course so as to be covered by the Red Cross insurance. This condition was met, so that for the past several years a member of the Thomas H. Slater faculty drives his car to Red Cross Headquarters in the morning, leaves it there, and takes a station wagon and picks up the sightless children, takes them to Slater School, and at the end of the day retraces his steps. Today, therefore, there is an accredited resident school for sightless Negro children operated by the Atlanta Board of Education.

There is such a large number of children in attendance in the Atlanta Public School System representing parents who fall in the unskilled labor category, and others who are under-employed, that they come to school without adequate funds with which to purchase lunches. Indeed, some come without having had a nutritious breakfast. In order to make milk available to these undernourished children, there has been established in the Public School System what is known as the "Ira Jarrell Milk Fund." This fund is supported by voluntary contributions from football games and other charitable gestures.

The Atlanta Chapter of Frontiers of America organized and sponsored East–West Football and East–West Basketball Classics and Clinics. The project had a twofold purpose: the Clinic was to provide an opportunity for coaches in the Negro high schools to participate in a two day coaching seminar under the sponsorship of coaching staffs that had coached national championship teams.

The first year, the head coaches of the University of Georgia, Georgia Tech, A&I University of Tennessee, and their staffs supervised the Clinic. The second year, the coaching staffs of Auburn,

Alabama, Polytechnic Institute, and For Valley College supervised the coaches.

The second purpose was to organize funds through a competition of football teams composed of star players representing Archer, Turner, Booker Washington, and Fulton High on the West; and Price, Carver, David T. Howard, and Trinity, of Decatur, on the East.

The major portion of the proceeds from these games was contributed toward the "Ira Jarrell Milk Fund." During the two years the games were sponsored by the Atlanta Chapter of Frontiers of America, three thousand dollars was contributed to the "Ira Jarrell Milk Fund" each year.

Because of demands made upon the Atlanta Chapter of Frontiers of America by the Georgia Intercollegiate Association which were not acceptable to the Frontiers, the Chapter released its promotional relationship to the project, and the contribution to the Milk Fund the first year that the G.I.A. sponsored the game was one thousand dollars. This controversy therefore cut the underprivileged Negro children two thousand dollars worth of milk, at wholesale prices.

The writer also organized Chapters in Miami, Florida, Nashville, Tennessee, and Fort Valley, Georgia. Shortly after the Chapter was organized in Miami the President of the Chapter, who happened to be a lawyer, approached the federal judge and asked if he would assemble a three-judge tribunal for the purpose of passing on the constitutionality of segregated bus transportation. The court replied that it did not need the collective opinion of two other magistrates but that he, on his own, would hold that segregation on buses in Miami was unconstitutional, and so he held, and Negroes in Miami are no longer segregated in bus transportation.

By coincidence, the President of the National Chapter was a lawyer. At the time the Chapter was organized, discrimination was employed in the cafeteria at the airport. It appeared that the cafeteria at the Nashville Airport, unlike the cafeteria at many other airports, was operated by the City and not by private concessionaires. The National Chapter threatened to bring the City into court, and as a result of that threat, the cafeteria desegregated its eating facilities.

These are typical examples of the evidence of acute unmet needs that may exist in any community on the one hand, and the extent to which they may be met on the other by organizations dedicated toward exposing, revealing, and satisfying unmet needs to the extent that its collective resources vouchsafe.

In appreciation of the spirit of universal cooperation received from the Atlanta public, the following is an open letter that was written on the day following the first East–West Game:

As President of the Atlanta Chapter of Frontiers of America, I wish to express for its membership appreciation to all of the identifiable organizations and individuals who contributed so significantly toward the overwhelming success of the history, if not epoch-making, humanitarian enterprise. I am reliably informed that on no other occasion, including the dedicatory program, were there as many people in the Herndon Stadium sitting and standing as there were last night to witness the first Gate City All-Star Football Classic.

The hoarse cheering multitude represented people of all ages from six to ninety moving on all cultural levels and falling in many different income brackets. It is difficult under the circumstances to know where to begin first expressing thanks and appreciation. Since, however, people are more important than things, I shall start with people.

To the parents and sponsors of the Queen contestants and to the members of the All-Star Queen Contest and to the contestants themselves, our thanks go uninhibited.

To Chief Jenkins, Lieutenant Reynolds, and the members of the Police Department whose gratuitous services were so necessary and contributed so immeasurably to the behavior pattern of the countless throng of sports enthusiasts, we owe an unpayable debt of gratitude. The writer has attended all kinds of functions around the world, governmental and private, on local, state, regional, national, and international levels, but he has never observed a police force more alert and more considerate in the handling of the well-behaved or ill-behaved persons than was characteristic of Chief Jenkins' staff in and around the Herndon Stadium.

To the upwards of twelve thousand cheering fans, congratulations on the orderliness of your behavior and to the extent that your support to this ALL-STAR Classic was a surprising success, we are most grateful.

To the coaches and member of the East–West ALL-STAR squads, you can never know how grateful we are to the excellent performance, to the cooperative attitude exercised, and to the painstaking earnestness which characterized your behavior at every point of contact.

To the publisher, the editorial staff, and sports writers of the *Atlanta Daily World*, we can only say that both your news and editorial coverage was most magnificent and invaluable. To say more would weaken the statement above; to say less would be a misrepresentation.

We are very much indebted to photographers Kelly, Caruthers, and Adams for the unlimited number of pictures they made as their contribution toward the success of this initial venture.

To the H. S. Murphy Publishing Company, had it not been for the free printing of our initial program schedule we might not have gotten "off the ground."

To the Yates & Milton Drug Stores and Paschal Brothers, we want to tell you how much your facilities as a distribution point contributed toward this effort also.

To Ralph Long, as long as you are long, you'll never come up short. Thank-you.

To Miss Carolyn Long, if you continue your momentum, Father Long will have to get out of the way or get run over. Yours news stories were action-compelling.

To Ralph Robinson, do you still have a job? How understanding and tolerant some people can be!

To Mrs. McPherson, do I understand you to say that Mac is still around? What endurance!

I know that P. J. Woods is crooning in the ears of his secretary, Mrs. Jency Booker, this theme song: "I'll be glad when this game is over, you rascal you."

To coaches Robert Dodd, Wally Butts, and Howard Gentry of the coaching staffs of the University of Georgia, Georgia Tech, and Tennessee A. & I and their associates; we want to emphasize a fact that is otherwise obvious, that without your unlimited and unrestrained services in the Coaching Clinic, nothing that followed in terms of the ALL-STAR Football Game would have been meaningful or history-making.

Turning to the Institutions and Business Concerns, we really pour out our thanks to:

Sears Roebuck & Company

Morris Brown College

Atlanta Board of Education

Atlanta Constitution

Bailey Theatre Corporation

The Waluhaje Hotel Management

A & P Food Stores

George Muse Clothing Store

King Hardware
Colonial Stores
Zachary
Rich's, Inc.
Coca-Cola Bottling & Coca-Cola Company
F.W. Woolworth
Davison–Paxon
National Manufacture & Stores Corp.
The Georgia Teachers Association
Fulton County Board of Education
Georgia Insurance Service
Georgia Interscholastic Organization
Principals of the Schools of Greater Atlanta
And All Others Who Helped In Any Way

Finally, to the Members of the Atlanta Chapter of Frontiers of America who worked hard night and day and to those who did not work hard either night or day, thank you so much for your inspired presence and stimulating well wishes. Amen.

XVIII

Fund Raising and Speeches

M ost of my public life has been involved in positions and job assignments which required public speaking before student bodies at high school and college levels; before church congregations and other religious organizations; before civic and fraternal organizations as well as legislative bodies.

Five years of this period were devoted exclusively to fund-raising campaigns. As Field Secretary of Tuskegee Institute, my time and energies were utilized in speaking before Rotary, Civitan, Lions, and Kiwanis clubs, Chambers of Commerce, and church congregations and interviewing philanthropic individuals and public-spirited citizens. There were few white congregations of the Protestant persuasion from Poughkeepsie to Buffalo, whose membership included persons of considerable financial ability, before which I did not speak during that period, nor was there a sizable percentage of individuals who were included among the persons of affluence and generosity that I did not see personally or communicate with otherwise.

When I was Principal of Voorhees Institute it became necessary for me to secure a considerable amount of money to cover expenses from the general public in the North and East, and the approach was corresponding to that referred to above. Because of the amount of money it was necessary for me to raise in this fashion, one hundred per cent of the time was spent in white communities because Negroes did not have the kind of money I was looking for.

As Senior Promotional Specialist of the United States Treasury, as Public Relations Consultant of the American Red Cross, and as Information Specialist of the Office of Price Stabilization, public speaking continued to occupy a considerable portion of my time in one or more of the ways described above.

I had the opportunity of appearing before most of the major organizations in the Negro community in all sections of the nation, including their churches, schools, and fraternal, business, and professional organizations, and also including varied and sundry civic, social, and welfare organizations. Under these circumstances it would be difficult to determine which public appearance was the most far-reaching in its ultimate consequences or history-making in its potential.

Copies of the speeches I have made would fill a volume consisting of thousands of pages. Through a process of elimination, I am including copies of four speeches, largely because of the circumstances under which they were delivered and the time element which made it necessary for some things to be said which, if said under some other circumstance, and at another time, would perhaps have been less meaningful.

Jackson, Tennessee
May 27, 1948

THE COMPARATIVE SIGNIFICANCE
OF THE UNIT BEHAVIOR OF MINORITY GROUPS
IN THE WORLD TODAY

During World War II, a larger percentage of the people throughout the world was either actively or inactively, either directly or indirectly, engaged in or affected by military conflict among the belligerent nations than was ever true in the history of this world.

War is an expensive business, not only from a point of view of natural resources but also from a viewpoint of human resources. The financial cost to the United States alone was upwards of 352 billions of dollars. During 1944, this Government was spending in connection with the war effort at a rate of one hundred fifty thousand dollars a minute; more than nine million dollars per hour; more than two hundred million dollars a day; more than six billion dollars a month, and more than seventy-eight billion dollars a year. This was more money than the government spent for everything from the time George Washington was elected president to 1940.

Three years after the cessation of battle, the victor nations have been unable to formulate a peace treaty agreeable to all the participants. Because in this world, "MIGHT IS RIGHT", the responsibility for formulating articles of agreement for what we choose to call "permanent peace" becomes the responsibility of the larger nations. Of course, the size of a nation, like the size of an individual, may not indicate superior wisdom or intelligence.

The consideration given smaller nations and minority groups will be determined very largely by the extent to which the behavior of minorities fits into or complies with the framework agreed upon by the majorities. By the same token, each individual member of a minority group, as we think in terms of his unit behavior, becomes a significant entity in the total evaluation of the national or group status of that minority. There are some aspects in which all minorities are similar.

First, concerning all minorities, regardless of who they are or where they are—it only matters if they are disadvantaged by reason of the comparative smallness of their numbers. Second, the extent to which a minority is disadvantaged depends upon its comparative superior educational attainment, financial prestige, or political control. Third, a minority not superior to the majority in the directions above indicated must depend very largely upon the crystallization of public opinion on its behalf for the justice, equity, and fair dealing it receives at the hands of the majority group.

The reason the Japanese were put into concentration camps after Pearl Harbor and the German–American citizens or the Italian–American citizens were not put in concentration camps when we were at war with both Germany and Italy was not that the Italians and Germans were white and the Japanese were brown—and not white—it was because there were only a hundred thousand Japanese residing in a concentrated community and easy of identification. If there had been twenty million Japanese in the United States, they would not have been put in concentration camps, because we could not have built camps large enough to contain them. By the same token, if there had been twenty-five million instead of six hundred thousand, Hitler would not have made a tirade on Jews.

The comparative smallness of numbers not only welcomes but invites exploitation in times of intercultural conflicts. Minorities, therefore, must employ all known strategies and devise every conceivable type of survival economy. A minority ought to demonstrate how the democratic processes which it seeks to enjoy with members of the majority on a parity can operate within its own intra-group culture. Being more specific, the Negro in America who is constantly demanding that the democratic processes be operative, so far as they guarantee his equal participation in the social heritage, ought to eliminate non-democratic processes within his own group. I have seen as many Hitlers among Negro college presidents as I have seen in any other group. I have seen as much totalitarian behavior, as relates to the latitude over which a particular Negro had jurisdiction, as I have read about existing anywhere else in the world. Negro Greek-letter fraternities for example, whose members are demanding democratic participation are unable to federate on a single constructive enterprise lest they lose their identity.

On domestic soil as well as in foreign countries, religious denominations compete for numerical representation and participation and operate, therefore, starvation missionary outposts because they have not developed the skills of cooperation and been able to consolidate their energies in a cooperative enterprise, and yet those same people are most vocal in demanding that democracy shall obtain interculturally. Majorities who exploit minorities and deny them equality of opportunity justify their programs of exploitation by the character they give the minorities. A substandard wage is justified on the basis that Negroes are lazy and shiftless. A differential in salary scale or double economic standard of wages is justified on the basis of comparative equality of Negro teachers or wage earners. Segregation is justified on the ground that the Negro is uncouth, he is boisterous, he is untidy, he is socially awkward and difficult of assimilation. A minority must refute these allegations, if they are not based upon a sound scientific and racial foundation. This means the eliminating of what we call, for want of a better name, racial earmarks from every aspect of our behavior.

The streets on which we live, the houses in which we live, the buildings in which we teach or preach, in terms of our economic resources, must be no different from the buildings or streets or neighborhoods occupied by any other group of American citizens. We must become so skilled and proficient in our vocations and professions that the unit production of our members will be equal to the unit production of the members of any other group of citizens who are employed under similar circumstances. In this fashion we will remove all justification for any differential predicated upon race and make it obvious that any type of discrimination imposed represents calculative injustices and downright cursedness on the part of the perpetrator.

Minorities must identify themselves with and become acutely interested in the difficulties encountered by other minorities around the world. Any social evil conceived or born in remote India, in interior Africa, or on the plains of Bethlehem, unless exterminated in the origin of its birth, may spread to every corner of the earth. Members of minorities and weaker peoples everywhere must become so sensitized to injustices that they will show a disposition to federate their efforts and seek to find common denominators for the purpose of eliminating any manifestation of injustices anywhere and everywhere.

Through federated efforts, minorities may become a majority and by so doing a democratic culture can evolve. It may be possible to save and conserve our civilization. We must, in the very nature of the case, depend upon educated Negroes to supply the kind of leadership which a followership ought to demand. All of the members of the graduating class who can afford to secure additional skills and equipment should do so, because an A.B. degree today is hardly equal to what a high school diploma was twenty-five years ago.

We must produce the kind of thinkers in this group of ours, representing a disadvantaged and socially disinherited minority, that will make a substantial and compelling contribution toward building a new economic society, a new social order, a new political philosophy, a new spiritual vitality, a new moral concept and steadfastness of moral purpose which so far as we are concerned will be predicated upon a minority-group strategy of a surviving economy in a competitive civilization.

PIONEERING IN BUSINESS ENTERPRISE DURING THE FIRST HALF OF THE TWENTIETH CENTURY
DEDICATORY ADDRESS OF THE HOME OFFICE
AMERICAN WOODMEN, DENVER, COLORADO
(By Jesse O. Thomas)

Mr. Master of Ceremonies, His Honor, The Mayor, distinguished platform guests, members of the office, field and administrative staffs of the American Woodmen, Ladies and Gentlemen, I wish in the first instance to express my appreciation to Dr. J.W. Haywood, who submitted my name to be included among those who were to participate in this Dedicatory Program on this auspicious and eventful occasion. I wish, in that same connection, to express my thanks to the members of the Program or Arrangement Committee who ratified Dr. Haywood's submission. I want to congratulate the officers of the American Woodmen for bringing to concrete reality the dream of the founders and the men and women who, in the days when slow was the pace, saw this magnificent building in process of becoming, and to felicitate the dreamers of yesteryears who gave birth to this organization and nurtured it through the days of liquid diet until it could partake of solid food.

It is an unusual satisfaction as well as an unusual honor for me to address a group of insurance folk whose policies cover twenty-five states and the District of Columbia—twice as much territory as that of any other single Negro-directed insurance business in the United States!

It is an unusual satisfaction for me to address an organization, now *forty-nine* years old, that represents the fourth oldest body of Negro-directed insurance in the world, and which has shown a steady and solid growth for the entire period of forty years during which its affairs have been under the present management.

It is an unusual satisfaction to me to stand here in the magnificent new home which you are dedicating today—the home which you have built for the great family of American Woodmen—one of the few organizational groups in the field of Negro business that has kept in step with progress in terms of recognition of the right of women to participate in every activity—not as auxiliaries or second class members—but fully, on equal terms with the male membership, and sharing with them the same privileges and opportunities. American Woodmen, I salute you!

Taking Stock

And now, may I be permitted to pause a moment, to look back, briefly, with you, at the beginnings of insurance organizations among Negroes. What was the need—the motivation—that led eventually to the formation of the forty-four member companies of the National Negro Insurance Association representing more than a billion dollars of insurance, in force among more than four and one half million policyholders, in twenty-nine states and the District of Columbia, with assets in excess of one hundred fifteen million dollars?

There was very little activity going on in the field of business among Negroes in the United States before the turn of the century. In 1900, when Booker Washington organized the National Negro Business League in Boston, Massachusetts, almost none of the business enterprises now in control of Negroes were in existence. All of the Negro banks and most of the insurance companies now operated by Negroes came into existence since the organization of the National Negro Business

League. The National Bar Association, the National Funeral Directors Association, the National Bankers Association, and the National Negro Insurance Association all grew out of the National Negro Business League.

We Are Poor Folk; Poor Folk Need Insurance

First and foremost, let us take as our point of departure the fact that insurance, in some form, is the only security available to the poor man in time of stress—and since most of us are poor and insecure in terms of amount of income, and of type and tenure of employment, we are "naturals" for insurance.

It must also be realized that with the turn of the century ninety-seven per cent of Negroes were employed in domestic and personal service and engaged in agricultural pursuits. This meant that the majority of them were in areas where they were victims of a double economic standard and a differentiated salary scale or wage rate. The nature of their employment placed them, therefore in a substandard category. They were called upon to so allocate this substandard wage to meet the subsistence demands of the family for survival. They were, most of them, purchasing a home for the first time, they were building their churches and supporting to the limit of their ability their educational institutions, which they regarded as having primary demands upon their resources; all of which left only a few pennies to insure themselves and their families against the hazards of old age, ill-health, and the consequences of death. These pioneers, therefore, had to rely upon the collection of a penny here, a nickel there, a dime yonder, as their weekly intake from an overworked and underpaid clientele. They so husbanded these imaginary resources that month by month and year by year they were able to add a desk, a typewriter, a chair, a clerk, an agent, a cashier, a supervisor, and a District Manager until today, in terms of administrative structure and scientific management, these companies compare favorably with their contemporaries in the great "White World."

Since 1787

M. S. Stuart, writing on Negro insurance in *The Crisis*, nearly a decade ago, pointed out that "church relief societies, crude but effective units," were organized by free Negroes in the North as early as 1787, and Joseph A. Pierce, statistical authority, in his admirable and exhaustive volume on Negro business, cites the "fundamental and important business experience gained by Negroes through the organization and conduct of these secret and beneficial societies."

"In a definite sense," continues Pierce, "free Negroes of the North were as greatly in need of mutual aid as those living under the influence of the Southern slave economy. Thus the precarious economic condition of the free Negroes led to the organization of the many mutual societies in the North and the South."

"The leaders of these organizations," he says (and the emphasis is mine) "had neither insurance knowledge nor training. They operated the societies on the basis of a small initiation fee and small periodic payments—arbitrarily determined." But he concludes his comment on the early beneficial societies with this significant statement:

"These rather uncomplicated efforts, however, laid the foundation for the structure of what is now the largest, most successful, and longest sustained business conducted by Negroes—life insurance," and by way of explanation cited this bit of sound business philosophy from the pen of a Negro insurance executive:"

"...Only those social and economic devices that are founded in the natural necessities of human existence find a permanent place in the progress of the human race."

This Is Behind Today's Insurance

There we have the motivation which has built up the Negro insurance business of 1950.

These were its beginnings—solidly rooted in necessity. So! While the oldest of our present-day insurance businesses, the Southern Aid Society of Virginia, now has fifty-six years of continuous operation back of it, its runner-up, Richmond Beneficial, has fifty-five, the substantial North Carolina Mutual fifty-one, and the Afro–American of Jacksonville forty-nine. Negroes have actually been working at some form of security through insurance for one hundred and sixty-three years.

The Timbers of Necessity Still Carry the Weight

In 1950 the solid, seasoned timbers of necessity are still carrying the weight of the growth and improvements and adaptations which distinguish today's modern insurance institutions from their humble forebears.

What Are the Principal Changes?

What are these changes? What do the years show? What, for instance, has taken place in the forty-five years since Atlanta Life, then a little church assessment society, was purchased by the pioneering A.F. Herndon from Pastors J.A. Hopkins and J. James Bryant and opened as a mutual non-assessment company, with Mr. Herndon, one clerk, and one agent? What has taken place in the half century since the venerable C. C.

Spaulding, head of North Carolina Mutual's two hundred-million-dollar insurance business first began tramping the highways and byways of the Tar Heel State, selling insurance from door to door?

What has taken place in the forty-nine years since the articles of corporation were filed, here, for the Supreme Court of the American Woodmen? And in the forty years since Cassius White, Granville Norman, and Lawrence Lightner took over the fortunes of your Association with assets of less than nine thousand dollars and a membership under two thousand, to increase both assets and membership tenfold in the first five years of their management—to acquire assets of one and one-fourth millions, a membership of over fifty-eight thousand, and one hundred fifty field workers, at the time of Mr. White's passing, thirteen years after this remarkable trio "took over"; and from up to your own 1950 milepost, when your Woodmen's assets are listed at six millions?

The Changes as I See Them

As I look back, with you, over the changes of this vital period, I see them in such factors as type of company, kinds of insurance written, dollar value of insurance written, number of policyholders, dividends, physical spread of operations, surpluses, extent and standards of employment, and *efficiency of operation*—quite a change from the "uncomplicated efforts" of the little beneficial society of 1787 or of 1905.

Why the Changes?

What happened? As I see it, these changes reflect, first of all, the stepped-up tempo of life throughout America, in the first half of this century. They reflect the coming of the common use of the telephone, and the modish dress and prettied-up hair of rural women who now buy beauty products as well as laying mash with their butter and egg money; and their fathers and brothers fix the price of their produce from the market reports on the air.

The changes we are looking at reflect increased incomes at the lower levels of our economy as well as higher up. They reflect sharpened attention to basic values in living, due in large part to stimulating affiliations with labor unions, civic and trade organizations, and broadened church activities.

Finally, they reflect corresponding changes in the needs of the average family—urban, village, or rural—in a society increasingly complex, increasingly demanding, and highly competitive: the need for better housing, better clothes, better education, better working equipment, and better medical attention.

The Kind of Insurance Now Written

Now, at the risk of "carrying coals to Cardiff," may I point to a few facts to which I shall refer later (but not much later) in this discussion. Preliminary figures of the National Negro Life Insurance Association, for 1950, show 4,600,000 policyholders for the member companies, as against 3,940,000 for 1945. I am competently advised that the distribution of policies by kinds of insurance has not changed to any appreciable extent in that period. In 1945, then, 3,860,000 of the total 3,940,000 policies were industrial, with a sprinkling of health and accident policies. Under 250,000 were "ordinary" or endowment, and fewer than a dozen were group policies. One company recently reported writing "many ninety-year contracts."

Amounts of Insurance Written

As of 1945, three Negro companies had better than fifty million dollars each in policies-in-force. Three others had from thirty to fifty millions each; four had twenty to thirty millions each; and seven had ten to twenty millions.

The increase already cited in the total insurance reported by the Association during the past five years would, of course, change these figures somewhat. But at this point let me quote Pierce again on the fact that (a) nearly half of the forty-four member companies had less than fifty thousand policies in force as of December 31, 1945, while thirteen and a half per cent had more than two hundred thousand; and (b) that it was estimated that just one of the large American insurance companies alone carried twice the total in policy value *on Negro lives*, as the combined total for all forty-four Negro companies included in the Association. What is the implication?

What's Ahead?

The never-to-be-forgotten book written by the late Dr. Hoffman, statistician of the Prudential Life Insurance Company, entitled *The Racial Traits and Tendencies of the American Negro*, did the race almost irreparable injury in the insurance market of America. In this book, Dr. Hoffman predicted, on the basis of the abnormally high death rate of Negroes at that time, that in one hundred years from that date tuberculosis alone would solve the Negro problem in America. Through the National Negro Health Week campaign, initiated by the late Booker Washington and other educational media, the Negro was made acutely conscious of his high rate of mortality and morbidity and the extent to which a large percentage of Negroes were dying, not only from curable diseases but many from preventable diseases. He began to apply the new acquired information to his health habits and moved into better health zones to the extent that thirty years after Dr. Hoffman wrote his book the Negro death rate was lower than the white death rate was when Dr. Hoffman wrote the book, and the rate is still going down. Anybody who is taking any comfort in the hope that the Negro is going to disappear from the American scene in the manner prophesied by Dr. Hoffman will find himself seriously disappointed. The Negro is here to stay as long as posterity gives to the world newborn babes, the prophets of doom to the contrary notwithstanding.

Friends, the implication concerns the origins of the insurance business, with Negroes dying like flies all over the lot, and the church beneficiaries saving the day for the neglected and the distressed (Woodson, estimated as high as twenty-five to forty per cent in some communities, right after Emancipation); and today's impressive advances in lowered disease and mortality rates vastly increased life expectancy, and the expanding needs and wants of a Negro population looking up in the world and wanting, each and every day, more and more of the same kinds of things that everyone else wants—in other words, wanting security in terms of their neighbors' security, and being uncomfortable until they get it.

Integration

It also concerns that integration for which we have been praying hard and about which we have been beating our drums up and down the highways.

Mrs. Mary McLeod Bethune, a lady whom I consider one of the wisest of our elder statesmen, had something to say about INTEGRATION not long ago. She reminded us that integration is a "two-way street"; that it is not painless; that it is going to call for giving up some of the *priorities of segregation,* such as getting S–13—that split drawing-room they used to hand out for the price of a lower berth, to keep us out of sight; such as letting more white students into so-called "Negro" schools (of course they want to come!) while we are getting more Negro students and *teachers* into the other schools. And she also pointed out that it is going to mean taking the "For Negroes Only" sign down from our businesses. Those are strong words, but the lady used them and I am thinking about them. I am also thinking very hard about Gunnar Myrdal's conclusions on Negro financial operations in his American Dilemma, because my own mind follows the same trend. Myrdal says—and here I quote:

"The Negro-managed bank and insurance company will not get away from the fact that the Negroes are poor and the segregated Negro community cannot offer any range of investment opportunities such as that investment risk can minimize."

He goes on even further to say: "Indeed, it is difficult to see a real future for a segregated Negro financial system."

With his final conclusion few of us will agree, but it is food for thought that should give us the intestinal stamina to wrench ourselves loose from fixed patterns and consider the future of Negro business with a greater degree of objectivity. Here is Myrdal's final comment on the subject:

"Basically, it (a segregated Negro financial system) is nothing but a poor substitute for what the Negroes really need: employment of Negroes in white-dominated financial institutions and more consideration for them as insurance or credit seekers."

There are points on which I agree and others on which I definitely disagree with Myrdal. He is correct, or course, about the limiting effects of segregation on Negro business. But interestingly (to me, at least), my points of disagreement are those based on his partial acceptance of segregation as a permanent pattern, or rather, I might say, his acceptance of "partial segregation" as a permanent pattern. Hence, he says "white-dominated" when I mean no such thing.

I do believe, however, that we would indeed be cutting off our noses to spite our faces if we failed to include in our businesses persons with exceptional experience in the fields we are exploring and attempting to develop, simply because those persons are not of our race. Neither do I believe that wisdom lies in scorning the dollar resources of entrepreneurs whose hands are not the same color as mine. Neither do I believe that a predominately Negro-operated business, seeking to expand, should attempt, in any way, to limit itself to Negro patronage.

And along with the comments of Mrs. Bethune and of the late Edwin Embree on integration in education, I believe that when we begin to remove our own barriers—defense barriers already becoming outmoded—we shall, by the same token, stimulate and expand the development of all our businesses.

A New Philosophy

Carrying over Embree's protest at the support given to the perpetuation of segregation in all its manifestations by the vested interests of Negro teachers, Negro preachers, and Negro business in the pattern of segregation, I find myself once more quoting from the profound and factual presentation of Joseph Pierce, who opens his discussion of a philosophy for Negro business with this thought:

"Running like a theme through these pages is the dilemma of the Negro business man who as a Negro disapproves of racial segregation but as a business man has vested interest in segregation because it creates a convenient market for his goods and services. This dilemma has led to confusion in the thinking of business people on the importance of race as an aggravating factor in the problems of Negro business, and has created conflicting opinions on the broad objective of Negro business."

"Among other things," says Pierce, "it has led to proposals that Negroes should establish a separate and self-sufficient Negro economy. *But Negro business cannot, with advantage to itself and to the Negro race, operate as an economic shut-in.*"

He quotes Will W. Alexander on "Our Conflicting Racial Policies," in Bucklin Moon's *Primer for White Folks*: "To adopt economic segregation as a means of solving the economic problems of Negroes bears on its very face the stamp of futility." And again, "there can be no *adequate* provision for the economic life of these thirteen million Americans except as they share in the general economic life of the country."

"There exists a great need," Pierce urges, "for the indoctrination of actual and prospective business people with—a philosophy based on the general premise that Negro business, if it is to achieve the fullest development possible in the American economy, must completely partake of the characteristics of American business and that it must not be limited in *its patronage to one race, in its location to Negro communities*, and in its lines of business to service establishments and retail stores. In short, the general need of Negro business men is an *inclusive* philosophy of business, which, when put to work, will have as its goal the complete integration of Negro business into the general American economy."

As techniques of such integration of business, Myrdal's suggestion of the entrance of Negroes into existing corporate businesses again arises, as do Negro-managed corporation outlets, a device coming more and more commonly into use; the formation of Negro-white partnerships, also now occurring with increased frequency, with the same idea which we have previously presented here, of creating larger resources for capital and greater stimulation of bi-racial patronage.

As the late T. Arnold Hill, long-time Urban League official, put it, the coming technique should be directed toward "interracial business—owned by white and colored capital, managed by white and colored officers, and sustained by white and colored patrons—which would provide positions for white and colored workers."

And instances of Negro–white business cooperation have been multiplying rapidly even in the short space of three years since the publication of Dr. Pierce's book.

Examples of Negro–White Business and Professional Cooperation

In Washington, where I spend most of my time as a Red Cross official, the District Theaters (formerly the Lichtman Theaters) have been operated for years on a white-capital, Negro-management basis, with Rufus Byars, veteran theater man, in immediate charge of the entire group. The Giant Market food chain, at several Washington stores, employ Negroes in capacities such as assistant managers, cashiers, clerks, section heads, and concessionaires, on a fifty-fifty basis with white employees.

Laundry and ice-cream chains also have many Negro managers. Several dime stores and smaller department stores have Negro clerks and window dressers.

The Thom McAn shoe stores, in New York, were among the earliest establishments to make this democratic experiment.

Conversely, a number of our leading Negro newspapers have sensibly hired white persons on both technical and editorial staffs for many years, and the famous Pacific Coast architect, Paul Williams, has consistently maintained a mixed staff since he first opened business to design homes and business structures for patrons of all races. Incidentally, the New Golden State Mutual Insurance Building in Los Angeles, costing eight hundred thousand dollars, is a Paul Williams production. The June issue of *Our World* tells the story of "Dynamite" Jackson's transition from fighter to businessman. Dynamite's partner at the Paradise Lounge in Hollywood is a white businessman.

In Government

Government, which has become more and more conscious of the need for *doing* integration and not just talking about it, has for a long time, now, hired Negroes—not by any means to cover up its shortcomings, as implied and even charged by some of our experts in bitterness, but to help its various branches to meet and understand the racial problems posed—including that of integration through all operational levels of these same departments. Progress has definitely been made in this direction, although we are well aware of a long road ahead. Probably the most pertinent example of integration in government to which we may look with great encouragement and satisfaction is that of Col. Campbell C. Johnson—no longer a "race" employee, but Assistant to General Hershey at Selective Service in full charge of all organizations: personnel, both military and civilian; space, records, supplies, statistics, publications, and alien and minority group programs.

That is a long way from the desks of the old "race relations advisers" who broke ice in the early 'thirties, important as they undoubtedly were. They started the trend, but they did not encompass it! Progress does not have an end.

Professional Organizations

Professional organizations are following the same trend—not without debate—but as the result of healthy debate. Even in the Deep South, the Florida Medical Association has opened its doors. The American Association of University Women has opened its doors, with a Southern woman leading the fight for democracy. The American Medical Association has lowered its barriers.

Not All Is Sweetness and Light

Not all is sweetness and light—nor most of it; but toeholds are becoming more numerous—people are reading more and listening more and understanding more. If everything were perfect, we would need no FEPC; and if we were hopelessly rooted in segregation, an FEPC wouldn't work. Neither is true. We *do* need an FEPC, and wherever one has been established, it *has* worked. The response shows that American minds are opening—with proper stimulation.

We Must Lead

But mind you! *We* must *lead*! We, who ourselves have been disadvantaged by failure of others to keep in step with the democratic process, should be the first to demonstrate our own belief in it—by practicing it!

Please do not misunderstand me. I do not say that a business may not logically be racial or "national" due to its locality, so long as we have ghettoes, or so long as we tend to "colonize" in like groups, but it should keep an open door. The Negro business entrepreneurs should make their stock available in the open market, and should encourage their own stockholders to buy in the open market.

In all these areas—business, professional, or educational—we will get *the feeling of belonging* through mutual participation, by knowing that everything that happens is of concern to us, and therefore, making it our concern. We have protested much, and rightly so, for those things to which all Americans are entitled. But I firmly believe that if we can down our own suspicions, and open our own doors wider, we stand to acquire more, and achieve more, with less protestation.

IN OUR OWN PRACTICE OF EDUCATION AND BUSINESS AND CIVIC ENTERPRISE we must set the example. IN THOSE INSTITUTIONS WHICH WE CALL OUR OWN, *we* must set the *pace* and the *direction*.

From this mid-century vantage point in retrospect, we are persuaded that this has been in many respects the most fascinating as well as the most devastating half-century in the history of the world. In terms of industrialization, in terms of mechanization, in terms of transportation, in terms of communication, and in terms of television, this has been the most epoch-making half-century in the history of organized society, in the history of the world; and yet when we consider that there have been two World Wars fought during this half-century, we are forced to conclude that the progress in human relationships has not paralleled the advance made in the other areas of our culture. This conclusion forces us to re-examine our skills, our tools, our philosophy, our attitudes, and our objectives.

As we recognize significant trends that are making themselves manifest in different departments of our culture, we are forced to conclude that in the second half of the twentieth century we shall contemplate a total market rather than a Negro business. The State Medical Association of Florida has deleted from its Constitution the word "white" and has thus invited into its membership any physician certified to practice medicine by the Board of Examiners. The State Nurses Association of Florida not only welcomed Negro nurses to bona fide membership but elected a Negro woman to membership on the executive committee and chose her as their representative to attend an International Nursing Convention in Sweden. The institutions of higher learning in Kentucky have opened their door to Negroes on all academic levels from freshmen to graduate school. The States of Arkansas and Oklahoma have Negroes registered in graduate institutions on an integrated basis. The State Teachers Associations of Missouri merged and became one association, distributing the administrative responsibilities among members of the two groups on a parity. These are a few of the evidences of significant changes that have taken place in America's social pattern.

Let me repeat, all Negro leadership—business and otherwise—have and are giving support to the President's Civil Rights Program, which includes Fair Employment Practice— which contemplates that prospective employees shall not be denied opportunity to market their skills on the basis of race, religion, or national origin. This means, if it means anything at all, that Negro businessmen shall not only contemplate the total market and include among their customers every shade of the community's complexion, but that they shall also invite capital of all of the elements of the community in support and expansion of their businesses and shall extend employment opportunities to qualified persons, regardless of accident of birth. We cannot have integration in education, in medical science, in the military, and in all the areas referred to above and then have segregation in business.

Business controlled by Negroes, or in which Negroes have the majority of stock, in the second half of the twentieth century, if it is not to go against the ocean-like current of public opinion, must contemplate integration. This is basic to a new concept which we must quickly acquire, and that is a sense of belonging and a sense of ownership. The Negro must regard America as his country, not himself as a visitor here to be tolerated and patronized in a spirit of condescension on the part of others who have less right to claim America than he. All that anybody has done to give their children the right of ownership, our forefathers did. They not only felled the trees and built the railroads; they fertilized the soil with their bones; they watered the fields with their sweat and tears; they irrigated the land with their blood. We must recognize our social heritage and in all relationships—business and otherwise—behave as if we are not naturalized but natural-born American citizens.

In that spirit, we can sing with all of the children of all the people, not in the spirit of inhibition and restraint, but in the spirit of identification and parity participation: "MY COUNTRY, 'TIS OF THEE, SWEET LAND OF LIBERTY, OF THEE I SING: LAND WHERE MY FATHERS DIED, LAND OF THE PILGRIMS' PRIDE, FROM EVERY MOUNTAINSIDE, LET FREEEDOM RING."

Now, that must mean every mountain. It must mean, not only the White Mountains of New Hampshire and Vermont; not only the Catskill Mountains of New York; not only the Allegheny Mountains of Pennsylvania and the Rocky Mountains of Montana; but, so far as Negro America is concerned, it must also mean the Blue Ridge Mountains of Virginia, the Ozark Mountains of Kentucky, the Lookout Mountain of Tennessee, and the Stone Mountain of Georgia.

FROM EVERY MOUNTAINSIDE—LET FREEDOM RING!

TEXT OF AN ADDRESS TO BE DELIVERED BY JESSE O. THOMAS, OF THE OFFICE OF PRICE STABILIZATION, AT DELAWARE STATE COLLEGE, DOVER, DELAWARE, FEBRUARY 26, 1952.

It is indeed a pleasure to be with you here at Delaware State College today.

I feel completely at home here. President Thomason and I were schoolmates in the New York School of Social Work many years ago. My sister-in-law, Louise Smith, was head of the Department of Economics in 1940–1941, and her husband, Dyke Smith, was athletic coach. I might add that Delaware State had an unbeaten championship team that year. So you can understand why I have been especially interested in your college for some time and have felt a closeness to it.

During most of my adult life I have been associated, in one way or another, with students and teachers. I enjoy the intellectual stimulation which comes to me when I visit colleges and universities throughout this broad land of ours. At all the institutions I visit, I find a deep interest in the complex problems which face our society today.

Everyone agrees that a democracy cannot work smoothly unless it has the support of an educated, responsible public. Those who are fortunate enough to receive college training have a duty and an opportunity. More and more, they are becoming leaders in their communities. In this period of national crisis, their influence is of greater importance than it has ever been. They should, therefore, make every effort to understand and help their government in its various programs designed to deal with the present grave emergency.

The Office of Price Stabilization, which I represent here today, is a part of this government emergency program. (It has been charged with a difficult, highly important task—to keep the fires of inflation from destroying our basic economy.)

Before we talk about the methods, the how and why of this program, let us discuss first what we mean by the word "inflation."

The dictionary describes inflation as "puffed up, swollen out of proportion." When our government refers to inflation, the meaning is about the same—swollen out of proportion. Inflation comes when there is too much money in terms of what there is to buy, and people bid up the process of the things they want. Too much money chasing too few goods and a disposition on the part of the people to get what they want at any price are the main causes of inflation.

When inflation was at its height in Germany during the 1920's, workers used to race out of their shops at night to exchange their wages for almost anything they could get—old shoes, kitchen knives, handkerchiefs. Money, as such, lost its value. Finally, in order to buy meat, you had to pay with goods. While all of this may seem far away and a bit impossible to us here, let me remind you that we could have had a disastrous inflation in the United States, too, if we had not taken steps to prevent it. It may never have reached the scale it did in Germany, but it could have been bad enough.

When war broke out in Korea in June, 1950, prices and wages were fairly stable in this country. We looked forward to a long period of prosperity and comfort.

Then—what happened?

Our nice, comfortable feeling disappeared. We remembered what happened after Pearl Harbor when prices shot up and shortages developed. Fearing another period of shortages and high prices, we went on a buying spree. No one would catch us napping this time!

Mr. and Mrs. America rushed out to buy refrigerators, rugs, automobiles, new clothes, sheets—all sorts of things we needed—or thought we would need or want.

Businessmen increased their stocks and manufacturers loaded up on raw materials or dipped into what they had in order to meet the sudden new demand for goods. Prices shot up. Costs also skyrocketed. This in turn brought higher prices. Inflation was on the move.

In the next six months living costs rose eight per cent, food prices over eleven per cent, and clothing almost eight and one-half per cent. House furnishings jumped thirteen and one-half per cent! All of us began to feel the pinch. While we can possibly get along without new clothes and house furnishings, we have to eat, and inflation really cuts into our food budgets.

In the same way high prices hit the individual, inflation also endangers our defense effort. General Marshall has estimated that out of the first thirty-five billion dollars we appropriated for defense after the outbreak of the Korean War, seven billion was lost to inflation. Think of what that means: two dollars out of every ten you paid for defense was wasted because of high prices.

This could not go on. We had to do something!

In January, 1951, your Government froze the prices of most goods and services.

Mr. and Mrs. America relaxed. We stopped our hoarding, our buying spree, because we no longer worried about what might happen to prices. We knew there would be no immediate scarcities. Soon the price freeze took a firm grip on our national economy, and prices began to level off. The cost of living in general has been held to a 2.9 per cent rise since last winter. Compare that to the eight per cent rise in the post-Korea period.

O.P.S. does not claim all the credit for putting the handcuffs on inflation in 1951. There were many factors. People all over the nation helped by increasing their savings and using restraint in their buying. The federal government made use of credit restrictions, taxes, controls on productions, and controls on wages, as well as price controls. But the fact stands that the wave of scare buying, speculation, and frenzied price increases did not stop until after the general price freeze.

The freeze was a temporary action, designed to meet an emergency situation. But the very suddenness of the freeze caught some businessmen between high costs and frozen prices. Those who had tried to do their patriotic duty and hold the price line found they were in a bad spot compared to others who had taken advantage of the buying spree to hike prices. Those who had not stocked up at lower cost found that they must reorder at higher prices. In order to relieve those price lags and squeezes, O.P.S. immediately started work on regulations tailored to fit individual industries and businesses.

In the course of these later operations, some prices were rolled back while others were rolled forward. This, too, was inevitable.

The basis of a sound stabilization program must be equal and fair treatment for all. No businessman should be allowed to take undue advantage over a competitor. That is a basic principle of our democratic process.

In my work on the Hoover Flood Commission during the Mississippi flood crisis of 1927, I had occasion to travel along both sides of that great river from Memphis to New Orleans. I saw what had happened to the system of dikes and levees which in normal years hold back the water. But when *real* floods came and the river rose above its normal level, these levees were not enough. Villages and farms were washed out, leaving devastation behind.

So it is with our national economy. When a flood of money pours through the economy during a period of increased defense buildup, the ordinary barriers are not enough. We must take extra precautions—build higher dikes and more dams against the pressures of inflation.

We siphon off a part of this new flood that comes with military expansion through taxation, credit control, and the sale of bonds, to encourage more savings. We embark on a program of price stabilization.

What do we mean by this word "stabilization"?

Let's consult Webster once more. The dictionary says that stabilization means *balance*. The pressures that come with increased production must be held in check—they must be kept in balance.

In a way, this process can be compared to the way we use one of those steam cookers that stores are advertising so widely these days. As I understand it—not from personal experience, of course—you place your vegetables or whatever it is you want to cook in the kettle with some water, clamp on the lid, and wait. When steam begins to pour through the small center vent, you put on a cap and, after the indicator reaches the cooking mark, adjust the fire. The manufacturer knows that he must provide safety measures, for it is impossible to guess at the exact pressure that will build up inside the kettle. To prevent explosion, he places a small valve in the lid, allowing extra stream to escape, a little at a time, without disturbing the cooking process. If you are careless and forget to turn down the heat, pressure builds up, the cap and safety valve blow off, and you have soup all over the ceiling.

That is about what would happen to our economy without stabilization. Prices would get out of control, bringing ruin to our national economy.

If we could guarantee a slow, even flow of defense orders and output, and at the same time maintain the necessary production of civilian goods to meet the extra demands, all would go smoothly. But this is where the difficulty arises. Our defense program must have priority. Some phases of production run ahead of others. There are material shortages. Certain goods must be diverted from civilian channels to meet our national goals. Others must be obtained abroad or at higher prices.

With the armed forces buying food and clothing, providing transportation and housing, armaments, and all the hundreds of other items they will need, there are bound to be pressures. We have been investing in national security at a rate of over forty billion dollars a year. By the end of 1952, this rate is expected to be twenty billion dollars higher. Much of this money will go into the hands of consumers as wages. But it will be many months before production can be expanded to meet both defense and civilian needs. Meanwhile, without effective stabilization, people would bid against one another for things they want, and that would lead to higher prices.

We must be prepared. We must protect our national security and our national economy.

What, then, is your job in the stabilization program?

As college students, you represent the most highly trained large segment of our population. I need not explain that it is to your personal advantage to fight inflation. For the more your families must spend as the result of high prices, the less there would be left for your tuition, books, and college living expenses. Also, I have not forgotten that there are other expensive sides to a college education. Dances, club and fraternity initiation fees, clothing, and travel usually are paid out of the family pocketbook.

But I am thinking mostly of a less selfish aspect of the problem. Many of you here today are, or will be, teachers. You certainly realize that you are entering one of the most influential professions in the country. So it is up to you to study and understand how inflation could destroy the foundations of American life. I ask that you inform yourselves on all aspects of the price stabilization program. I ask that you also to study ways and means of getting this message to others so they, too, will have a realistic view of the perils which face us.

For your own welfare—for the welfare of your families, your communities, your nation—you must fight inflation!

There are five simple tasks every student and teacher can perform—now!

Avoid scare buying.
Pay no more than ceiling prices.
Fight waste everywhere.
Do not hoard.
Save all you can, –buy defense bonds.

Let's keep America strong!

"Wings Over Jordan" Program
Dayton, Ohio
October 20, 1940

THIRTIETH ANNIVERSARY OF THE
NATIONAL URBAN LEAGUE

The Board and Staff members of the National Urban League, as well as those occupying corresponding positions in the forty-five local branches of the League located in twenty-seven states of the nation, are grateful to Doctor Settle, originator of "Wings Over Jordan," and are appreciative of the facilities of the Columbia Broadcasting Company for the opportunity to give this brief historical resumé to our friends of the radio audience.

Thirty years ago, Mrs. Ruth Standish Baldwin, widow of the late president of the Long Island Railroad, called together a small group of civic-minded white and colored citizens to her New York home to consider means by which the social conditions of the Negro in our cities might be improved.

It was in this atmosphere of cooperating citizenship that the Urban League Movement was born, the objectives of which were formally adopted as follows:

1. Seek cooperation of welfare movements in efforts to apply to the Negro urban population the benefits of modern social service.

2. Investigate carefully and scientifically the manifestation among Negroes of antisocial and destructive social and economic forces—marshalling data factually (always honestly) and so convincingly that always practical programs of amelioration may be obvious and thus be assured of public support.

3. Train Negro social workers (there were no Negro trained social workers then) so that they, themselves, might not only accelerate social work among their own people but pool their resources with those of white social workers for the good of humanity in general. (Ninety-two men and women have received training in accredited schools of social work through fellowships provided by the National Urban League. In addition, the League was primarily responsible for the establishment of the Atlanta School of Social Work, from which approximately two hundred seventy-five men and women have been graduated.)

In 1911, the staff consisted of one full-time and two part-time members with a total budget of eighty-five hundred dollars. In the past three decades, this movement has expanded until today there are employed in the forty-five branches some two hundred fifty trained men and women and the aggregate current expenditures amount to more than one-half million dollars.

In addition to the work of the Administration, embracing the supervision and coordination of the activities of the entire movement, the national organization has the following departments:

INDUSTRIAL RELATIONS, which concentrates on labor adjustment and vocational guidance through maintaining contacts with personnel management in industry and conducting an annual Vocational Opportunity Campaign. Through this Campaign, Negro youth are sensitized on occupational and vocational problems which they must encounter for economic adjustment. In the annual Vocational Opportunity Campaign seventy-five thousand or more students in the high schools and colleges are reached directly. This Department also attempts to make the Negro intelligent respecting the history of organized labor and the technique of collective bargaining.

RESEARCH, which gathers and disseminates authentic information concerning the Negro. This material is widely sought after by students and writers, who regard the National Urban League as the principal source of current reliable data on the sociological conditions of Negroes in our cities. This Department has made special surveys in ninety-seven cities at the request of local committees who wish to use this information as a basis for programs of adjustment.

The official organ of the National Urban League is OPPORTUNITY: *The Journal of Negro Life,* which enjoys the reputation of being one of the best publications of its kind and has wide circulation among the libraries, community centers, and professors and students of the Social Sciences.

A few days ago, Eugene Kinckle Jones, Executive Secretary of the National Urban League, in his address before the delegates in attendance at our Thirtieth Annual Conference at Green Pastures Camp near Jackson, Mississippi, stated that the Urban League Movement had passed through three distinct periods and is now entering upon the fourth:

The first, 1910–1917, was devoted to promotional activities, employment, and welfare service in industry;

The second, 1917–1929, was largely devoted to economic expansion, labor adjustment, and seeking job opportunities for the Negroes who had migrated to the large industrial centers and urban communities of the North and West. (In a single year, the League secured twenty-five thousand jobs for Negroes, many of them in new types of industries in which Negroes had not previously been employed.)

The third, 1930–1939, the facilities of the League were very largely employed in providing survival techniques during this period of protracted unemployment and widespread depression.

The fourth stage is that which we are now called upon to enter—helping to merge the gifts and talents of Negroes with those of the country at large to produce the greatest possible unity in the nation's effort to prepare itself against the encroachment of totalitarianism.

As was true during World War Number One, in this present crisis the League Movement will throw the full force of its energies and strength behind the nation's defense program as it seeks to have Negro youth included on equal footing and participating with other race elements in the training programs of national preparedness.

The National Urban League, located at 1133 Broadway, New York City, has a governing board of forty white and colored citizens representing the progressive elements of our population lead by L. Hollingsworth Wood as its President. The motto of the League is: "Not Alms, but Opportunity," and the spirit in which it works is expressed in a statement of Mrs. Baldwin: "Let us work not as colored people nor as white people for the narrow benefit of any group alone, but together, as American Citizens, for the common good of our common city, our common country."

During the First World War, the National Urban League cooperated closely with the War Industry Board, the United States Employment Service, and with federal, state, and municipal officials as well as representatives of private industry in our program of national defense. We are placing at the disposal of our government today the personnel of our national organization and its forty-five affiliated branches in strategic industrial centers throughout the nation in this threatening emergency.

The United States today is the last nonbelligerent of the great democracies. In days like these, the public coordination of all national resources demands the united support of all agencies and the unlimited participation in all sections of our population as contemplated in the American Bill of Rights and granted by our Federal Constitution and all of its amendments.

In the last analysis, the status of the Negro and of his inalienable rights is the final test of whether we can unflinchingly and conscientiously face the world in our claims to the right to defend true Democracy as a living force and the "American Way."

XIX

Mexico City
(Smothered with Hospitality and Embarrassed with Kindness)

I have received a lot of public attention and have been given many honors in my public life at home and abroad. Sometimes I have felt that in some particular instant, I have been given more consideration than I deserved. I have never, however, been a recipient of as many sustained and varying expressions of hospitality and cordiality as were bestowed upon Mrs. Thomas and me by the officials of the Mexican Red Cross, from the Director General to the elevator pilot, which characterized our experiences from the capitol of the republic.

Mrs. Thomas and I compared notes, as related to our experiences throughout our lives, and concluded that neither of us had ever experienced anything approximating this mass demonstration of hospitality and good fellowship.

The Director General of the Red Cross of the Mexican Republic, Dr. A. J. Quijano, had been advised by the international section of the American Red Cross of our contemplated visit to Mexico. Dr. Quijano was ill upon our arrival, but alerted the members of his national staff and members of the local delegation.

One morning Mrs. Thomas and I were coming down on the elevator of our hotel and were told by the pilot, "There are twenty cars of Red Cross people waiting for you downstairs." On reaching the ground floor we were met by this deputized delegation. Some were in uniform indicating their rank in the motor crops. Upon presentation of their cards, those in civilian clothes were recognized through their membership on the national committee or official position by the national delegation.

This motorcade took us through the city to see many points of beauty and also many points of historical significance. Of particular interest was the Mexican Red Cross hospital. The National Red Cross Council was the governing body for the republic. It was composed of a chairman and twenty-five members. Each city had its own council. These members were elected to promote and obtain funds for the delegation.

There was in Mexico City a ladies' committee of one hundred and fifty who worked for the hospital. The nurses, who gave their services, were under the direction of this committee.

There were three resident physicians who gave eight hours per day and had charge of the eighty or ninety doctors who served as interns.

As soon as the nurses completed their training, they were usually placed in good positions.

There was a special room for first aid kits and coats for the ambulance drivers.

Twice a year a campaign was put on to raise funds for the operation of the delegation.

The following day we were taken thirty-five miles to see the archaeological City of Teotihuacan and to see the pyramids of the Sun and Moon known as one of the seven wonders of the world. These masses of rock and mortar were constructed with geometrical perfection that has amazed modern man. There is no accurate description of how this ancient man conceived and constructed these pyramids without any machinery or modern facilities. While there, we also visited the museum of the National Historical Institute of Anthropology, which is located at the base of the Pyramid of the Sun.

At a short distance away there is an ancient cave that is now being utilized as a cafeteria and night club.

The next day our trip at first took us through the exclusive residential section occupied by the "Four Hundred," known as Chapultepec Heights. One example of the grandeur of these homes will suffice. The widow of a brother of one of the recent ex-governors had acquired a block square on which to build her home. Her mansion faced the front side of the block and her servants' quarters faced the opposite side. Incidentally, the servants' quarters looked like a New York apartment house.

After this pleasant ride we were taken to a reception in our honor, at the palatial residence of Señor Leandro Cuevas, who was Director General of ambulance services of the Republic of Mexico. And here we met "Mexico in Person." We leave the rest to your imagination.

The morning after this heart-warming reception we were scheduled to leave the city. We returned to our hotel from the Sanborn Restaurant, which was the eating place and social center for tourists, to find our perpetual hosts again in evidence, ready to pilot us to the highway, and in the meantime presenting Mrs. Thomas with a bouquet of red carnations.

The piloting motorcade was led by a Mexican Red Cross ambulance. Instead of taking us to the highway, as we had supposed they would do, they led us twenty-two miles beyond the city limits and bade us goodbye after a few pictures were made. As soon as I prepared to take over the steering wheel of my car, the siren of the ambulance was opened and filled the air—what a surprise! By this time both of us were so overwhelmed by personal and social attention, we were dizzy.

Puebla Red Cross

The Puebla Red Cross Hospital was in operation twenty-four hours per day. The organization was in process of enlarging its quarters and facilities. In the new plan provisions were made for the residence of a supervisory Nun personnel. Their quarters were to be provided with every modern creature comfort. The new plan contemplated departmentalizing the resident patients on the basis of sex and age. They planned to have on the medical staff at least one specialist for each of the known diseases. Provisions were also made for a nurses' training unit. They had some twenty-odd physicians, each of whom gave an hour of volunteer service daily. Sleeping accommodations were provided for physicians who found it necessary for them to remain overnight on account of the critical condition of patients in their care.

The hospital had three ambulances. Two operated in the city of Puebla and one was known as the road ambulance. The road ambulance brought patients who were victims of any kind of accident, from any part of the state, who were in need of hospitalization. Victims of any type of emergency called the Red Cross for ambulance service. The Red Cross, however, did not accept persons suffering from contagious diseases. Through the use of its discretionary power, some patients, because of their economic position, were referred to private hospitals. Others, as a result of the nature of their illness, were referred to the municipal charity hospital.

A police guard was stationed at the hospital to assume custody of patients whose hospitalization resulted from some type of episode where there had been a violation of the law, as soon as the patient had recovered to the point where the physician recommended his discharge.

Only the Red Cross and the police department owned ambulances. All services were volunteer except ambulance drivers and part of the custodial personnel, including the cooks and repairmen.

The Red Cross charged an ambulance fee for the transportation of patients. However, no patient was denied ambulance service if he was unable to pay the fee charged.

The organization operated on funds secured through volunteer contributions. Among its equipment were found X-ray machines, necessary instruments in the operating room, and, in fact, all the facilities used in a well-managed hospital.

Puebla is one of the oldest cities in the Republic of Mexico. It is fourth in size and importance. A governor of Puebla is elected for five years. In 1948 the governor, Beteacuer, had served three years but was greatly disliked, according to one of the city guides. The governor's mansion was a pink stucco, and what one could see of the grounds behind the pink wall was beautiful and impressive.

One Gonzales, a textile merchant, was reputed to be the richest man in the city. His home was as attractive as the governor's mansion.

The industries were: glass blowing, pottery, straw hat and tile making, onyx carving, silver smithing, and textile manufacturing.

Around the Main Square or Plaza

The Cathedral in Mexico City was begun in 1671 and completed in 1813. As you faced the Cathedral, the National Pawn Shop was to the left. It covered a block and was formerly the private home of Montezuma, the Emperor. To the right stood the Superior Court of Justice of Mexico City, next to which was the Palace or office of the President. Just opposite the Cathedral, or to your back, was the City Hall. The Bank of Mexico was back of the famous Sanborn Restaurant. Next to the Bank was the Post Office. The section in which the rich Americans lived was typical. It was called Chapultepec Heights. There were approximately sixty-two thousand Americans in Mexico City. There were two other residential areas that corresponded in beauty and affluence to the American section, known as the French and Spanish communities.

The usual pay for servants, who gave six days per week, one day off, with room and board, was about ten dollars per month. The American families, who had three or four servants, paid less than they would for one servant in the U.S.A.

Against these three exclusive, financially restricted areas as a background was cast ninety per cent of the population, representing a population under housed, underfed, and under clothed, of the more than three million inhabitants of the City of Mexico. It is safe to guess that at least two and one-half million fell in the category of the under housed, inadequately clothed and obviously suffering from malnutrition.

From what one could see from the highway, he was convinced that the peasant population was no exception to the general rule described above.

The Shrine of the Virgin—Santa Maria de Guadalupe—was built in 1531 and rebuilt in 1934. Pilgrims came from approximately all the states in the republic to worship at this shrine. All day long the worshipers were milling through the church as they left their pennies.

There were three large pipe organs in the church. The bases of all the columns were bronze. The windows were imported from Italy. The many huge chandeliers were gifts of the people. The crown of the Virgin in the main chancel was of platinum and precious stones. A new crown replaces the one on the Virgin every fifty years. The special chair in which the Bishop of Mexico sat when he went for special services was of gold. The rail at the Altar of Santa Maria was of pure silver, and the chairs within were hand carved of black mahogany.

The Castle, which would represent the White House in the U.S.A., was near Chapultepec Park and was called Chapultepec

Castle. ("Chapultepec" means grasshopper in the Aztec language,)

Cortez destroyed everything that could be found that was built by the Indians.

Maximilian was sent by the Spanish to rule Mexico, and ruled three years. His wife, Carlotta Amelia, was one of the most beautiful women in the world. After Maximilian was slain, she lost her mind shortly thereafter but lived many years in confinement. She had every possible luxury during the reign of her husband. Her bathtub was of solid marble. The birds and flowers carved on the wall around the tub were painted in delicate pastel shades. Her bedroom and dressing room furniture were still in excellent condition; they were imported from France. The huge mirror in her dressing room was in a frame of gold. Carlotta loved music. In the music room there were two grand pianos, in good condition, that were sent to Carlotta from Germany in 1864. Carlotta had two carriages. A special carriage, used for the city, was trimmed in gold and satin. The one for long distance trips was more sturdy and could be completely closed.

Diaz ruled Mexico for thirty-one years. At present, the president may serve only one term of six years. He may not succeed himself, but may be re-elected after some other president has served.

Riding in a Red Cross Ambulance

During an inspection trip of the various departments of the Red Cross general hospital in Mexico City, a call was received from the police department, saying that a serious accident had occurred at the intersection of two of the busiest streets in the downtown section of the city.

Prior to this emergency call, members of the ambulance corps had attempted, through their limited English vocabulary, to explain to me how the ambulance corps functioned. Upon reception of this emergency call, the Director General of the ambulance corps had a bright idea. He suggested that I accompany the ambulance on this "pick up" call. The suggestion was accepted, and in a matter of seconds, the driver, a doctor, two stretcher bearers, and I were moving down the crowded streets of the capitol of the republic at the rate of fifty-five miles per hour. With one foot first on the accelerator, then on the brakes, and weaving through traffic, with the siren open, this white ambulance with the Red Cross insignia on the top, sides, and back, sped to the scene of the accident.

After the doctor had given the accident victim first aid treatment, he was placed in the ambulance, and with what seemed to me as accelerated speed, returned to the hospital.

Further commenting on the experience, it was a thrill of a lifetime, and anybody who has a weak heart has no business making an experimental or other trips, in a Red Cross ambulance in the streets of Mexico City during business hours.

Welcomed to the State of Tamaulipas by Governor Garate

I admit that I have not had too much experience with governors. I can understand how, when the legislature is in session and a governor may be interested in getting some pet measure given favorable action, or some bill he opposes killed, or when he has a bill on his desk that he is both afraid to sign or not to sign, he might remain in his office beyond "union hours." I was not prepared, however, for the surprise that awaited Mrs. Thomas and me when we were taken by our hosts, Drs. Manuel G. Hinojosa and C. Forre, president and secretary, respectively, of the Victoria Red Cross to the governor's office at eight o'clock at night to find the chief executive in his shirt sleeves working as if it were noonday.

His reception room and outer corridors were occupied with politicians, private citizens, and business and professional men of all grades in terms of cultural levels, waiting to see the governor.

Without any previous appointment, when the governor was advised by his secretary that these two local Red Cross officials in company of the Public Relations Consultant of the American Red Cross wished to see him, priority status was immediately given, and this international Red Cross combination was invited into the governor's private office. We were given a welcome in English, which Mrs. Thomas acknowledged in Spanish. Notwithstanding that some forty or fifty people were waiting to see the governor, he reflected no impatience. On the contrary, he talked leisurely with the local Red Cross officials as they sought to give him the international implications of this official visit of the representative of the American National Red Cross.

From the governor's office we were taken to inspect the new Red Cross hospital that would bid fair to serve, when completed, the people of Tamaulipas.

After a sumptuous dinner at the Florida Café, we were taken to the air-conditioned Sierra Gorda Hotel, the finest hostelry in the city of Victoria.

Monterrey, Nuevo Leon

Following a delightful conference with the President of the Monterrey delegation (chapter) of the Mexican Red Cross, the Executive Officer of the Red Cross presented me with an autographed souvenir booklet of the city of Monterrey. When I reached my hotel and examined my prized gift, I discovered that every word in the souvenir booklet was printed or written in Spanish, and that I would not be able to evaluate this gift until I learned some Spanish or had it translated into the "mother tongue."

Therefore, I have resolved to acquire a Spanish vocabulary for this and other reasons obvious to anyone privileged to travel through the Republic of Mexico, where there is no discrimination predicated upon accident of birth.

XX

Conclusion of the Whole Matter

All of my public life has been associated with positions which required constant and unlimited travel. Some of the assignments not only made it necessary for me to travel in every state in the Union, but on several occasions the job requirement took me out of the continental United States into foreign countries. I suppose it would be a factual statement to say that perhaps no one thirty days in some forty-odd years did I remain in one city or local political subdivision. This means that for that period I lived on planes, on trains, on boats, and in automobiles, both day and night, traveling on both intra and interstate and international errands.

I am very grateful for the fact that not on a single occasion was I involved in a serious accident. I am also grateful for the fact that, for the forty-odd years, I was employed every hour without being forced to take advantage of one day's sick leave.

The above outline becomes significant when we come to evaluating the extent that it was necessary to husband my financial resources or judiciously allocate my buying power. To accomplish this it was imperative to have a "helpmate"—a wife who counted the pennies, not once, but several times before deciding which penny should be spent for what. I was most fortunate in the person chosen, and the one who agreed to become my companion. She also was a graduate of Tuskegee Institute, Class of 1914. Prior to entering Tuskegee Institute she had studied at both Bishop and Wiley Colleges, Marshall, Texas. Her name was Nellie Ida Mitchell. I first met her on the occasion of a visit to Tuskegee while serving the Institute as Field Secretary, with headquarters in Rochester, New York. The nature of the visit was to witness Commencement Exercises and to have a conference with Dr. Washington and his secretary, Dr. Scott, as we laid plans for a campaign to raise ninety thousand dollars in a thirty-day period for the purpose of liquidating an obligation in connection with the installation of a central heating plant. We were married on August 1, 1917, at high noon, in Marshall, Texas.

Both of our experiences had been similar as relates to the responsibility that we had either assumed or which had been forced upon us to provide a leadership responsibility for the other members of our respective families. This experience had 'schooled" us for correcting the welfare status of both of our family governments, jointly accepting responsibility for the house-living and for the working opportunities as well as the educational advantages of the members of the families on both sides of the equation.

Mrs. Thomas was the oldest daughter in a family of eight daughters and two sons. Not too long after we were married, both her parents died. We assumed the guardianship responsibility for the members of the two families that had not reached adulthood. Some of them were at the elementary-school level; others were at the high school level. With such economic assistance and parental supervision as we were able to provide, all of those who had the ambition and desire completed their college work and assumed responsible positions as productive citizens in educational and professional categories. The degree of economic security which we enjoy is credited primarily to the judicious manner in which Mrs. Thomas differentiated in the allocation of our buying power.

To our union was born one daughter (Anne Amanda), later a student at Oglethorpe Elementary School (a private institution) at Atlanta University Laboratory School, Spelman College, and Columbia University. She received her Bachelor's degree with an English major at Spelman College when she was nineteen years of age and her Master's degree in Personnel Administration from Columbia University when she was twenty. She is married and the mother of two daughters, Nell Anne Braxton and Rosemary Haru Braxton. Her husband, John T. Braxton, received his Bachelor's degree from Morris Brown College and his Master's degree in Physical Education form New York University. They now reside on the campus of Tougaloo Christian College, where he is director of Physical Education. Mrs. Braxton is employed as Counselor at Brinkley High School in Jackson, Mississippi, which is some seven miles from the college campus. The two daughters are now enrolled as members of the Freshman and Sophomore classes of Spelman College.

During the past three summers they have been participating in an interracial camp experience in the Catskill Mountains in the State of New York. On the basis of their aptitude, the older girl has been employed as senior counselor and the younger girl occupies a corresponding position in the junior division.

The impact of the parity participation of all of the family units has been a great source of encouraging reassurance of satisfactory dividends resulting from the investment of conscientious and sometimes sacrificial efforts on the part of persons dedicated to the fulfillment of a group endeavor for high attainment. The total result supplied driving power and regenerated energy to keep striving.

EPILOGUE

Philosophy of Life

Referring again to what was said at the beginning of this narrative, my case does not appear unique from a point of view of
obscurity of birth, economic instability, or the lowly social estate
of my ancestors. It was not the fact that Jesus was born in a manger,
in itself, that enabled him to revolutionize the moral concept and
spiritual vitality of mankind across the centuries. There were many
people born before Jesus' time, and others have been born since
the morning stars sang together, in environments less desirable
than a manger. It is what one does after birth, regardless of the circumstances surrounding his entrance into this world, that counts.

If there is any justification in writing this personal history, it
will emanate from the conclusion that may be drawn by illustrating that it is possible for the most socially disinherited individual
to make some contribution toward the sum total of human welfare if he will diligently utilize consistently all the resources at his
command.

As a guiding influence in my life, I have developed for my own
motivation a philosophy of life. This philosophy is predicated upon
two fundamental theories, as far as I am concerned: First, I believe
that duty belongs to man, and destiny to God; second, I believe
that at the point of creation, in terms of social unit and moral
worth, everybody is equal. That does not mean that a child born in
an alley of unfed and ill-housed parents has an opportunity equal
to that of a child born in a mansion.

I also believe that one person becomes better than another on the basis of conduct and usefulness, rather than by accident of birth.

These conclusions were responsible for my attitude toward people. I have never been able to regard anybody as my superior simply because he was a member of a certain club or a member of a certain race. If an individual ever reflects more sense than I have or more character than I have, and makes a larger contribution to social progress than I make, I accept that individual as my superior; it does not matter who he is, or where he is. The idea that one person is superior to another because he belongs to a certain race, church, or club never found any acceptance in my appreciation. On the question of interracial contacts, I frequently have to pinch myself to keep from laughing in the face of a white person who, by every means of measurement, is inferior to me but assumes an attitude of condescension. I find this to be true of a large number of colored people. It would be quite a revelation to white America if it had an opportunity of knowing how it is evaluated by Negroes in terms of comparative status. One does not have to be brilliant or endowed with superior talent to become a useful and effective unit of society. It is my firm conviction that nature in its nonprejudicial distribution of talent has endowed every normal human being with potentialities to develop into a recognized member of the body politic.

With constant application, dogged determination, and unreserved energy, an individual with limited native talent may achieve extraordinary distinction. If he believes in himself, in his fellow man, and in the Creator and accepts defeat as tuition or as a training or disciplinary process, he will be a hard person to count out of the game. He may frequently be down, but he is never out.

I have never wasted much time wishing that I was like somebody else. I may wish for the opportunity that someone else has been given to improve my skills or demonstrate my ability. I have so often heard my associates, classmates, and work mates express a wish that they had somebody else's hair, legs, eyes, nose; or express the craving for some other person's wealth, position, car, income, social position, or financial status. Sometimes they justify an attitude of resignation or defeatism because they do not have the things someone else possesses or enjoys.

I do not believe that there is any person who has not encountered some serious physical or mental handicap or some major misfortune of some other kind, but who, if he will take the time to discover the one or more unique talents which he possesses, through constant application will succeed in making himself felt as a useful member of society. It is my belief that in every human being there is a spark of divinity. This explains to me the nonpredictability of every human being; it explains why a Booker T. Washington can be discovered in a sulfur or coal mine—why Booker T. Washington, born without a name, now lives in the Hall of Fame; how a Thomas Edison can give a new meaning of light to the world, even though he had never entered a high school; how a Ralph Bunche can emerge from the broken home of parents in the lowest income bracket; and how a George Carver can emerge from a slave market to membership on the faculty of a state university. It explains how a Mary McLeod Bethune can ascend from a cotton plantation in South Carolina to become appraised as one of the twelve great women of America; and how Henry Ford can come out of obscurity and put the whole world on wheels. Conversely, it explains how some persons born on Fifth Avenue, New York, or in Buckingham, England, can end up in the slums.

Neither anthropologists, psychiatrists, psychologists, nor anyone else can predict, without errors of inaccuracy, basing their conclusions or prophecy on circumstances of birth, racial identity, or heredity, the destiny of any individual.

In the most prejudicial or unsympathetic community, if one will "stay in the box and pitch until the last half of the ninth inning, he will strike somebody out at the plate." I believe one will find that in the most nonappreciative environment, even the most hostile community, there will be found a sizable percentage of the inhabitants ready to give recognition to a job well done.

Many games are won and history made in the fifty-ninth of the sixty minutes to play. What little recognition I have received or what little success I have attained has resulted from my fundamental conviction that I had a contribution to make toward advancing the world in my generation, in the direction toward which all creation moves, which I could not expect anybody else to make.

Index